OBAMA, CLINTON, PALIN

Obama, Clinton, Palin

Making History in Election 2008

EDITED BY
LIETTE GIDLOW

UNIVERSITY OF ILLINOIS PRESS
Urbana, Chicago, and Springfield

© 2011 by the Board of Trustees
of the University of Illinois
All rights reserved
Manufactured in the United States of America
1 2 3 4 5 C P 5 4 3 2 1
∞ This book is printed on acid-free paper.

Library of Congress Cataloging-in-Publication Data
Obama, Clinton, Palin : making history in election 2008 / edited by Liette Gidlow.
    p.   cm.
Includes bibliographical references and index.
ISBN 978-0-252-03660-6 (cloth : acid-free paper)
ISBN 978-0-252-07830-9 (paper : acid-free paper)
1. Presidents—United States—Election—2008. 2. Obama, Barack.
3. Clinton, Hillary Rodham. 4. Palin, Sarah, 1964–
5. Presidential candidates—United States—Biography.
6. Political campaigns—United States—History—21st century.
7. United States—Race relations—Political aspects—History—21st century.
8. Women—Political activity—United States—History—21st century.
9. United States—Politics and government—2001–2009.
I. Gidlow, Liette Patricia.
E906.O23   2011
324.973'0931—dc23   2011019908

For
Max and Sam,
agents of change

CONTENTS

Acknowledgments ix

Introduction: Taking the Long View of Election 2008 1
Liette Gidlow

PART I. REPRESENTATIONS: IS HILLARY MAN ENOUGH? IS BARACK BLACK ENOUGH? IS MICHELLE THE NEW JACQUELINE KENNEDY?

1. Hillary Rodham Clinton, the Race Question, and the "Masculine Mystique" 19
Kathryn Kish Sklar

2. Barack Obama and the Politics of Anger 26
Tiffany Ruby Patterson

3. Michelle Obama, the Media Circus, and America's Racial Obsession 39
Mitch Kachun

PART II. HISTORICAL PRECEDENTS, OR HOW ELECTION 2008 BEGAN BEFORE THE CIVIL WAR

4. The 2008 Election, Black Women's Politics, and the Long Civil Rights Movement 53
Glenda Elizabeth Gilmore

5. The Forgotten Legacy of Shirley Chisholm: Race versus Gender in the 2008 Democratic Primaries 66
Tera W. Hunter

6. Hillary Clinton's Candidacy in Historical and Global Context   86
   Susan M. Hartmann

7. Defining a Maverick: Putting Palin in the Context of Western Women's Political History   94
   Melanie Gustafson

8. Populist Currents in the 2008 Presidential Campaign   105
   Ronald P. Formisano

PART III. LEGACIES: DEMOCRACY UNDERMINED? FEMINISM REDEFINED?

9. Obama 2.0: Farewell to the Federal Campaign Finance System and the Secret Ballot?   125
   Paula Baker

10. Political Feminism and the Problem of Sarah Palin   137
    Catherine E. Rymph

Conclusion: The Difference that "Difference" Makes   149
Elisabeth Israels Perry

Historical Timeline   167

Contributors   169

Index   171

ACKNOWLEDGMENTS

This project began spontaneously, progressed on faith, and happily has come to completion with the assistance of many people.

The members of the 2008 Berkshire Conference program committee responded nimbly when I asked to organize and lead a panel on the remarkable Democratic primary season then under way. Ann Little in particular facilitated this late change in the program. The atmosphere in that session was electric, the auditorium at the University of Minnesota filled to bursting. The thoughtful, informed, and impassioned discussion that followed was a model of both civic and civil discourse. I thank all who contributed that day, especially Tera Hunter, Kitty Sklar, Mitch Kachun, and Susan Hartmann, who served among the panelists and also elected to write for this volume.

Working with each of the scholars whose essays appear in the pages that follow was a genuine pleasure. The press's readers offered thoughtful suggestions for improvement. Louise Newman's recommendations for reorganizing the chapters proved especially helpful. Danielle McGuire helped me sharpen the prose in the introduction.

Joan Catapano expertly guided this project in the early stages at Illinois. Jennifer Clark shepherded it through the production process. Angela Wesley Hardin provided skillful copyediting. Matthew Smith designed the cover image.

Two of the essays that follow appeared elsewhere in earlier versions. My thanks to Claire Moses for permission to use Kitty Sklar's article, "A Women's History Report Card on Hillary Rodham Clinton's Presidential Primary Campaign, 2008," *Feminist Studies* 34$^{1}/_{2}$ (Spring/Summer 2008): 315–22. Cambridge University Press permitted the reprint of Ronald P. Formisano's "Populist Currents in the 2008 Presidential Campaign," *Journal of Policy History* 22 (April 2010): 237–55. Special thanks to Ron for his support in acquiring the rights from Cambridge.

Elizabeth Theis and Toni Lupro, our babysitters and friends, gave me time to complete this work. My husband, Adam Sakel, has been supportive in every way. Our children, now four and three, believe everything is possible. They are my favorite agents of change.

OBAMA, CLINTON, PALIN

INTRODUCTION

Taking the Long View of Election 2008

Liette Gidlow

It was an awkward situation. In their first side-by-side appearance as rivals for the Democratic presidential nomination, Senators Barack Obama and Hillary Clinton gathered in March 2007 in Selma, Alabama, with crowds of supporters and well-wishers. Forty-two years earlier, some six hundred activists, most of them black, had tried to march from Selma to Montgomery to press President Lyndon Johnson and Congress to enact a law to remedy decades of disfranchisement. In the bloody clash that erupted on the Edmund Pettus Bridge, state and local police attacked the marchers with batons, horsewhips, and tear gas, injuring seventy-eight people. Now, commemorating that march at the beginning of what would become the most hotly contested primary the Democratic Party had ever experienced, the competing candidates walked the line between recognizing the solemnity of the sacrifices made there and vying for the votes of an African American electorate that could decide the nomination. Both candidates acknowledged their debt to the brave men and women who had walked the bridge before them, and both candidates connected their personal histories to the history of that moment and place. As Hillary Clinton put it to a group at the First Baptist Church, the Voting Rights Act was "giving Senator Obama the chance to run for President of the United States, and by its logic and spirit, . . . yes, it's giving me that chance, too."[1]

Election 2008 made history in numerous ways. By the middle of January it was clear that the Democratic Party was going to nominate either the first African American or the first woman to head the ticket of any major political party. This Democratic nomination was also the first since the creation of the modern primary system in the 1970s to be decided not by voters in the primary process, but by select party "superdelegates" at the convention. The Republicans made history of their own by choosing Sarah Palin, the governor of Alaska and the first female named to a Republican presidential ticket, to run with party nominee Senator John McCain of Arizona. Both parties took advantage of new cell phone and Internet technologies, and the Democrats were especially effective in using them to raise money, communicate with supporters, and turn out voters. Together the parties shattered old fund-raising records and took campaign spending to new heights. Of course, the most striking historical development of the 2008 election was the outcome. When Senator Obama won, he broke the presidential color line.

Election 2008 made American history, but it was also a product of American history. Obama, Clinton, and Palin smashed through some of the most enduring barriers to high political office, but they did not come out of nowhere. The historians whose work appears in this volume show that though the campaigns of 2008 pointed to a new future in American politics, they also had deep roots in stories of the American past—inspiring accounts of families working hard and moving up; painful narratives of bigotry and discrimination; stirring tales of the American West as the frontier of freedom; and controversial chronicles of the 1960s, with their competing legacies of justice and division. The candidates' successes demonstrated their ability to adopt and adapt familiar stories and tested tactics, and Americans' understandings of the past framed the way they understood the election of 2008.

Barack Obama's ascent to the highest office in the land may have seemed the most improbable journey of the three. Born to a white mother and African father, raised by his mother and grandparents in Indonesia and Hawaii, and endowed with an uncommon name, the future president was unknown enough to the American public that as recently as 2004—on his return trip home from giving the keynote address at the Democratic National Convention in Boston—he was pulled out of the airport screening line for an extended security check. Three years into his Senate term, Obama declared that "the ways of Washington must change" and launched his presidential bid from the steps of the historic Illinois state capitol at Springfield. Adopting a mantra of "change" in the midst of a lingering war and a stalling economy, Obama took his campaign to Iowa and began to reinvent old paths to power—organizing supporters and raising heaps of money—through the use of the interactive Web and the latest in mobile technologies.[2]

It was deeply ironic that in her contest with Obama, Hillary Clinton got tagged as the "Establishment" candidate, for Clinton's candidacy, too, truly broke new ground. The first woman to compete plausibly for a major party nomination, Clinton had a long history of trailblazing. After graduating from Yale Law School and marrying Bill Clinton, she became the first female partner at the Rose Law Firm in Little Rock, the oldest law firm west of the Mississippi. Clinton was the first former First Lady to run for office and the first woman elected to statewide office in New York. And yet her eight years as First Lady gave her candidacy a whiff of incumbency, especially when she argued that her years in the White House, together with her tenure in the Senate and her decades of policy advocacy on behalf of women and children, gave her the edge in "experience." In a year in which voters demanded a new direction, it was hard for Clinton to make the case that she was the candidate of change. The photographs of her the night she lost the Iowa caucuses captured her dilemma perfectly: there she stood, positioned between her ex-president husband and an official from his administration, telling supporters that "America needs a new beginning."[3]

That Iowa evening kicked off what turned out to be the most hotly contested series of presidential primaries since the current system was put into place in 1972. After the Iowa caucuses, the other candidates for the Democratic nomination, including John Edwards, Bill Richardson, and Joe Biden, quickly dropped out as the contest narrowed into a horse race between Senators Obama and Clinton. These two split the opening contests; Obama won Iowa, and five days later, Clinton won New Hampshire. Then they split a patchwork of contests in the balance of the month, with Clinton picking up Michigan, Nevada, and Florida and Obama winning decisively in South Carolina. Even Super Tuesday on February 5 proved indecisive. Obama proved his national appeal by winning fourteen races, including Minnesota, Kansas, Alabama, Georgia, and even far western states such as Utah and Idaho. Clinton picked up ten primary wins including vote-rich California, New Jersey, and her home state of New York. But Clinton did not win another primary in February as Obama put together a string of ten victories from Washington state to the Virgin Islands. Between March and the last contests in June, both candidates won multiple victories; Clinton picked up the prized states of Texas, Ohio, and Pennsylvania, but Obama continued to accumulate wins and ran close enough in many of the states he lost to amass greater numbers of delegates. The results on the last day of the primary season, June 3, reprised the story of the delegate math: the two candidates split the contests, Clinton picking up South Dakota and Obama winning Montana. Obama's delegate total edged out Clinton's, but even Obama fell short of the number of delegates needed to secure the nomination. Remarkably, the full six-month run of the caucus and primary season failed to pick the party's nominee.

For the first time, the Democratic nomination rested on the votes of the party's superdelegates, an elite cadre of current and former elected officials and party leaders who, since 1980, have cast about 20 percent of the delegate votes at the Democratic national convention. As the spring wore on, the superdelegates broke for Obama. Representative John Lewis's (D-GA) change of heart foretold the outcome. An icon of the civil rights movement and longtime friend of the Clintons, Lewis had endorsed Hillary in the fall but in mid-February switched his allegiance to Obama. In the midst of Obama's string of primary wins, Lewis concluded that "something is happening in America, and people are prepared and ready to make that great leap." Most of the other superdelegates came to the same conclusion, and, faced with both the harsh reality of a delegate count that favored her opponent and enormous pressure to spare the party a convention fight, on June 8 Clinton announced that she would suspend her campaign.[4]

Unelected superdelegates and elected delegates convened in Denver in August to nominate Barack Obama and heal the rift. Speaker after speaker stressed that the time had come for unity. Michelle Obama sounded that theme in her address on the convention's opening night. Her husband, she assured, "knows that thread that connects us—our belief in America's promise, our commitment to our children's future—... is strong enough to hold us together as one nation even when we disagree." Taking her turn on the convention stage, Hillary declared that she was "a proud supporter of Barack Obama" and urged Democrats, "whether you voted for me or voted for Barack, ... to unite as a single party with a single purpose." All the same, some Clinton supporters remained wary, even bitter. Karen O'Connor, the director of the Women and Politics Institute at American University, summarized their disappointment. "If [Hillary's] 18 million votes is not enough, what does it take in the Democratic Party to get a woman on the ticket?"[5]

The Republican Party immediately began to exploit that frustration. Unlike Obama, Senator McCain had sailed to his party's nomination easily, dispatching rivals Mike Huckabee, Mitt Romney, and Rudy Giuliani early in the primary season. By August, the biggest remaining question on the Republican side concerned McCain's choice of a running mate. Seeking to blunt Obama's convention bounce, McCain announced his choice the day after Obama accepted the Democratic nomination and stunned pundits and party regulars by selecting the little-known Governor Palin. The first woman nominated to the Republican ticket and the first woman nominated to a major party ticket since the Democrats nominated Geraldine Ferraro for vice president in 1984, Palin focused attention squarely on the gender issue. A self-described feminist, Palin noted in her inaugural appearance with McCain that Hillary's campaign was over, "but it turns out the women of America aren't finished yet!" Though critics quickly targeted Palin's lack of experience in foreign policy and national security matters, the pro-life working mother triggered a surge in Republican fund-raising and proved enormously popular with the party's evangelical faithful. Palin drew the largest Republican crowds of the campaign—larger than McCain did—and infused new energy into the Republican effort.[6]

Both sides energized, the nominees launched their fall campaigns. Though the contest was hard fought, the Democratic ticket began the general election season with a lead in the polls and never looked back. In early and mid-September, the candidates crisscrossed the country, trading jabs over their competing proposals to help the ailing economy, bring peace to Iraq and Afghanistan, and improve health care. But the economy soon dominated the nation's political agenda as Wall Street slipped into a crisis that threatened the stability of the international financial system. In a stunning two weeks in September, several of the nation's largest mortgage underwriters, investment banks, and insurers, from Fannie Mae and Freddie Mac to Lehman Brothers and AIG (American International Group), teetered on the brink of insolvency and, in Lehman's case, collapsed. As the Treasury Department and the Federal Reserve struggled to stabilize the system, McCain tried to revive his flagging campaign with a high-stakes gamble, declaring on September 24 that he would suspend his campaign, including the first of the scheduled debates with Obama, in order to return to Washington to broker a bipartisan compromise on an emergency bank bailout bill. Just one day later he reinstated his campaign schedule, declaring that congressional compromise was imminent. But congressional negotiations then crashed; the candidates debated that weekend, as scheduled; and bailout legislation wasn't passed for another week and a half. When this "Hail Mary pass," as Rep. Barney Frank (D-MA) termed it, failed to revive the McCain campaign, Republicans struggled to rebrand their candidate. Was he a maverick or a statesman? A nonpartisan leader or the leader of his party? Did he stand for change or for gritty perseverance? Meanwhile, Obama deftly adapted his message of change to the new economic realities. It was time, Obama told a rally in North Carolina on the 29th of October, to "'turn the page' on an era of 'greed and irresponsibility.'" As his campaign slogan had put it all along, it was "time for change."[7]

And change there was. The outcome of the 2008 presidential election was truly historic. A black president was something that many Americans, black and white, never thought they would see. Theologian, historian, and civil rights veteran Vincent Harding summed it up as a conundrum: an African American president, even after his election was a fact, was "impossible." On election night, Jesse Jackson could not hold back tears. He stood in

Chicago's Grant Park with thousands of others when president-elect Obama walked out with his family to address the crowd. Jackson himself had run for the presidency twice and won more than seven million primary votes in 1988, making him the most successful black candidate to that point. Jackson, however, had also stood with Martin Luther King, Jr. in 1968 on the balcony of the Lorraine Motel in Memphis at the very moment King was gunned down. Few could appreciate as Jackson could just how historic Senator Obama's win was.[8]

A historic event not only breaks new ground; it also connects the present with the past. For all that was new about the Obama, Clinton, and Palin candidacies, the 2008 election drew deeply on the patterns of America's political, racial, and gendered past. For African American men and women and for white women, that past was defined both by systematic exclusion from the official body politic and by generations of struggle to establish their legitimacy as citizens and gain access to political power. For all the candidates, the 2008 contest was framed by the nation's historic political structures and cultures—the two-party system and the histories of each party; the "rules of the road" governing everything from the Electoral College to fund-raising; and the myths, stories, and ideologies that shaped how Americans interpreted the candidates and the campaigns.

W. E. B. Du Bois called it the problem of "twoness," the difficulty of being at once "an American" and "a Negro." African Americans have had to assert that they were rightful citizens from the nation's founding, when the Constitution itself set the value of an enslaved black as but three-fifths of a person for purposes of electoral representation. Any doubts about whether African Americans were citizens before the Civil War were settled in the negative by the Supreme Court's *Dred Scott* decision in 1857. The postwar Fourteenth (1868) and Fifteenth (1870) amendments established that "all persons born or naturalized in the United States" are "citizens" and made African Americans eligible for suffrage, and for a few short years the freedmen voted in great numbers for the Republican "party of Lincoln" and elite black men held political office, including seats in Congress. Over time, however, even constitutional amendments failed to guarantee equal rights. In the bitter environment of the post-emancipation South, the right to participate in elections and hold political office proved short-lived once federal troops withdrew. Bolstered by Supreme Court decisions in the 1870s that rendered key provisions of the Fourteenth and Fifteenth amendments meaningless, white supremacists imposed Jim Crow over a period of decades with systematic campaigns of terror and lynching and used the Democratic Party to secure their gains. At the turn of the century, white supremacists enshrined disfranchisement in new state constitutions. That, they expected, would guarantee white supremacy for good.[9]

African Americans, however, fought back at every turn. In the century between emancipation and the civil rights victories of the 1950s and 1960s, they defended their families and property from attack. They sought justice in the courts. They migrated to cities in the South, North, and West in search of safety and opportunity. They sought spiritual strength in churches of their own and acquired educations in new schools and colleges. They testified before congressional committees, wrote public officials, and protested to press for change. Middle-class black women in particular created reform organizations to improve their communities and sought out progressive white women as allies. Black men eagerly sought out military service in the two world wars to prove their fitness for the rights and obligations of citizenship. Despite these constant challenges, however, white supremacy held fast until the mid-twentieth century, when black freedom movements gained traction.

White women's exclusions from political power followed a different path. Until well into the nineteenth century, the prevailing idea that male heads of households cast ballots on behalf of the family unit made woman suffrage nearly unthinkable. At the first woman's rights convention in 1848 at Seneca Falls, New York, the assembled women and men unanimously agreed to resolutions calling for "an overthrowing of the [male] monopoly of the pulpit" and for equal access for women to "the various trades, professions, and commerce." Elizabeth Cady Stanton's resolution calling for woman suffrage, however, provoked intense debate. Though it passed by a narrow margin, even as fierce an advocate of women's rights as Lucretia Mott had urged Stanton to withdraw it. "Thou will make us ridiculous," the Quaker Mott warned. "We must go slowly." When in the years after the Civil War the Fourteenth Amendment expressly limited some civic protections to men and the Fifteenth Amendment protected citizens from disfranchisement on the basis of race but not sex, suffragists organized, campaigned, and rallied. A few radicals, such as Susan B. Anthony, protested their exclusion by attempting to vote anyway.

Piecemeal suffrage victories in the 1890s and early 1900s enfranchised women for some elections or in some territories and states. Though many places permitted women to vote in school board elections and western states in particular granted white women a broad suffrage, even these gains were reversed in some locations by state legislatures or the courts. Progressive activists established women's roles as civic reformers and secured a place for women in government agencies, especially city governments, and the

Nineteenth Amendment, ratified in 1920, expanded woman suffrage broadly. A few exceptional women, such as Democrat Eleanor Roosevelt, Democratic strategist Belle Moskowitz, and Republican Harriet Taylor Upton, exercised substantial power within their party organizations, yet in the decades after ratification of the Nineteenth Amendment, women remained largely outside the halls of political power. Few women achieved elected office, much less high office, and many poor women and women of color continued to face obstacles to casting ballots.[10]

The freedom movements of the 1950s, 1960s, and 1970s dramatically expanded the opportunities available to white women and to men and women of color. Civil rights activists sacrificed blood and treasure to push back the reach of Jim Crow in schools, transportation, and public accommodations. They won sweeping victories when Congress passed the Civil Rights Act of 1964, which outlawed many discriminatory practices, and the Voting Rights Act of 1965, which established federal protections for voting. The Civil Rights Act benefited white women, too, because it prohibited discrimination on the basis of sex as well as race. In the second half of the decade, the women's liberation movement swelled and pressed the case for women's freedom in legislatures, the courts, and the streets. Feminist activists succeeded in securing greater reproductive freedom and fuller access to higher education, the workplace, and military service.

Men and women of color and white women took advantage of new opportunities for political participation and leadership. Blacks largely credited the Democratic Party of the 1960s with civil rights gains and rewarded Democratic candidates with their votes. Between 1964 and 1969, voter registration for African Americans in the South jumped from 35 percent to 65 percent. In 1967, Richard Hatcher in Gary, Indiana, and Carl Stokes in Cleveland became the first of a growing number of black mayors elected in northern cities. Leading feminist activists, black and white, at first worked closely with leaders in both parties through, for example, the bipartisan National Women's Political Caucus formed in 1971, but they soon found the Democratic Party much more responsive to their efforts. In the wake of the 1968 Democratic convention debacle in Chicago, activists pushed through new rules that changed the composition of the party's leadership for good, resulting in equal representation of women among the elected delegates to the party's quadrennial nominating conventions. The number of women elected to Congress jumped from twelve in 1966 to twenty-one in 1976, and most of them were Democrats. In 1972, their number included a handful of women of color, all Democrats: Barbara Jordan, Yvonne Burke, and

Cardiss Collins joined Patsy Mink (elected in 1964) and Shirley Chisholm (elected in 1968).[11]

Even as new constituencies gained access to political power through Democratic channels, the rightward tilt of American politics since the mid-1970s opened up opportunities for conservative women, too, most of whom were white. The Republican Party gained strength in the South in the aftermath of the civil rights victories, but it also picked up votes in the North over unpopular policies of forced busing and affirmative action. Mobilized by opposition to the U.S. Supreme Court's *Roe v. Wade* decision (1973), the effort to ratify the Equal Rights Amendment (ERA), and the Reagan revolution, conservative women organized through evangelical churches and antifeminist organizations and gained ground in the Republican Party, sending women such as Lynn Martin of Illinois and Paula Hawkins of Florida to Congress in 1980 and Barbara Vucanovich of Nevada in 1982.

Through the 1980s and 1990s, white women and African Americans, both women and men, continued to strengthen crucial political networks and move up in party organizations. Feminist strategists, combing through electoral results after state legislatures failed to ratify the ERA, discovered the emergence in 1980 of a "gender gap" in which women were both more likely to vote and more likely to vote Democratic than men. The gender gap helped Rep. Geraldine Ferraro (D-NY) secure the vice presidential spot on the 1984 Democratic ticket, but Ferraro was unable to rescue Walter Mondale's flagging campaign. The number of black members of the House expanded to twenty-three in 1986, and yet only five African-American women served there before 1990. Nineteen-ninety-two was dubbed "The Year of the Woman" as fifty-five women swept into Congress, including ten African American women and the first African American woman elected to the Senate, Carol Moseley Braun of Illinois.[12]

This is the political context in which Obama, Clinton, and Palin launched their bids for national office. Obama, whose first election win took him to the Illinois Senate in 1996, jumped to the U.S. Senate in 2004, becoming only the fifth African American to serve there. Clinton, whose 2000 bid for the Senate was her first race in her own right, became the first woman elected to that office from New York. Palin, a former small-town mayor, defeated an incumbent governor in 2006 to become the first female governor of Alaska and the youngest person to hold that office.

Certainly the history of these candidates' prior runs for office shaped their 2008 campaigns for president. But all of this history—the centuries of the political exclusion of white women and African American women and men; the struggles and setbacks as they created places for themselves in civic life as citizens, voters, party leaders, and elected officials; shifting political values and the changing fortunes and identities of the Democratic and Republican parties—shaped the conduct and meaning of the 2008 election. Obama, Clinton, and Palin could not have become serious candidates without the expansion of political opportunities over time, and above all the gains made by the freedom movements of the mid-twentieth century, but their successes in 2008 were hardly simple American success stories, happy highlights in an unceasing, distinctly American push for progress.

Rather, Obama's presence as a prominent candidate evoked the nation's complicated history of race relations, of enslavement and freedom, of Jim Crow and civil rights, of blackness and biraciality. Inevitably, conversations swirled around race even as his campaign tried to avoid the issue. The explosion of the Jeremiah Wright controversy in February prompted Obama to bring matters of race to the fore as he frankly described the "complexities of race in this country" as "a part of our union that we have yet to perfect." Clinton's candidacy seemed to some the pinnacle of feminist achievement, but Clinton kept her distance from feminist groups and touted parts of her résumé, such as her experience on the Senate Armed Services Committee, that countered charges of weakness that had held back female candidates for the presidency before. The extended primary contest between Obama and Clinton threatened to rip apart the coalition of white liberals, black civil rights advocates, organized labor, and feminists that had seemed to function as a liberal consensus since the early 1970s. And even though Palin was clearly a conservative, she seemed to many the very embodiment of feminist success—a powerful, independent woman who was also an attractive wife and loving mother, the iconic woman who "has it all." While these candidates were breaking barriers, they also were juggling the familiar tasks of a presidential bid—the need to raise enormous sums of money, to organize supporters, to master party machinery, and ultimately to win votes—even as those tasks were being transformed by new media technologies. For all that was new about the 2008 election, the past was inescapably present.[13]

The presence of the past in the 2008 election is the focus of the essays that follow. The essays in Part I explore how the candidates challenged, negotiated, manipulated, and sometimes reinforced historical stereotypes of gender and race that had long been used to justify the exclusion of white and black women and black men from civic life. Never had the American public been asked to re-imagine so completely what national leadership looks like, and historical stereotypes inevitably mediated the ways in which the candidates presented themselves, the media represented them, and the public understood them. If national leadership has historically looked masculine and white, then just what does a candidate do to help the public envision leadership as female or black? How does a white female or black male candidate "act presidential," anyway?

Kathryn Kish Sklar (Chapter 1) explores the intricate connections between the politics of gender, race, and class in Clinton's presidential bid. Leading nineteenth-century feminists such as Angelina Grimké, the daughter of South Carolina slaveholders who became one of the most popular public speakers in the antebellum North, championed both antiracism and antisexism, refusing to privilege the freedom of one group at the expense of another. Sklar argues that in 2008, Clinton made a different choice. In her determination to pass the "masculinity test" for commander in chief, Clinton molded herself into the candidate for "hard-working Americans, white Americans," failing the "race test" and setting back the cause of unity and justice for all Americans.[14]

Tiffany Ruby Patterson (Chapter 2) considers the Jeremiah Wright controversy against the background of historical stereotypes of black men as angry, irrational, and dangerous, stereotypes that have long been used to call into question the fitness of African Americans for full citizenship. She concludes that while Obama, as a candidate in 2008 and as president afterward, may need to deal with racial injustice dispassionately, genuine healing can take place only after African Americans are able to give full voice to their anger over generations of wrongs done.

Mitch Kachun (Chapter 3) shifts the focus to Michelle Obama, a figure whose family's experiences of enslavement, emancipation, and northward migration make her nearly as important a cultural figure as her husband. Kachun explains how media coverage of Michelle Obama during the campaign was shaped not only by Americans' expectations of prospective First Ladies, but by a long history of powerful stereotypes of black women and their bodies.

The essays in Part II make the case that the 2008 election took place within the context of American histories of freedom struggles, feminism, westward expansion, and the politics of "the people," histories that in some cases date back to before the Civil War.

Glenda Elizabeth Gilmore (Chapter 4) uncovers the significance of African American women's high voter turnout in the 2008 election. Black women's power as voters in 2008, she argues, originates in their political activism in the first half of the twentieth century. Here Gilmore offers a major new synthesis of African American women's politics by arguing that their efforts evolved from the "politics of association" (1900–1920) to the "politics of citizenship" (1920–30) to the "politics of community" (1930–40) to the "politics of protest" (1940–50). Barack Obama's victory, then, is in part the result of long-term efforts by black women to undo the damage inflicted by disfranchisement more than a century ago.

Tera W. Hunter (Chapter 5) sets up the basic dilemma of the Democratic primary contest: how would the competition between an African American man and a white woman affect the liberal coalition of African Americans, white liberals, feminists, and organized labor in place since the 1970s? Hunter decries the deterioration of the Democratic race into a debate over which group, African Americans or women, was more aggrieved and reminds us of the historical consequences of division. In the Civil War era, a progressive coalition of blacks and whites, women and men, succeeded in putting antislavery at the center of the nation's political agenda, only to split apart after the war in the debates over which group would get the vote first, a split that opened the way to nearly a century of Jim Crow, lynching, and the most egregious forms of discrimination. The Democratic Party would do better, Hunter argues, to recall instead the legacy of Shirley Chisholm, who in 1972 ran a principled campaign for president on a platform of antiracist, antisexist, pro-labor, and pro-peace policies.

Susan M. Hartmann (Chapter 6) analyzes the ways in which Clinton's campaign both built upon and departed from the campaigns of previous female contenders for the presidency, including Victoria Woodhull, Margaret Chase Smith, and Patricia Schroeder. Clinton's comparative success, Hartmann argues, can be explained by her unprecedented ability to raise funds and mobilize party networks. Her failure to win the presidency and join the ranks of Margaret Thatcher, Angela Merkel, and other female heads of state can be explained in part by the peculiar demands of presidential elections in the American constitutional system.

Melanie Gustafson (Chapter 7) assesses the Palin campaign as an exercise in political storytelling. In this media-saturated age in which party labels may not tell us much about a candidate, personal biography has become a key way that the public comes to "know" a candidate. Gustafson argues that the most effective storytelling for the Palin candidacy focused on her background as a westerner. By highlighting Palin's big-game hunting on the Alaskan frontier and her "maverick" record of reform in the state house, Republican operatives tried to embed Palin in a long line of stories of presidential candidates and the American West, from Teddy Roosevelt, the Rough-riding "cowboy president," to the wood-splitting, horseback-riding Ronald Reagan. Attentive as they were to the political possibilities of Palin's identity as a westerner, Gustafson shows that the Republican campaign never fully dealt with her identity as a western *woman*, despite the rich history of women's political advancement in the West, the region in which American women first won the right to vote and first held high political office.

Ronald P. Formisano (Chapter 8) highlights the populist strains in the 2008 campaigns and connects them to the nation's long history of politics "for the people." When "Joe the Plumber" heckled Obama in Toledo, when Clinton hoisted a brew at a bar in Indiana, when Palin proudly introduced herself to the nation as a "hockey mom," they were participating in a tradition of populist electoral appeals that can be traced back to the Whig Party's "Log Cabin and Hard Cider" campaign of 1840. Though populist campaigning took a digital turn in 2008 with the emergence of campaigning via interactive digital communications technologies, Formisano concludes that, as in the past, the populist rhetoric of the 2008 campaigns often had very little to do with policies that promoted the greatest good for the greatest number.

The essays in Part III explore some of the legacies of the 2008 election, not all of which were intended by either the candidates or the public at large. Paula Baker (Chapter 9) takes a critical look at the Internet fundraising techniques the Obama campaign perfected and argues that such techniques, combined with federal campaign contribution reporting requirements, pose an important challenge to political values that Americans have long embraced. Not only do the stunning amounts raised render obsolete the nation's four-decades-old system of public campaign financing; the fact that much of this money was raised from a large number of small donors, and that these donors can be readily identified in online campaign finance reports, challenges one of the most important innovations in the electoral process of the late nineteenth century, the secret ballot.

Catherine E. Rymph (Chapter 10) suggests that it is Palin's candidacy, rather than Clinton's, that gives us the better measure of the impact of the feminist movement of the past forty years. Rymph considers the seeming contradiction of a feminist, pro-life Republican and recalls a time, as recent as the mid-1970s, when feminist women filled the party's highest leadership roles. Rymph argues that Palin's ongoing popularity shows how profoundly the feminist movement has changed American values, for even conservative men and women who have long decried feminism enthusiastically embraced this working mother who prefers to be called "Ms."

The concluding essay by Elisabeth Israels Perry explores whether the categories of difference that set Americans apart from one another will ever, or should ever, cease to figure in assessments of a person's qualifications for office. Perry reflects upon what the essays in this collection can teach us about the stereotypes that surfaced during the 2008 campaign, the influence of past political struggles of white women and women and men of color on the election results, and the possible effect of that experience on future presidential races and on the larger political culture within which we live. Arguing that the elimination of categories of difference is neither reasonable nor necessarily desirable, Perry suggests that the acknowledgment of and respect for difference might be a better goal.

Together these authors illuminate how the 2008 presidential election both connects to and departs from the course of American history. They also look to the future. Obama, Clinton, and Palin continue to enjoy opportunities to make history. President Obama continues to promote a sweeping agenda to restore growth to a faltering economy and shift to a post-fossil-fuel future. Secretary of State Clinton continues to work to bring peace to the world's most troubled regions, especially the Middle East. Governor Palin has become the most visible champion of the powerful Tea Party movement, and she is the only person whom 70 percent of Republicans say they could vote for in a future presidential election. All three remain important public figures, and so these essays are hardly the last word. They do, however, help us make sense of a critical period in recent American history, a period that shapes our present and is sure to shape our future.

Notes

1. "Obama, Clinton Mark Infamous Civil Rights Clash," CNN, March 5, 2007, http://www.cnn.com.

2. "Senator Obama's Announcement," *New York Times*, February 10, 2007, http://www.nytimes.com.

3. "Hillary Clinton's Caucus Speech," *New York Times*, January 3, 2008, http://www.nytimes.com. For the visual, see the MSNBC news coverage of Clinton's concession speech captured at http://www.youtube.com/watch?v=dTn9WRiaqqw.

4. Jeff Zeleny and Patrick Healy, "Black Leader, a Clinton Ally, Tilts to Obama," *New York Times*, February 15, 2008, http://www.nytimes.com.

5. Adam Nagourney, "Appeals Evoking American Dream Rally Democrats," *New York Times*, August 26, 2008, http://www.nytimes.com; Patrick Healy, "Clinton Rallies Her Troops to Fight for Obama," August 27, 2008, http://www.nytimes.com; Kate Zernike, "Can You Cross Out 'Hillary' and Write 'Sarah'?" *New York Times*, August 30, 2008, http://www.nytimes.com.

6. Michael Cooper and Elisabeth Bumiller, "Alaskan Is McCain's Choice; First Woman on GOP Ticket," *New York Times*, August 29, 2008, http://www.nytimes.com.

7. Elisabeth Bumiller and Michael Cooper, "Obama Rebuffs McCain on Debate

Delay," *New York Times,* September 24, 2008, http://www.nytimes.com; Peter Baker and Jeff Zeleny, "Obama Repeats a Campaign Staple: Time for Change," *New York Times,* October 29, 2008, http://www.nytimes.com.

8. Vincent Harding, "Fannie Lou Hamer, Martin Luther King, and Obama's Other Ancestors," talk moderated at the University of Michigan–Dearborn, May 12, 2009.

9. W. E. B. Du Bois, *The Souls of Black Folk* (New York: Penguin Putnam, 1995), 45.

10. Nancy Hewitt articulates this point beautifully. See "From Seneca Falls to Suffrage? Reimagining a 'Master' Narrative in U.S. Women's History," in Nancy A. Hewitt, ed., *No Permanent Waves: Recasting Histories of U.S. Feminism* (New Brunswick, N.J.: Rutgers University Press, 2010), 15–38.

11. Steven F. Lawson, *Black Ballots: Voting Rights in the South, 1944–1969* (New York: Columbia University Press, 1976), 331; "Women in Congress," http://womenincongress.house.gov.

12. "Women in Congress," http://womenincongress.house.gov.

13. "Barack Obama's Speech on Race," *New York Times,* March 18, 2008, http://www.nytimes.com.

14. Kathy Kiely and Jill Lawrence, "Clinton Makes Case for Wide Appeal," *USA Today,* May 8, 2008, http://www.usatoday.com.

PART I
REPRESENTATIONS

Is Hillary Man Enough?
Is Barack Black Enough?
Is Michelle the New Jacqueline Kennedy?

CHAPTER 1

Hillary Rodham Clinton, the Race Question, and the "Masculine Mystique"

Kathryn Kish Sklar

How can we best place Hillary Clinton's primary campaign in historical perspective—what were its precedents, and what might unfold from it?[1] Of course, it's impossible to speak about her candidacy without also thinking about Barack Obama's—and once you start thinking about gender and race, can class be far behind?

Future historians might agree that Clinton's campaign revolved around three questions.

First, on the "woman question" Clinton's candidacy built on the gradual change that took place over two generations since 1930; she consolidated those changes into a permanent base for women presidential candidates in the future.

Second, on the "race question" Clinton's campaign built on the historic precedent of 1869 in which white women competed with Black men for the right to vote. Her example shows that future women candidates for president—Black or white—need to seek an alternative precedent for white feminists' history on the race question.

Third, Clinton's campaign prompts us to ask the "gender question" as well as the "woman question" and the "race question"—and ask questions about the relationship between gender and class. Why has gender remained so prominent in American politics and class so submerged in the past half century? How might the gender question be answered differently in the future?

On the "woman question," I agree with Katha Pollitt, who wrote in *The Nation* on June 6, 2008, "Thank you, Hillary, for opening the door for other women." Pollitt thought that "because [Clinton] normalized the concept of a woman running for President, she made it easier for women to run for every office, including the White House. That is one reason women and men of every party and candidate preference, and every ethnicity too, owe Hillary Clinton a standing ovation, even if they can't stand her."[2]

Jo Freeman charted changes in public opinion polls from 1930 to 1990. In 1937 only a third of respondents were willing to vote for a woman for president. By 1945 that figure grew to 50 percent. In 1972 (elevated by the Second Wave) it grew to 70 percent. And in 1990 it reached 90 percent, where it has stayed.[3]

So when Hillary Clinton's candidacy emerged in 2006, it built on seventy years of gradual change in public opinion with regard to women candidates for president.

But, of course, her candidacy was about more than "the woman question." Race, too, was deeply involved. And on this question Clinton failed to establish a path for future white women candidates. Her claim that more hardworking "white" Americans were voting for her exemplified her effort to use race to her advantage in ways that forever tarnished her reputation.[4]

What was she thinking?

Perhaps the historic precedent of 1869 was in her mind. That iconic moment shaped the woman suffrage movement for decades thereafter and has usually been interpreted as pitting the suffrage of white women against Black men. But if we step back and look at the broader context of that moment, we see that its origins in 1837 offer a more usable past for future women presidential candidates.

In 1869 the woman suffrage movement tried to find a place in the politics of the post–Civil War era. After a bloody Civil War accomplished the abolition of slavery, the Fifteenth Amendment to the Constitution was debated. Adopted in 1870, it declared: "The right of citizens of the United States to vote shall not be denied or abridged by the United States or by any State on account of race, color, or previous condition of servitude."

Suffragists were divided over this revolutionary amendment, which for the first time created a "national" citizenship. One group, led by Elizabeth Cady Stanton and Susan B. Anthony, decided not to support it because they wanted "sex" to be included in the protected categories. In 1869 they formed the National Woman Suffrage Association in New York and launched a periodical called *Revolution*. Feminist historians have generally seen them as radical in their insistence on women's rights. Another group, headed by Lucy Stone and Elizabeth Blackwell, supported the amendment and in 1869 formed the American Woman Suffrage Association in Boston. Feminist historians have generally seen them as more conservative.[5] Yet new views of these groups see them as quite similar, more mainstream than radical or conservative. If we measure radical change as the willingness to welcome the participation of Black women, neither group qualifies. Famously, from 1869 forward, Black women formed their own suffrage movement in local groups separate from these white national organizations.[6]

Yet these suffrage groups grew out of a moment of revolutionary change in 1837—when the women's rights movement first emerged to claim an equal place for women in American public life. A good way to measure their radical impulse is to notice that these 1837 white women condemned racism. Indeed, they generated a social justice legacy that American feminists have drawn on ever since.

Why was 1837 a more innovative moment than 1869 for white women's political achievements related to racial justice? Gerda Lerner answered that question forty years ago. Angelina Grimké led women in the antislavery movement to claim equal participation in American public life—as public speakers and movement leaders. Raised in a wealthy South Carolina slaveholding family, Grimké moved north in 1829 and became a fabulously popular antislavery speaker who, when attempts were made to silence her, insisted on her right to speak in public, declaring that "whatever is morally right for a man to do is morally right for a woman."[7]

Grimké's revolutionary leadership came out of a context in which antislavery women were courageous and well organized because they had to be. They and their male colleagues were seen as threats to the social order in the North as well as the South because that order depended on the profits generated by slavery. Their lives were constantly at risk. William Lloyd Garrison was dragged around Boston by a mob that placed a noose around his neck in 1835.

But rather than be silenced by this context, antislavery women spoke out. They held three unprecedented national conventions, beginning in 1837, when they asserted women's rights and condemned racism. Especially noteworthy is the way they drew on spiritual traditions to frame their revolution. They needed all the help they could get, and they drew on a higher law to assert women's rights and condemn racism.[8]

At the 1837 convention, their women's rights resolution declared: "The time has come for woman to move in that sphere which Providence has assigned her and no longer remain satisfied in the circumscribed limits with which corrupt custom and a perverted application of Scripture has encircled her."[9] Their antiracism resolution declared: "This convention do firmly believe that the existence of an unnatural prejudice against our colored population, ... is crushing them to the earth in our nominally Free States ... and ... we deem it a duty for every woman to pray to be delivered from such an unholy feeling."[10] Thus in this antiracist moment women were challenging entire patterns of the social order—the rule of white over Black as well as the rule of men over women—and they did so by asserting a higher law.

Women took the lead in this campaign against racism. Antislavery men did not meet in multiracial groups; it was too dangerous. In 1838, the second time women met in a national convention that drew white and Black women together, a mob estimated at ten thousand men burned the hall where they were meeting to the ground. They escaped with their lives by walking through the mob, white women on each side of every Black woman.[11]

The suffrage movement grew out of these social forces. The first women's rights convention, held in Seneca Falls, New York, in 1848, was convened by women who had met each other in the antislavery movement.

Yet the women's rights convention movement did not continue the campaign against racism that had begun in the antislavery movement. We know it did not, because we have the printed proceedings of about fifteen women's rights conventions held between 1848 and 1869.[12]

A search of these documents reveals only a single trace of the 1837 sentiment against northern racism, a resolution discussed at the women's rights convention in Worcester, Massachusetts, in 1850, which supported "equality before the law, without distinction of sex or color." No similar resolution appeared in any subsequent women's rights convention in the 1850s and 1860s, and the Worcester resolution unleashed a postconvention debate in which one convention leader declared, "The convention was not called to discuss the rights of color; and we think it was altogether irrelevant and unwise to introduce the question."[13]

Although former slave Sojourner Truth spoke at some of these women's rights conventions, nothing like the 1837 resolution appeared after 1850. Why not?

The best answer, in my view, is that because the women's rights conventions focused on secular, political issues, like married women's property rights, rather than the large moral issue of slavery, they did not need to cultivate the spiritual strength that informed the antislavery women, and, lacking that strength, they took the easy route of not challenging racism. Instead, they set their sights on non-utopian goals.[14]

Nevertheless, other groups of women did draw on the 1837 revolutionary legacy of challenging racism. For example, Josephine Griffing led a group of women in Washington, D.C., in the 1860s, which mobilized material support for recently freed slaves. She stood up to male reformers who insisted she was creating dependency by providing clothes, schooling, employment, and food.[15]

The legacy of 1837 is all around us today in the coalitions that feminists built across race. That legacy offers a foundation for future presidential candidates and allows us to see coalitions that are not visible when we focus on 1869. Hillary Clinton's ignominious missteps on race might have been avoided if she had taken to heart the brave example of 1837.

Another broader historical perspective might help future women candidates navigate another minefield in American politics—the gender question and its relationship to class. If Clinton did superbly on the woman question, and poorly on the race question, how did she fare on the gender question?

One doesn't have to be postmodern or Maureen Dowd to question Hillary's identity as a "woman." Many of her supporters within the political establishment viewed her as a surrogate for Bill. But since she self-identified as a "woman," and many of her grassroots supporters thought she represented "women," we can take her at her word and conclude that despite her imperfect record on women's issues, she demonstrated that a woman can stand the heat of our grueling political process and "perform" as well as any man.

In fact we can say that she "performed" especially well as a woman pretending to be a man. However, in that regard, her candidacy reminds us of the dominance of what we might call "the masculine mystique" in our political discourse.

Since at least 1964, that mystique has been aggressively asserted by the right wing of the Republican Party as part of their effort to obscure their class agenda. The "masculine mystique" has been crucial to their success in shifting wealth upward and in privatizing and impoverishing our commons. Beginning with Goldwater in 1964, and continuing more successfully with Ronald Reagan, Bush the father, and Bush the son, the masculine mystique has become a staple characteristic of American presidential campaigns. Dukakis and Kerry crucially failed masculinity tests, Dukakis with headgear in a tank, and Kerry windsurfing. Dukakis failed to appear fierce enough. And Kerry revealed his elite perspective on sports.

Hillary Clinton sustained the masculine mystique when she tried to discredit Obama as too feminine to be president. She campaigned as a woman, but she consistently made passing the masculinity test her top priority. When she entered the Senate in 2000, she sought a place on the Senate Armed Services Committee. When she supported the invasion of Iraq and refused to acknowledge the error of her judgment, she chose muscle flexing over reality testing. And when her campaign emphasized her capacities as a commander in chief who could answer the red telephone better than Obama and "obliterate" Iran, she proved her willingness to use muscle flexing as an electoral tactic.

Yet Clinton's embrace of "the masculine mystique" and militarist priorities left her behind the new curve that Obama created when he championed antiwar opinion. And her stance made many feminists realize that they couldn't support her just because she was a woman.

Hillary answered the "woman question" by showing that women can compete, but she failed the "race question" by choosing competition over coalition. And she failed the "gender question" by allowing the masculine mystique to distort her political agenda and obscure the class agendas of right-wing Republicans. She couldn't make a "gender" speech equivalent to Obama's "race" speech because she was herself playing a game of gender deception.

Thus the challenge for the next woman candidate—especially one who campaigns as a progressive—will be to demonstrate more than endurance and competence. She will need to meet the race question by drawing on the legacy of cross-race coalitions that enriches the history of women of all races in the United States. And perhaps her greatest boost to progressive agendas will be to expose the "masculine mystique" as dysfunctional and show us how to champion priorities based on human rather than macho values.

Notes

1. An earlier version of this essay was presented at "Two Historic Candidacies," Berkshire Conference in Women's History, June 14, 2008, Minneapolis, Minnesota.

2. Katha Pollitt, "Iron My Skirt," *The Nation,* June 5, 2008.

3. Jo Freeman, *We Will Be Heard: Women's Struggles for Political Power in the United States* (Lanham, Md.: Rowman and Littlefield, 2008), 102–3.

4. Kate Phillips, "Clinton Touts White Support," *New York Times,* May 8, 2006.

5. Ellen Dubois, *Feminism and Suffrage: The Emergence of an Independent Women's Movement in America, 1848–1869* (Ithaca, N.Y.: Cornell University Press, 1999).

6. See Gaylynn Welch, "Local and National Forces Shaping the American Woman Suffrage Movement, 1870–1890" (PhD dissertation, State University of New York, Binghamton, 2008) and Rosalyn Terborg-Penn, "Discontented Black Feminists: Prelude and Postscript to the Passage of the Nineteenth Amendment," in Lois Scharf and Joan Jensen, eds., *Decades of Discontent: The Women's Movement, 1920–1940* (Westport, Conn.: Greenwood Press, 1983).

7. Gerda Lerner, *The Grimké Sisters of South Carolina: Pioneers for Women's Rights and Abolition,* updated and rev. ed. (Chapel Hill: University of North Carolina Press, 2004), 139.

8. Kathryn Kish Sklar, "'The Throne of My Heart': Religion, Oratory, and Transat-

lantic Community in Angelina Grimké's Launching of Women's Rights, 1828–1838," in Kathryn Kish Sklar and James Brewer Stewart, eds., *Women's Rights and Transatlantic Antislavery in the Era of Emancipation* (New Haven, Conn.: Yale University Press, 2007), 211–41.

9. *Proceedings of the Anti-Slavery Convention of American Women, Held in the City of New-York, May 9th, 10th, 11th, and 12th, 1837* (New York: William S. Dorr, 1837), 9.

10. *Ibid.*, 13.

11. Sklar, *Women's Rights Emerges within the Antislavery Movement, 1830–1870* (New York: Bedford/St. Martin's, 2000); Gerda Lerner, "The Grimké Sisters and the Struggle against Race Prejudice," *Journal of Negro History* 26 (October 1963): 277–91.

12. See Nancy Isenberg, *Sex and Citizenship in Antebellum America* (Chapel Hill: University of North Carolina Press, 1998). No historical monograph, however, has yet focused on these printed proceedings.

13. *The Proceedings of the Woman's Rights Convention, Held at Worcester, October 23d and 24th, 1850* (Boston: Prentiss and Sawyer, 1851), 15; Jane Grey Swisshelm, "The Worcester Convention," *(Baltimore) Saturday Visiter* (November 2, 1850): 166. See also John McClymer, "How Do Contemporary Newspaper Accounts of the 1850 Worcester Woman's Rights Convention Enhance Our Understanding of the Issues Debated at That Meeting?" *Women and Social Movements in the United States, 1600–2000* 10, no. 1 (March 2006). The proceedings of women's rights conventions, 1848–69, are available as searchable, full-text sources on *Women and Social Movements*.

14. For more on the women's rights conventions of 1848–69, see Sklar, *Women's Rights Emerges within the Antislavery Movement*, 165–204.

15. Carol Faulkner, *Women's Radical Reconstruction: The Freedmen's Aid Movement* (Philadelphia: University of Pennsylvania Press, 2004).

CHAPTER 2

Barack Obama and the Politics of Anger

Tiffany Ruby Patterson

"God damn America!" blared from YouTube videos, CNN, MSNBC, Fox News, and many other media outlets in early 2008, in the heat of the presidential primary season. Black rage was making a frontal assault on America's consciousness. The sermons of a Chicago minister, Rev. Jeremiah Wright, exploded onto the nightly news and Internet blogs and remained there round the clock for months, pushing network ratings over the top as Americans pondered his particular understanding of God and the nation.

Wright, the former pastor of Trinity United Church of Christ, was no ordinary minister: he was the pastor of Barack Obama's church, the senator's mentor and friend. It was his relationship with Obama that catapulted Wright from obscurity to national prominence. Night after night, media gurus and pundits expressed outrage over the political interpretation of life in America for Afro-Americans and what that meant for a black candidate for the presidency as explained by an irate Wright, who minced no words and tempered no emotion. In one particularly incendiary sermon, Wright explained that Obama was not rich, white, or privileged and therefore did not fit the mold of the proper candidate for the presidency. Obama's opponents—Hillary Clinton and Rudy Giuliani—did. They *were* rich, white, and privileged. Hillary never endured her own people saying she was not white enough for the job (as some blacks argued that Obama was not black enough for the job). Hillary, Wright charged, never had a cab pass her up on a New York street because of her color. Most important of all, he reminded his audience, including those who were white, America left a legacy of horror that has shaped the lived experiences of blacks in America, a legacy for which America has not atoned.

Digging into biblical scripture, Wright declared that God will damn America for killing innocent people in Japan and Vietnam. But he expressed deep gratitude for serving a God who knows what it means to live in a society where black people are oppressed and yet teaches them to love their enemies. Wright trained his anger on blacks, as well, those he described who "don't get it." As the congregation cheered in agreement and approval, America was shocked! They had just discovered that there are black people in America who are still mad as hell!

This chapter examines how the Wright controversy placed racial matters and black rage at the center of the 2008 presidential campaign for several months, threatening to derail Barack Obama's bid for the most powerful office in the world. Early in the campaign, Obama and his staff avoided racial matters by focusing on the plight of the middle class and the working poor. There was no acknowledgment that those classes were refracted through race and gender, or that some groups within the middle class and working poor experienced the added burdens of racial oppression. Displaying his characteristic calm demeanor, Obama resisted any hint of anger or rage over the historic issues confronting black Americans. Indeed, in his well-known autobiography, *Dreams from My Father*, published more than a decade before his presidential bid, he had rejected those black thinkers and leaders, such as W. E. B. Du Bois, who failed to overcome their anger and disappointment and embraced instead those, such as Malcolm X, who found reasons for hope. More than a decade before he declared his candidacy for the presidency, a period in which he was tutored in his faith by Jeremiah Wright, Obama was already focused on a hopeful future for America.

But the Wright episode opened old wounds for Afro-Americans and reminded the American public that racial matters are ubiquitous in the American psyche and in its social and political realities. It was a reminder for Obama, as well. The Wright episode brought the issues of race front and center in the campaign and forced candidate Obama to reckon with the realities of America's racial past. Wright's rage and anger seemed to offer no hope for change, and few could bear to listen long enough to hear the anguish and the love that infused his rage and seeming hopelessness. To become blind with anger can indeed lead to hopelessness becoming part of the problem if anger is all one has to offer. But Wright offered much more. His political activity in Chicago and within religious circles suggests a belief in the possibility for change despite his growing frustrations. Indeed, Obama found inspiration in that same community and in Trinity church. Yet those who heard excerpts from Wright's sermons and who were predisposed to reject black anger out of hand understood Wright's rage as anti-American. Others, who believed that anger is always incompatible with efforts to make change, understood Wright's rage as hopelessness. Wright's rage, and the political reactions to it, created a dilemma for Obama.

When Obama delivered his speech "A More Perfect Union," on March 18, 2008, in Philadelphia, he had to confront the conundrum of race and racism in American society in order to challenge Wright's vision and insist on a hopeful future for America. The following comments will briefly consider the Wright controversy in historical perspective, examining his critiques of American society and U.S. imperial policy in relationship to the American jeremiadic traditions. The American jeremiad is an oratorical tradition that has, at least since the days of Jefferson, cried out warnings of the consequences of America's racial injustices, a tradition that the black church has long cultivated. The next section examines Obama's response to the Wright controversy and challenges his assertion that black rage and white anger are generated from the same source of oppression and that both are always counterproductive. Though racism's corrosive damage has touched immigrants and other people of color, most found a way to sidestep this racism by becoming white, an avenue not open to Afro-Americans. Finally, this essay concludes by suggesting that Afro-Americans, like all Americans, must be allowed a hearing in this country in whatever voice they choose. If we want hope for true racial reconciliation, we are obligated to listen.

The Wright Controversy and the Jeremiad Tradition

Jeremiah Wright became a household name when portions of several of his sermons migrated from the blogosphere to mainstream media. Before that, he was not a public figure but was well known in the religious community and among political activists. A decorated former U.S. Marine, Wright was born to a middle-class family, the son of a respected Baptist minister and a schoolteacher in Germantown, Philadelphia. By all accounts, Wright's life journey prepared him to expect success. He was educated at Virginia Union University, Howard University, the University of Chicago, and the United Theological Seminary. He served his country in the marine corps and the navy. Trained as a cardiopulmonary technician at the national Naval Medical Center in Bethesda, Maryland, Wright was part of the medical team that cared for President Lyndon B. Johnson after his 1966 surgery.

When Wright became pastor of Trinity United Church of Christ in Chicago in 1972, it was a small congregation of 250 people, with only about 90 who regularly attended. After three decades under his leadership, the church grew to become one of the largest in the United Church of Christ denomination, a mostly white group, boasting a membership of 8,000.[1] This growth was certainly a measure of Wright's personal success. Many of his congregants also achieved personal success, none more glaring than Barack Obama, who joined in 1992. But the vast majority of Wright's people, and so many within his view, remained shut out from America's promise. Located on the South Side of Chicago, Trinity placed Wright in the heart of the blight that plagued so many Afro-American communities.[2]

Within religious circles, Wright rose to national leadership as he led his congregation in addressing the impoverished world of the inner city, the disparities in housing, education, and economic opportunities. His church had grown to be a significant voice in Chicago politics and social justice movements, as well as a leading religious institution. Wright was not shy about mixing his spiritual messages with political analysis, and he made that plain in the fiery sermon in which he warned that America's racial sins could lead only to damnation and ruin. In the ears of mainstream America, however, his message of "God damn America" smacked of anti-Americanism. How could Obama attend such a church? As Maureen Dowd sneered, Wright was "wackadoodle."[3]

From January 1 to May 4, 2008, the Wright controversy was the most frequently reported news item, receiving roughly three to eight times more attention than did the second most frequently reported item, how the superdelegates were aligning in the primary process. It was covered four to nine times more heavily than John McCain's ties to lobbyists. Wright and his views received an avalanche of coverage compared to the meager attention given to the views of John Hagee, Pat Robertson, and Rod Parsley, all controversial and exceedingly right-wing clerics with a relationship to McCain, all personalities with outlandish beliefs. Media Matters for America reports that between February 27 and April 30—the 27th having been the date on which Hagee endorsed McCain in San Antonio while McCain was campaigning with Parsley in Ohio—the *New York Times* and *Washington Post* "published more than 12 times as many articles mentioning Wright and Obama as they did mentioning Hagee and McCain. In terms of editorials and op-eds, the ratio was even greater—more than 15 to 1."[4]

What had Wright said to attract this much attention? Phrases cut from several sermons outraged Americans. Media pundits claimed that he said that America deserved the attacks on September 11, though what he actually said was that 9/11 was *predictable*. He screamed from the pulpit that America was getting back what it had done to so many for so many years. He offered a laundry list of America's sins: America dropped bombs on Hiroshima and Nagasaki killing more people than those killed in the towers at the Trade Center and "never batted an eye"; 9/11 was not the worst attack of terrorism on American soil because thousands have been lynched in America and the nation was settled through genocidal wars against millions of indigenous people; thousands of Afro-Americans are imprisoned with unfair sentences for similar crimes committed by whites who receive lighter sentences; slavery, for which there has been no redress, built this country as millions remained shut out of America's promise.[5]

Of course, these assessments are true and well documented. Wright emphasized that this nation has treated Afro-Americans not as citizens or as humans and that slavery, segregation, ethnic cleansing, unjustified imprisonment, and economic injustice are testimony to the historical and continuing oppression that has destroyed so many black lives and continues to scar Afro-Americans.[6] Americans were horrified when they heard him say, "God damn America," out of context. What he did say was that God *will* damn America and any nation that carries out such crimes.[7] Not only is this message in keeping with the prophetic tradition in Afro-American thought, it is well within the genre of the American jeremiad, a form of speaking perfected by Jonathan Edwards, considered the most important religious thinker in American history. According to linguist Geneva Smitherman, "The jeremiad is a speech, sermon, or other form of public discourse in which the speaker critiques the society for its misdeeds and wrongdoings while holding out hope that this fall from Grace can be reversed if the country corrects its behavior and lives up to its divine mandate." The jeremiad renders a judgment upon those who transgress the moral codes of a nation, community, or group. A sermon with both biblical and political purposes, the jeremiad was a call to grace by seventeenth-century Puritans, who believed they were God's chosen people, "called by God to establish a new order, to create in this New World a nation that would be a symbol of liberty, freedom, and hope for peoples around the globe." Like the Puritans, Afro-Americans believed they were God's chosen, and the Black Jeremiad was their protest against slavery.[8] Though a doleful complaint, "the jeremiad's dark portrayal of current society never questioned America's promise and destiny," says David Howard-Pitney in his study entitled *The African American Jeremiad*.[9]

These judgments have been delivered by some of America's most illustrious leaders, including Thomas Jefferson, Frederick Douglass, and Martin Luther King, over the past two centuries. Two examples bear repeating. Commenting on the impact of slavery on the morals and manners of slaveholders, Jefferson, also a slaveholder and a man corrupted by slavery, opined:

> And can the liberties of a nation be thought secure when we have removed their only firm basis, a conviction in the minds of the people that these liberties are

the gift of God? That they are not to be violated but with his wrath? Indeed I tremble for my country when I reflect that God is just: that his justice cannot sleep for ever: that considering numbers, nature and natural means only, a revolution of the wheel of fortune, an exchange of situation is among possible events; that it may become probable by supernatural interference! The almighty has no attribute which can take side with us in such a contest.[10]

Frederick Douglass, too, condemned America's treatment of Afro-Americans. Invited by the by Rochester Ladies' Anti-Slavery Society to deliver a Fourth of July speech in 1852 commemorating the signing of the Declaration of Independence, he chose to deliver the speech on the fifth of July instead. It was a caustic assessment of America:

> What, to the American slave, is your 4th of July? I answer, a day that reveals to him more than all other days of the year, the gross injustice and cruelty to which he is the constant victim. To him your celebration is a sham; your boasted liberty an unholy license; your national greatness, swelling vanity; your sounds of rejoicing are empty and heartless; your shouts of liberty and equality, hollow mock; your prayers and hymns, your sermons and thanksgivings, with all your religious parade and solemnity, are to him mere bombast, fraud, deception, impiety, and hypocrisy—a thin veil to cover up crimes which would disgrace a nation of savages. There is not a nation of the earth guilty of practices more shocking and bloody than are the people of these United States at this very hour.[11]

Of course Jefferson's language is eloquent, with only a hint of some of the emotion that may have consumed him during the crafting of his statement. By contrast, Douglass, eloquent and moving in his language, undoubtedly expressed emotion in his oration that matched the fire in his words. He was speaking to an audience that was prepared to listen. Reverend Wright, too, was speaking to an audience that understood his words and passion. The American public, however, is unprepared for such cold and hard truths.

While one can argue with some of Wright's charges, such as his statement that America was the architect of the AIDS pandemic, most of his allegations are historically documented. Indeed, even the charge about the AIDS pandemic sounds plausible to Afro-Americans who are aware of the Tuskegee episode, where hundreds of black men infected with syphilis were denied treatment in a medical experiment carried out by the federal government.[12] White antiracist writer and activist Tim Wise is perceptive when he argues that "white folks have a hard time hearing these simple truths. We find it almost impossible to listen to an alternative version of reality." Wise is equally insightful when he argues that America has created a mountain of untruths to support the narrative of itself as the most democratic and just nation in the world. There is an arrogance of perfection in this country that will not permit that narrative to be critiqued, particularly from a group that has been one of its most debased victims.[13] Beyond the content of Wright's sermons, what most offended America and the media was Wright's tone, his unrelenting rage. He felt free to express his views in the sanctuary of his church. Americans cannot bear the anger of its victims. And for this travesty, he was demonized.

Candidate Obama had to confront the Wright issue and the question of race if he had any hope of becoming President Obama. But he avoided the issue of black rage. Wright gave complete voice to his rage over the historical treatment and current condition of Afro-Americans. By contrast, Obama was determined to play down the question of racism and to avoid the specter of the "angry black man," a politic decision, to be sure, considering that the presidency was at stake. Forced to comment on the Wright affair, he maintained his characteristic calm tone, severed his relationship with his church and with Wright, and blurred the question of black rage by equating it with white working-class anger. The collision of Wright's rage and Obama's calm, a collision created and manipulated by media and right-wing ideologues alike, threatened to derail Obama's candidacy in the Democratic primary, and thereby his opportunity to become president. Reverend Wright was driven by the history of unresolved racial tension and the continuing reality of racism in America. Senator Obama was constrained by that same tension and reality.

The attacks on Wright morphed into an attack on Obama. Obama was accused of sharing Wright's views, of being unpatriotic and unfit for office. His truthfulness was suspect when he claimed not to have heard these sermons. Even Hillary Clinton implied that he was not truthful and left the question open regarding his faith. Finally Obama condemned Wright, calling his comments "outrageous," full of "ridiculous propositions" that were "divisive and destructive," the product of a "very different vision of America."

Though much more can be said and needs to be said about this controversy, my concern here is the historical straitjacket that Afro-Americans have been in for two centuries regarding their freedom of speech. That jacket requires that the harsh truth of our lived experience be muted and that rage never be expressed forthrightly. The hurt and pain of racial oppression has had to be delivered only in eloquent language and always from the position of the supplicant.

This demand for an indirect or muted expression of anger was required in our writing and in our oration. This requirement has been predicated on the belief in our inferiority and doubt about our full humanity. Anger is an irrational emotion, to be sure, particularly if left unbridled, but it is also a very human and honest emotion. Given the degree of horror experienced by Afro-Americans, anger should be expected. But to display anger, it was feared, would suggest that we were less than rational.

In 1829, David Walker, a free black and abolitionist, addressed our right to express anger in his *Appeal* and rejected the idea that we should mute our rage over slavery and colonization. Indeed, Walker suggested that our captors should expect our rage. In "Blueprint for Negro Writing," published in 1937, Richard Wright demanded an end to prose that was "dressed in the kneepants of servility, curtsying to show that the Negro was not inferior, that he was human, and that he had a life comparable to that of other people." Though both these writers gave legitimacy to black rage, they also understood the perils of its expression in America. Hence, black writers, on the whole, exercised intense emotional control and public speakers followed suit. They understood that brutish rage was an indictment of our humanity and alleged to be the primary nature of the black character from slavery days to the present.

There are few spaces safe enough to release the pent-up frustrations and rage over our condition as black people. The hypocrisy inherent in the American narrative of a free and democratic society based on equality is deeply offensive to most Afro-Americans, though most will not say so in public. But in private, anger, resentment, and sometimes rage infect the atmosphere when the reality of our lived experience is the subject of the moment. Lettered intellectuals can play with words and pretty up horrific realities. But the need to be explicit remains. Our institutions, especially the church, were and continue to be the only safe place to unleash not only rage, but the hurt that comes with living in America. I recall seeing my mother cry in church on Sundays, and when I got the nerve to ask why she was crying, she replied, "Keep living child and you will, too." Yet I never saw her cry elsewhere, outside of funerals, while growing up. The church could contain all that we felt, our joys and our screams.

Jeremiah Wright allowed himself unmitigated release from the pulpit in front of a primarily black audience who fully understood his meaning. Once the media violated this sanctuary, a media bent on distortions without the tools or knowledge to understand the cultural space that they had entered, Wright became the perfect pariah to use against Obama.

It is important to note that Wright deserves critique just as he deserves defense in his right to speak. The media had no right to invade his church. He, on the other hand, was a disaster during his appearance at the Press Club in Washington, D.C. Stubborn and unprepared for the needling that most saw coming, he refused to listen to his peers, the clergy who suggested that he not go to that meeting. His distinctly masculine and egocentric pride took over, and he hurt himself and Obama. Obama was pushed into a position of either repudiating him or risking the election. Forced to choose between his pastor and political office, Obama found himself in an unfair predicament. The relationship between a pastor and parishioners is sacred. For Obama, it was even more. Wright brought him to his faith.[14]

Racism, White Anger, and Black Resistance

Obama delivered his speech in a climate charged by the uproar over Jeremiah Wright, the man he claimed as a spiritual mentor. He embraced his church, his pastor, and his community. "These people are a part of me. And they are part of America, this country that I love." For the first time in the campaign, he confronted the question of race directly: "race is an issue that I believe this nation cannot afford to ignore right now," he said, placing this issue in its historical context. "We need to remind ourselves that so many of the disparities that exist between the Afro-American community and the larger American community today can be traced directly to inequalities passed on from an earlier generation that suffered under the brutal legacy of slavery and Jim Crow." He continued to map the world that Wright came from. Legalized discrimination that blocked Afro-Americans from owning homes through denial of loans; exclusion from unions, police departments, fire departments; segregated education in inferior schools—all these things help to explain the economic conditions and achievement gaps for Afro-Americans. Lack of economic opportunity for black men, welfare policies that split families and render the community impoverished, even the absence of parks in neighborhoods "all helped to create a cycle of violence, blight and neglect that continues to haunt us." Obama also conceded that "for all those who scratched and clawed their way to get a piece of the American Dream, there were many who didn't make it—those who were ultimately defeated, in one way or another, by discrimination. That legacy of defeat was passed on to future generations." So was the "anger and the bitterness of those years." This was the real world of black existence that Wright railed against.

But as Obama tried to put this history into perspective, he compared the rage and bitterness of segments of the white community to Afro-Americans. "Most working and middle-class white Americans don't feel that they have been particularly privileged by their race. Their experience is the immigrant experience—as far as they're concerned no one handed them anything. They built it from scratch." Fair enough.

Obama wanted to be inclusive as he shifted from the cause of black rage to the bitterness and anger of working-class whites. While his assessment of this anger was perceptive, the reason for it stems from a very different historical source for whites than for Afro-Americans. White anger is part of a backlash that increased in the aftermath of the civil rights movement, a movement that tore down the walls of segregation and, despite its failures, went a long way in ending the most egregious forms of violence against blacks in this society. The civil rights movement leveled the playing field to a considerable extent, but it did not end racial discrimination. Many middle-class whites continue to view Afro-Americans through a racial lens, scapegoating them and their demands for equity as the cause of both *their* economic difficulties and the social transformations that brought crime to the inner cities. This is not to deny the impact of racism on segments of the white community.

Immigrants, too, have a history of suffering in this country. Who could forget the plight of Irish railroad workers in the 1870s, or the Italian dockworkers who were lynched in New Orleans in the 1890s, or the anti-Semitism leveled against Jews in the early twentieth century? But ethnics of European background not only ultimately benefited from their ability to move from an "off-white" status to the privileges of whiteness, they were and are free to express their anger when they feel discriminated against. Indeed, we are witnessing much of that anger in the Tea Party movement. However, modern-day immigrants of color, such as Mexicans, Puerto Ricans, and Middle Easterners, continue to suffer and, like Afro-Americans, find it difficult to express their anger regarding the racism that is often directed toward them in much the same way violence is directed toward blacks. Though they have been vocal in the past and are expressing their anger and discontent over issues like immigration and the building of mosques, they find themselves in an uphill battle. Given that Afro-Americans have made considerable noise about their condition, the struggle has been much more violent, longer, with fewer returns. In other words, Afro-Americans are punished for their anger as if the legacies of discrimination are no longer a factor in American society and we should be grateful for what we have gained and end our demand for equity.

Obama's speech was powerful in many respects and offers an approach to race and class matters that seeks to embrace the suffering of all poor people, a position advocated by Martin Luther King. But his view of history, like that of so many, is distorted in one significant way. The speech implies that anger, even righteous anger, should be left in the dustbin of the past. Yet he calls for white Americans to accept "that what ails the Afro-American community does not just exist in the minds of black people; that the legacy of discrimination—and current incidents of discrimination, while less overt than in the past—are real and must be addressed." But how can white Americans accept what ails the black community when they cannot listen to our anger?

The anger and rage of blacks stems from a very concrete history of terror and discrimination, while the anger of whites stems from a scapegoating of blacks and minorities rather than critiquing the greed in capitalism that sacrifices the working classes of all colors, a point Obama made in his speech when he said that "white resentments distracted attention from the real culprits of the middle-class squeeze—corporate culture rife with inside dealing, questionable accounting practices and short-term greed; a Washington dominated by lobbyists and special interests; economic policies that favor the few over the many." Obama's effort to bridge the divide between black and white is admirable, but the bridge can only be built out of bricks of truth.[15]

Obama is in a different position than Wright. He cannot lead with anger. This is the requirement of a national leader. But in repeating so often that his story is not possible anywhere else in the world but America, Obama unwittingly lets America off the hook. The fact that other slaveholding societies and the former colonial metropoles have not gone as far as America is not a testimony to American values, as he so often contends, but to the struggle of righteously indignant and justifiably raging Afro-Americans and progressives. Until America can bear to listen to its black citizens in all their registers, it will not be capable of making peace with its past.

Notes

1. "Jeremiah A. Wright, Jr. Biography," http://www.biography.com, and Eliott C. McLaughlin, "Reverend Wright More than Sound Bite, Obama's Ex-Pastor," April 29, 2008, http://www.cnn.com.

2. For studies of continuing poverty in Afro-American communities in the United States and Chicago, see Leon Litwack, *How Free Is Free? The Long Death of Jim Crow* (Cambridge, Mass.: Harvard University Press, 2009); Stephen Steinberg, *Turning Back: The Retreat from Racial Justice in American Thought and Policy* (Boston: Beacon Press, 1995) and his essay "The Myth of Concentrated Poverty" in Chester Hartman and Gregory D. Squires, eds., *The Integration Debate: Competing Futures for American Cities* (New York: Routledge, 2010); William Julius Wilson, *When*

Work Disappears: The World of the New Urban Poor (New York: Vintage Books, 1996). See also Will Guzzardi, "Poverty in Chicago: Recession Hits Poor, Uneducated, Minorities Hardest," May 6, 2010, http://www.huffingtonpost.com.

3. Maureen Dowd, "Haunting Obama's Dreams," *New York Times*, March 23, 2008, http://www.nytimes.com.

4. Ed Herman and David Peterson, "Jeremiah Wright in the Propaganda System," in *Dissident Voice: A Radical Newsletter in the Struggle for Peace and Social Justice*, September 18, 2008, http://dissidentvoice.org.

5. Tim Wise, "Jeremiah Wright, Barack Obama and the Unacceptability of Truth: Of National Lies and Racial America," in Alexander Cockburn and Jeffrey St. Clair., eds., *CounterPunch*, 2, http://www.counterpunch.org.

6. *Ibid.* See also Eliot Jaspin, *Buried in Bitter Waters: The Hidden History of Racial Cleansing in America* (New York: Basic Books, 2007).

7. Herman and Peterson, "Jeremiah Wright in the Propaganda System," 4.

8. Geneva Smitherman, "It's Been a Long Time Comin,' but Our Change Done Come," in Tracy Sharpley-Whiting, ed., *The Speech: Race and Barack Obama's "A More Perfect Union,"* (New York: Bloomsbury, 2009), 190. See also Alice Randall, "Barack in the Dirty, Dirty South," in Sharpley-Whiting, ed., *The Speech*, 210.

9. David Howard-Pitney, *The African American Jeremiad: Appeals for Justice in America* (Philadelphia: Temple University Press, 2005), 6. See also Sacvan Bercovitch, *The American Jeremiah* (Madison: University of Wisconsin Press, 1978), and Wilson Jeremiah Moses, *Black Messiahs and Uncle Toms: Social and Literary Manipulations of a Religious Myth* (University Park: Pennsylvania State University Press, 1982).

10. Merrill D. Peterson, ed., *Thomas Jefferson: Writings* (New York: Library of America, 1984), 289.

11. John Blassingame, John R. McKivigan, and Peter D. Hinks, eds., *The Frederick Douglass Papers*, ser. 1, vol. 2: Speeches, Debates, and Interviews, 1847–1854 (New Haven, Conn.: Yale University Press, 2000), 359–88.

12. For an excellent accounting of the Tuskegee syphilis episode, see the recent study by Susan Reverby, *Examining Tuskegee: The Infamous Syphilis Study and Its Legacy* (Chapel Hill: University of North Carolina Press, 2009), and the pioneering study by James H. Jones, *Bad Blood: The Tuskegee Syphilis Experiment*, rev. ed. (New York: Free Press, 1993).

13. Wise, "Jeremiah Wright, Barack Obama and the Unacceptability of Truth," 2–7.

14. See Obery Hendricks, "A More Perfect (High-Tech) Lynching: Obama, the Press, and Jeremiah Wright," in Sharpley-Whiting, *The Speech*, 155–83, for a discussion of the relationship between Jeremiah Wright and Barack Obama and the belief among many that Wright was unfairly demonized.

15. For history of the violence and discrimination against Afro-Americans, see the following: Douglas Blackmon, *Slavery by Any Other Name: The Re-Enslavement of Black Americans from the Civil War to World War II* (New York: Anchor Books, 2008); James W. Loewen, *Sundown Towns: A Hidden Dimension of American*

Racism (New York: Touchstone, 2006); Paul Ortiz, *The Hidden History of Black Organizing and White Violence in Florida from Reconstruction to the Bloody Election of 1920* (Los Angeles: University of California Press, 2005); Nan Elizabeth Woodruff, *American Congo: The African American Freedom Struggle in the Delta* (Cambridge, Mass.: Harvard University Press, 2003); James Allen, John Lewis, Leon Litwack, and Hilton Als, eds., *Without Sanctuary: Lynching Photography* (Santa Fe, N.M.: Twin Palms, 2001); Clyde Woods, *Development Arrested: The Blues and Plantation Power in the Mississippi Delta* (New York: Verso Press, 2000); and Leon F. Litwack, *Trouble in Mind: Black Southerners in the Age of Jim Crow* (New York: Knopf, 1998).

CHAPTER 3

Michelle Obama, the Media Circus, and America's Racial Obsession

Mitch Kachun

As momentous as it was for Americans to realize that a man of African descent had been elected president, for some it was just as meaningful that Barack Obama's wife, Michelle LaVaughn Robinson Obama, would become the first African American First Lady. In fact, in an important sense, her move to the White House might be even more historically meaningful than her husband's—for unlike her husband, Michelle Obama is a descendant of American slaves.

The *Washington Post* hardly can be said to have "broken" the story, since common sense alone was sufficient for most people to draw that conclusion, and the Robinson family clearly was cognizant of its connection with slavery. But the *Post*'s October 2, 2008, story, "A Family Tree Rooted in American Soil," offered genealogical and historical evidence that traced Mrs. Obama's family back to a specific plantation in South Carolina—apparently presenting information that even the Robinson family had not preserved or discovered. In a way that Barack Obama's story could not, *Post* writer Shailagh Murray observed, "Michelle Obama's family history—from slavery to Reconstruction to the Great Migration north—connects her to the essence of the African American experience."[1]

When Barack Obama declared his candidacy in 2007, American media commentators, Democratic and Republican opponents, and the American people rushed to gather information and take stock of this oddly named comet that had zoomed into the American political atmosphere. It did not take long before the candidate's wife was similarly thrust before the public and, with the possible exception of Hillary Clinton, scrutinized more extensively and more critically than any prospective First Lady in history. The *Post*'s genealogical research itself suggests the intensity of that scrutiny. The subsequent months of campaigning brought out the best and the worst of the

American people, the media, politicians, and political organizations. While praised and admired by many, Michelle Obama also became a target whose attackers utilized an ever-expanding twenty-four/seven cable news cycle and the unprecedented forum of the blogosphere to promulgate every sort of personal and political attack. In the process, they dredged up deep-seated stereotypes of African American women—the domineering "mammy," the hypersexualized "jezebel," the more recently minted "angry black woman"— and used them to construct an unappealing and even threatening image of the candidate's wife.

Before the mid-twentieth-century expansion of visual electronic media transformed American politics, presidential candidates' spouses could maintain a relatively low profile, both during the campaign and after the election. While earlier First Ladies such as Rachel Jackson and Eleanor Roosevelt had attracted considerable public attention, popular First Lady historian and biographer Carl Sferrazza Anthony argues that it was not until Jacqueline Kennedy that "the First Lady role alarmingly magnified from public persona into an exaggerated, larger-than-life image." By the early twenty-first century, national news media covering presidential campaigns had developed a sort of "journalistic shorthand" for discussing our "collective memory of the first lady institution." During the 2000 general election campaign, prospective First Ladies Tipper Gore and Laura Bush were discussed primarily in terms of their roles as escorts, advocates, and defenders of their husbands. Considerable attention was dedicated to the sacrifices they made in their careers and families to support their spouses' political ambitions, and their wariness in seeing their families take on the rigors of the campaign. There was also some discussion of each woman's charitable works or independent political and social agendas. And each was very much compared to the controversial outgoing First Lady, Hillary Clinton. To a large degree, both Bush and Gore were cast as the "anti-Hillary"—a woman who would support her husband, but who would not generate controversy or become an active policy adviser.[2]

In some respects, the twenty-first century has become the "post-Hillary" era with regard to public perceptions of the First Lady role. In 2004, First Lady Laura Bush and the challenger, Teresa Heinz Kerry, were again assessed largely in terms of how they compared with previous First Ladies. Would they approach their responsibilities in a "traditional" or "activist" manner? Would they be more like "Eleanor or Hillary, Bess or Mamie"? Each of these names—along with Jackie, Lady Bird, Pat, Betty, Rosalynn, Nancy, Barbara, and now Laura—conjures up certain images and associations in the American public imagination that, of course, belie the complexity and the human reality of the women themselves.³ As Michelle Obama entered this arena, she became virtually unique as a candidate's spouse. Not only was she the first African American vying to be First Lady on a major party ticket in a general election, but she also became the first to be so persistently compared with one of the most idealized First Ladies, and the woman who stimulated America's modern First Lady obsession: Jacqueline Kennedy.

The "Black Camelot" motif seemed to surface effortlessly in 2007 as a young, handsome, charismatic, and eloquent junior senator emerged as a candidate who inspired enthusiasm and hope in the American people. While both Obamas publicly discouraged such comparisons as unrealistic and irrelevant, many speculated that Michelle Obama and her husband's campaign in fact actively cultivated such an association. It didn't hurt that by 2008 both Senator Ted Kennedy and JFK's daughter Caroline Kennedy had placed the family's imprimatur on Barack Obama. *Vogue* editor-at-large André Leon Talley observed that "a black Camelot moment is the right moment for the Obamas" and that "the faux pearls, the A-line dresses, the Jackie flip are obviously all part of how [Michelle's] image strategy has evolved." Michelle's youth, attractiveness, and bearing may well have conjured images of Jackie with little assistance, but her choices of clothing, accessories, and hairstyle clinched the deal. Blogger "The Sweet 7" ran a June 2008 column featuring paired photographs of Michelle and Jackie (during her time as First Lady) wearing astoundingly similar fitted suits, solid-colored shifts, hairstyles, and pearl necklaces. With her "intelligence and graceful, sophisticated style," readers could plainly see, "Michelle O. is the black Jackie O." This attention to Michelle's "style" marked a significant departure from the minimal attention other recent candidates' spouses had received in that area. The online *New York Times* Fashion and Style section in January 2009 had a special segment devoted to Michelle, including links to *USA Today*, the *Chicago Tribune* (which called her "an American Fashion Icon"), and a Web site—Mrs. O—dedicated exclusively to following the fashion of the incoming First Lady.⁴

Shortly after the 2008 general election, another component of Michelle Obama's appearance drew the attention of the media—one which, to my knowledge, is virtually unique in modern presidential politics and which also brought racial attributes and attitudes front and center. In a November 18 column for Salon, Los Angeles–based journalist Erin Aubrey Kaplan expressed her great satisfaction that the new "First lady got back." "I'm a black woman," Kaplan wrote, "who never thought I'd see a powerful, beautiful female with a body like mine in the White House. Then I saw Michelle Obama—and her booty!" Kaplan purported to be writing in praise of the fact that Mrs. Obama possessed what she called "a solid, round, black, class-A *boo-tay*." In a campaign that made enormous efforts to mute race as a factor, "here was one clear signifier of blackness that couldn't be tamed, muted or otherwise made invisible." Kaplan argued that this most "vilified and fetishized" feature of black women's bodies would now be redeemed in a way that would negate centuries of racial, class, and status anxieties surrounding black physicality and sexuality. Others, not surprisingly, were offended and appalled by what Kaplan intended as a tribute. One black feminist blogger called Kaplan a "handmaiden of misogyny" and likened her to a "slave auctioneer . . . who decided to throw Michelle Obama up on the auction block so she could be one of the 'cool Black kids' this week over at Salon.com."[5]

That the ostensible praise of one black woman's physicality by another could be construed as such a negative and damaging message suggests the power that images of the black body—and black women—have long held in American culture. Michelle Obama's appearance, in fact, became the subject of blatantly nasty attacks from her husband's political opponents. Contributors to the pro–Hillary Clinton blog, Hillbuzz, consistently criticized Michelle for her physical appearance and fashion choices, with one post comparing her floral print dresses to sofa upholstery. Responding to rumors that Barack bought his wife a $30,000 diamond and rhodium ring, one writer suggested that "she doesn't have the class to carry off wearing a ring like that," while another opined, "I don't care what MOO-Bama wears . . . it won't make her look any better . . . well ok, maybe a burka. Now, she needs to work on those hips." To which the first poster rejoined, "A burka for mad michelle would work wonders."[6]

While these intensely mean-spirited personal comments may not represent most critics' tone and content, they do reflect the negative attention Michelle Obama has received from her husband's political opponents, independent bloggers and commentators, and even mainstream journalists. But these Hillbuzz criticisms, at least, do not appear to be inherently racial. They can be seen merely as another example in the long history of misogynist comments directed toward prominent women in the American public sphere. Ironically, these bloggers' own heroine, Hillary Clinton, endured very similar treatment as First Lady, U.S. senator, and presidential candidate. However, since early 2007 much of the public vilification of Michelle Obama has either overtly or subliminally drawn upon deeply rooted negative racial stereotypes of black women. Some even used Michelle's own comments to feed these fires. During the campaign, Michelle stated that America as a country was "just downright mean" and "guided by fear." She frankly discussed "the bitter legacy of racism and discrimination and oppression in this country" and what she called the "veil of impossibility" enshrouding many black Americans. As a black woman on the verge of moving into the White House, Michelle projected bemusement: "I'm not supposed to be here." These and other statements about America were interpreted by some as evidence that she did not fully appreciate the freedom and opportunity America offered and in fact was chastising America for its ongoing subversion of black opportunity. Such comments prompted the *National Review* to label her, on its June 2008 cover, "Mrs. Grievance." The magazine's White House correspondent, Byron York, called her "America's angriest would-be First Lady."[7] Less subtle critics simply branded her a racist.

That characterization was bolstered by selected excerpts from her 1985 Princeton senior thesis, "Princeton-Educated Blacks and the Black Community." This paper by a twenty-one-year-old woman more than two decades earlier was both trivialized as a "sophomoric, non-scholarly piece of drivel" and purposefully misrepresented as a reflection of the forty-four-year-old Michelle Obama's secret black separatist sensibility and agenda. Of course, it was neither. The thesis rather is a testimony to its time, reflecting a young black woman coming of age in an elite white-male-dominated institution during a perplexing period in the historical experiences of black Americans. As she benefited from affirmative action admission policies that gave her and many others entrée into the American professional class, millions of other African Americans remained mired in the poverty and quashed hopes of an urban America whose infrastructure had been gutted by decades of deindustrialization, neglect, and misguided public policy. There was good reason for Michelle Obama to feel that she was an outsider at Princeton—as she expressed it in the thesis, black first and a student second. There was also good reason for her to ponder elite-educated African Americans' dilemma, as they struggled with a kind of survivors' guilt, attempting to retain their identification with black culture and community while navigating an American higher-education system and business world defined by white cultural values. Her recognition in 1985 of distinct "White" and "Black" cultural worlds may not have sat well with many (especially many whites) in 2008, but it surely represents a thoughtful and valid investigation into the post–civil rights era in which she was coming of age.[8]

But the modern world of political maneuvering leaves little room for nuance or historical contextualization. As the thesis was cherry-picked for damning ideological tidbits, ludicrous accusations surfaced of Mrs. Obama allegedly "railing about whitey" at a Chicago women's forum. This charge was leveled first in May 2008 by a pro-Hillary blogger, and then picked up and disseminated in the blogosphere and on conservative talk radio and other mainstream media outlets. The existence of a tape was reportedly confirmed by numerous people, but the footage has yet to be seen or heard by the American public. Nonetheless, the pro-Hillary blog, Hillbuzz, was quick to accept the existence of the tape, condemning it as yet another example of "Michelle Obama's ranting and raving" and promising that, should Barack Obama be the Democratic nominee, the Republicans would coast to victory by "making Michelle Obama's anti-American, racist remarks the buzz of a general election campaign." Hillbuzz took this opportunity to remark further "that Michelle Obama is not known in Chicago as being a nice woman," adding the corroboration that "she's been rude, in person, to several of us at events held at the University of Chicago, so we have personally seen the 'real' Michelle in action."[9]

Thus emerged a relentless mission among many of Barack Obama's political opponents to expose an insidious "real Michelle" who was lurking beneath the smiling, friendly, stylish, down-to-earth, and all-American exterior the Obama campaign was presenting to the American public. African American comedienne Wanda Sykes called attention to the racial undertones of these insinuations in May 2009, during an appearance on *The Tonight Show with Jay Leno*. "There are, like, little subtle ways they, you know, they try to dance around the race issue," Sykes told Leno. "'Who is the real Michelle Obama? When will we see the real Michelle Obama?' And you know what they're saying is, when are we gonna see this? [Sykes then performs a stereotypical "angry black woman" head-shaking and finger-wagging gesture] . . . They're waiting for her to throw all his stuff out on the White House lawn . . . 'And you get the hell out my house' . . . That's what they're waiting for."[10]

Similarly, the Michelle whom readers encountered on Hillbuzz did not fit into the accepted frames of reference for prospective First Ladies. She was castigated even more savagely by anti-Obama blogs from the right. For example, the Obama File summed her up as "a depressing specimen of a post-modern class of victim—demanding, whining, self-absorbed, self-pitying, and infantile." The most fundamentally damning characterization was that Michelle was categorically un-American. Media coverage raised fears in many Americans that Michelle harbored a longstanding hatred of white America, a deep-seated bitterness, and a cynical view of America's ideals of freedom, equality, and justice. Even when playing an acceptable role by defending her husband against his detractors, critics chided her for appearing to blame any Americans daring to question Barack's credentials and qualifications for office. Her comment in a 2008 campaign appearance about being proud of her country for the first time in her adult life was connected by many observers with her sometimes critical comments about American society, decontextualized excerpts from her thesis, and her apparent penchant for "terrorist fist jabs." The message was that if Michelle could be compared with anyone, she was more an Angela Davis than a black Jackie O, more a stereotypical angry black woman than a potential First Lady. Even the infamous July 21, 2008, *New Yorker* cover, which intended to parody those irrational fears, was instead interpreted by many readers as confirming and validating them.[11]

Similarly, many felt that Michelle went beyond the accepted level of candidates' wives in expressing hesitancy to subject their families to the pressures and scrutiny of political campaigning and a potential move to the White House. The couple's two little girls' lives would be uprooted by the campaign and an election victory, and Michelle herself would be torn away from her Chicago home, family, and network of friends. Not to mention putting on hold her own professional ambitions and career aspirations. To many she seemed to dwell, far more than other wives, on what she termed the "inconvenience factor" in the decision to run. It was also widely reported that she held veto power over that decision and that she had made it clear that if the 2008 presidential campaign did not go the Obamas' way, there likely would not be another.

This attitude fed another image that some commentators used to construct Michelle as un-First-Lady-like—that of the domineering wife who publicly belittled her husband and who really wore the pants in the Obama family. This characterization played on a persistent variation of the "mammy" stereotype that has circulated in American culture since the nineteenth century: the "Sapphire" caricature. While the black mammy figure, both in slavery and afterward, was perceived as nurturing and protective of "her" white family, she was also frequently depicted in the twentieth century—perhaps most famously in the popular radio and television comedy *Amos 'n' Andy*—as a stern and heavy-handed controller of her black husband and family. This image of an inappropriately bossy Michelle was inadvertently supported by friends who referred to her as "the Taskmaster." One reported that in the Obama family, "Michelle is *totally* in control . . . She is friendly but very stern and sharp . . . and she is *very* involved in his decision making." As Barack Obama emerged as a seemingly flawless wunderkind in 2007, Michelle used campaign appearances to humanize her husband, saying he was too "snorey and stinky" for their daughters to cuddle with in bed, and telling stories about his poor bed-making skills and his inability to put his dirty socks in the hamper. Syndicated columnist Maureen Dowd worried in April 2007 that, rather than humanizing her husband, Michelle's "chiding was emasculating" and risked reducing this up-and-coming black leader to the status of "an undisciplined child." This image of the infantilized black male itself represents a deep and troubling component of America's racial legacy.[12]

Indeed, the white-dominated mainstream media—and Americans generally—were navigating a maze of cultural archetypes that have been deeply etched in Americans' racially tinged collective memory. Where did Michelle Obama "fit" in the range of stereotypes of black women? Was she a nurturing "mammy" devoted to protecting her family? Or a Sapphire—a domineering black woman bent on emasculating black men and controlling all who fell within her domain? Was she an "angry black woman" with a chip on her shoulder, casting blame for black Americans' oppressed status on an unnamed (but presumably white) "them"? With attention being directed even toward her "boo-tay" and Fox News referring to her as Barack's "baby mama"—a term implying a man's casual sexual consort who happened to have borne a child, rather than a life partner and devoted mother—Michelle has been associated implicitly with the "Jezebel" stereotype that casts black women as inherently wanton and hypersexualized harlots. One columnist termed this incident Fox News's "subliminal ghettoization of Michelle Obama." Was it—is it—possible for the American public to construct an image of Michelle Obama without at least subconscious reference to these powerful racial images?[13]

Michelle Obama is not unique for being placed in the media's crosshairs or for being oversimplified and reduced to a few narrowly defined stereotypes. Recent prospective First Ladies such as Hillary Clinton, Teresa Heinz Kerry, and Cindy McCain have garnered their fair share of harsh media scrutiny. But Michelle's identity as a black woman placed her in a uniquely complicated and vulnerable position. On the one hand, Michelle is a black Jackie Kennedy, an elegant and poised black woman destined to preside over a Black Camelot in the White House. She is the embodiment of black American upward mobility from slavery and Jim Crow through migration, civil rights, and education to professional and economic success. Even without her husband's political status, she is living a black American dream. She is a highly educated and highly skilled professional, an elegant and poised socialite, a compassionate and involved wife, mother, and homemaker. With her move into the White House, she became a powerful symbol of hope and possibility. At the same time, many of the racially charged negative images have persisted in American society well into her husband's presidency. In March 2009, conservative radio host Tammy Bruce mocked Michelle as pretentious, fake, and self-centered, and concluded that "we have trash in the White House." Shortly after the inauguration, Fox News commentator Juan Williams characterized Michelle as a potential liability to her husband because "she's got this Stokely Carmichael-in-a-designer-dress thing going. . . . Her instinct is to start with this blame America, you know, I'm the victim, and she'll go from being the new Jackie O to being something of an albatross." Michelle's physical appearance and fashion choices continued to fascinate the public, as evidenced by the inordinate attention she attracted in February 2009 for wearing sleeveless dresses that showed off her well-toned arms.[14]

During the campaign, though, the mainstream media seemed to back off from criticizing Michelle Obama by late summer 2008. This shift may have been partly due to the Obama campaign's efforts to exert more control over Michelle's public appearances and statements, but more than anything else it was because the media had a new female target—Republican vice presidential nominee Sarah Palin. While other essays in this volume assess Sarah Palin's impact on the American political scene, it bears noting here that the twenty-first-century media seems inordinately drawn to women in the political spotlight. And often not in a good way. African American women in recent national politics have certainly not been immune to criticism. During the 1990s, Anita Hill drew the ire of much of the nation for her allegations of misconduct against Supreme Court nominee Clarence Thomas. Around the same time, freshman California representative Maxine Waters rankled many in the white-male-dominated political establishment for her outspoken challenges to the status quo. Former Illinois senator Carol Moseley Braun and former Georgia representative Cynthia McKinney similarly endured criticism from politicians and pundits that seemed related to their race and gender as much as to their political positions. Whether black or white, politician or First Lady, from Hillary as First Lady to the outspoken candidate's wife Teresa Heinz Kerry, to Hillary as presidential contender, to Michelle to Sarah, the media seem to love having a woman to tear down.[15]

As Michelle Obama exercises her duties and defines her style and agenda as the nation's First Lady, her every move continues to be scrutinized. Some love her and some hate her. All modern First Ladies have faced similar risks. Yet Michelle Obama is different. As much as the Obamas, and to some extent the American people, want the Obama presidency to transcend race, in truth it cannot. Not yet. Michelle Obama, unlike her predecessors, will need to live with the added reality that she will for the foreseeable future be identified as America's first black First Lady. There seems little doubt that race will continue to play a role in the public perceptions surrounding Michelle Obama's tenure as First Lady. How these perceptions evolve during and beyond her occupancy of the White House will tell much about the woman, the nation she represents, and the legacy both will leave for future generations.

NOTES

1. Shailagh Murray, "A Family Tree Rooted in American Soil," *Washington Post*, October 2, 2008, http://www.washingtonpost.com.

2. Carl Sferrazza Anthony, *First Ladies, Volume II: The Saga of the Presidents' Wives and Their Power, 1961–1990* (New York: William Morrow, 1991), 44; Lisa M. Burns, "Collective Memory and the Candidates' Wives in the 2004 Presidential Campaign," *Rhetoric and Public Affairs,* special issue, *On the 2004 Presidential Election Campaign* 8, no. 4 (Winter 2005): 684–88; Betty Houchin Winfield and Barbara Friedman, "Gender Politics: New [or News?] Coverage of the Candidates' Wives in Campaign 2000," *Journal and Mass Communication Quarterly* 80, no. 3 (Autumn 2003): 548–66.

3. Burns, "Collective Memory and the Candidates' Wives," 684–88.

4. Talley quoted in Guy Trebay, "She Dresses to Win," *New York Times,* June 8, 2008, www.nytimes.com; "Black Camelot: Michelle Obama's Style," The Sweet 7, June 6, 2008, http://www.thesweet7.com ; "Michelle Obama's Fashion," *New York Times,* January 19, 2009, http://topics.nytimes.com; Mrs. O is located at http://www.mrs-o.org.

5. Erin Aubrey Kaplan, "First Lady Got Back," Salon, November 18, 2008, http://www.salon.com; "Michelle Obama's 'Booty' Put Up on the Auction Block by Salon.com," What About Our Daughters, November 18, 2008, http://www.whataboutourdaughters.com. While the tone and racialized nature of this discussion is unique, it should be noted that Jackie Kennedy stirred some controversy when paparazzi circulated photographs of her wearing swimsuits and other casual attire while she was vacationing with her Radziwill relatives in Italy in 1962. No First Lady had ever been represented in print wearing so little clothing. Many Americans were critical, while others praised her beauty and glamour and suggested that she had the makings of a Hollywood starlet. See Anthony, *First Ladies,* vol. 2, 76–77.

6. "Diamonds are Michelle Antoinette's Best Friends (While Appropriate Behavior Remains Her Worst Enemy)," Hillbuzz, December 1, 2008, http://hillbuzz.wordpress.com.

7. Byron York, "Michelle Obama Says 'Amen': America's Angriest Would-Be First Lady Wows 'Em in Charlotte," National Review Online, May 6, 2008, http://www.nationalreview.com; Lauren Collins, "The Other Obama: The Politics of Candor," *The New Yorker,* March 10, 2008, http://www.newyorker.com.

8. Jeffrey Ressner, "Michelle Obama Thesis Was on Racial Divide," *Politico,* http://www.politico.com; Dan Slater, "Campaign '08: Michelle Obama's Sidley Austin Years," *Wall Street Journal* (Law Blog), comment 5 by Colony14Author, http://blogs

.wsj.com/law/2008/06/23/campaign-08-michelle-obamas-sidley-austin-years; Sally Jacobs, "Learning to Be Michelle Obama," *Boston Globe*, June 15, 2008, http://www.bostonglobe.com.

9. "Michelle Obama Caught on Tape at Trinity United Making Racist Remarks," Hillbuzz, May 15, 2008, http://hillbuzz.blogspot.com.

10. Katherine Thompson, "Wanda Sykes Mocks Media's Michelle Coverage: 'They're Waiting for Weezy,'" Huffington Post, May 28, 2009, http://www.huffingtonpost.com; Vanessa Jones, "The Angry Black Woman," *Boston Globe*, April 20, 2004, http://www.bostonglobe.com.

11. "Michelle Obama," The Obama File, http://www.theobamafile.com/ObamaWife.htm; Diane Roberts, "Michelle Obama Endures Public Scrutiny," National Public Radio (NPR) *Weekend Edition*, Sunday, June 22, 2008, transcript at http://www.npr.org; Maureen Dowd, "Mincing Up Michelle," *New York Times*, June 11, 2009.

12. "Sapphire Caricature," Jim Crow Museum of Racist Memorabilia, http://www.ferris.edu/jimcrow/sapphire; Michael Powell and Jodi Kantor, "After Attacks, Michelle Obama Looks for a New Introduction," *New York Times*, June 18, 2008; Liza Mundy, *Michelle: A Biography* (New York, Simon and Schuster, 2008), 158, 183–84; Maureen Dowd, "She's Not Buttering Him Up," *New York Times*, April 25, 2007.

13. K. Emily Bond, "Who's Afraid of Michelle Obama?" *Bust* (October/November 2008): 56–59; Miles Marshall Lewis, "Baby Mama Drama," Salon, June 13, 2008, http://www.salon.com; "Jezebel Stereotype," Jim Crow Museum of Racist Memorabilia, http://www.ferris.edu/jimcrow/jezebel/.

14. Megan Slack, "Tammy Bruce Calls the Obamas 'Trash in the White House,'" Huffington Post, March 23, 2009, http://www.huffingtonpost.com; "Juan Williams Again Baselessly Attacked Michelle Obama, Claiming 'Her Instinct Is to Start with This "blame America" . . . stuff,'" MediaMatters, http://mediamatters.org/research/200901270002; "Up in Arms: Michelle Obama's Sleeveless Style Sparks Controversy," The Huffington Post, February 27, 2009, http://www.huffingtonpost.com.

15. Michael Powell and Jodi Kantor, "After Attacks, Michelle Obama Looks for a New Introduction," *New York Times*, June 18, 2008; James Forsyth, "Michelle Obama's Speech Was Cautious but Effective," The Spectator, Coffee House blog, http://www.spectator.co.uk/americano/1417786/michelle-obamas-speech-was-cautious-but-effective.thtml.

PART II
Historical Precedents, or How Election 2008 Began before the Civil War

CHAPTER 4

THE 2008 ELECTION, BLACK WOMEN'S POLITICS, AND THE LONG CIVIL RIGHTS MOVEMENT

Glenda Elizabeth Gilmore

In May 2009, the *New York Times* ran a story under this headline: "NO RACIAL GAP SEEN IN '08 VOTE TURNOUT" (Figure 1). Now, this *would have been* news, if only it had been true. It wasn't. The longstanding racial electoral gap in presidential elections, in which whites turn out to vote in higher percentages than other groups, narrowed to .9 percent but did not disappear. Black voter turnout was 65.2 percent, and white turnout was 66.1 percent. Thus, even though fewer blacks voted than whites, the *Times* reported that the gap "evaporated."[1]

The article continued: "black women turned out at a *higher* rate than any other racial, ethnic and gender group." This implies that black women did something *very* different from other identity groups in the election. In fact, at 68.8 percent, black women turned out in numbers only .8 percent higher than the next-highest group: white female eligible voters at 68 percent. The *Times* framed the article to imply that it's a trouncing when black women turn out in numbers .8 percent higher. However, when white people turn out in numbers .9 percent higher than black people, they aren't ahead; rather, "the longstanding gap between blacks and whites in voter participation evaporated in the presidential election."[2]

Figure 1. % Change in Voter Turnout Rates among Eligible Voters, 2008 and 2004

	2008	2004	% Change
ALL	63.6	63.8	−0.2
WHITE	66.1	67.2	−1.1
BLACK	65.2	60.3	4.9
HISPANIC	49.9	47.2	2.7
ASIAN	47.0	44.6	2.4

Source: Pew Center tabulations from the *Current Population Survey*, November Supplements Data

Looking at male voting patterns negates the story of the vanishing racial gap, as well. Of black male eligible voters, 60.7 percent turned out, 3.5 percent lower than the 64.2 percent turnout of white male eligible voters. Knowing that black men turned out in numbers 3.5 percent lower than white men did, with white voter turnout .9 percent higher than black voter turnout, one might question a headline that declares: "NO RACIAL GAP SEEN IN '08 VOTE TURNOUT." Perhaps this one would be more appropriate: "BLACK MEN'S TURNOUT LAGS AT POLLS, DESPITE BLACK MALE CANDIDATE FOR PRESIDENT" (Figure 2).

Certainly, Figure 2 indicates a receding tide of whiteness at the voting booth, but it also demonstrates three important points that go unmentioned in the *Times* story: the change has been evenly spread over two decades, it is incrementally small each year, and the white percentage decrease is due more to increases in Hispanic and Asian voting percentages than to a wave of black voters. The percentage of black voters (of those who actually cast votes in presidential elections) increased by only 2.3 percent in two decades, from 9.8 to 12.1 percent. Moreover, the Obama candidacy did not have a dramatic effect on the black vote share. The increase in the percentage of voters who were black between 1996 and 2000 was .9 percent, only slightly less than the 1.1 percent increase between 2004 and 2008. The *New York Times* headline might have read: "OBAMA CANDIDACY BRINGS ONLY A 1.1% INCREASE IN BLACK VOTE SHARE OVER 2004."

The Pew report upon which the *New York Times* story was based pointed out this fact, not mentioned in the *Times*: "The white share [of turnout] is the lowest ever, yet is still higher than the ... white share of the total U.S. population." Given the tone of the story, it is astonishing to discover that the white share of the total U.S. population is around 66 percent and that 76 percent of those who voted were white. Or by another measure, the white share of the voting-eligible population (adult citizens excluding felons) is 73.4 percent, yet 76.3 percent of the vote was white (Figure 3). Shouldn't

Figure 2. Voters by Race and Ethnicity (%): 1988 through 2008

	ASIAN	HISPANIC	BLACK	WHITE
1988		3.6	9.8	84.9
1992	1.2	3.8	9.9	84.6
1996	1.6	4.7	10.6	82.5
2000	1.8	5.4	11.5	80.7
2004	2.3	6.0	1.0	79.2
2008	2.5	7.4	12.1	76.3

Source: Pew Research Center

Figure 3. 2008 Actual Voters by Race and Ethnicity (%) compared to Voting Eligible Population (VEP) by Race and Ethnicity (%)

	% VOTERS	% VEP
ASIAN	2.5	3.4
HISPANIC	7.4	9.5
BLACK	12.1	11.8
WHITE	76.3	73.4

Source: *Pew Research Center*

that headline have read: "2008: WHITE PEOPLE STILL VOTE IN DISPROPORTIONATE NUMBERS"?

The real news wasn't that black women so far outdistanced other racial and gender groups, but that they turned out in greater percentages than they had in the past. Of eligible black women, 68.8 percent turned out to vote, an increase of 5.1 percent over 2004. It seems that 95 percent of them voted for Obama. Given that a higher percentage of eligible black women voters turned out than in recent years, you might ask if a greater percentage of those women voted for Obama than voted for Al Gore or John Kerry. If you did ask, you would have a hard time finding an answer, because historically there has been little analysis of black women's voting behavior.

For example, the few who *were* watching black women voters in the past two presidential elections found compelling indications that they would be a decisive factor in the 2008 election, perhaps even without Barack Obama's candidacy. Two weeks after the 2000 Gore/Bush debacle, political scientist Yvonne Scruggs-Leftwich wrote an article titled "Significance of Black Women's Vote Ignored." She argued that "the swing-vote power of the African-American women's vote has historically been largely overlooked, dismissed or relegated to footnote status, although it has determined key races." She proved that without black women's votes in the 2000 election, Al Gore would have lost Pennsylvania, Illinois, California, and possibly six more states. Moreover, it appears that in the year 2000, more than 90 percent of black women voted for Gore, that there was a record turnout of black women, and that black men's turnout lagged.[3]

In other words, all of the factors that resulted in Obama's sweep among black women voters were already in place for Gore, who was clearly not a handsome young black man endorsed by Oprah. After the 2000 election, Scruggs-Leftwich warned that polling data detailing black voter participation is "scant, late, [and] underused" by reporters. She suggested to Democrats that if they studied black women's voting behavior, they might gain insights into "future successful strategies for voter education and mobilization."[4] Few took her up on that suggestion.[5]

If the big media story of 2008—black women's voting patterns—was already old news in 2000, what was the new news? The very last paragraph of the *New York Times* story gives us a clue: there was "a distinct regional pattern in the state-by-state increases of turnout. From 2004 to 2008, the greatest increases in turnout rates were in Southern states with large black eligible voter populations: Mississippi, 8%; Georgia, 7.5%; North Carolina, 6.1%; Louisiana 6.0%; D.C., 6.9%."[6]

Six southern states set turnout records in 2008: those identified in the previous paragraph, plus Alabama and Virginia.[7] The dramatic increases are attributed to a dramatic rise in Democratic—and especially African American—voters in the southern states. North Carolina, Georgia, and Virginia showed the biggest jumps in Democratic voters in the South.

In the key state of North Carolina, Obama won by a mere 14,177 votes. According to the only exit-poll analysis available for the state, "an extraordinary 95% of the state's registered African-American voters turned out, with Obama carrying an unprecedented 100% of African-American females and African-Americans age 18 to 29. Comparatively, the overall turnout of all eligible voters in North Carolina was 69%."[8] In North Carolina's Wake County, Barack Obama won 57 percent of the votes, a crucial victory in this populous county that includes the state capitol. Anna Julia Cooper, a nineteenth-century black feminist from Wake County, wrote in 1892, "Only the black woman can say 'when and where I enter, in the quiet, undisputed dignity of my womanhood, without violence and without suing or special patronage, then and there the whole Negro race enters with me.'"[9] Anna Julia Cooper predicted that black women's full participation in public life would signal true opportunity for all African Americans, but she had no idea that it would take one hundred years to recognize that promise. Black women made a crucial difference in Barack Obama's election.

Thus a more accurate *New York Times* headline might have read, "IT TOOK OVER A CENTURY TO OVERCOME DISFRANCHISEMENT." That triumph is directly linked to an incremental reversal of voting procedures that were originally put into place in southern states at the turn of the twentieth century. From 1890 until 1908, the former Confederate states disfranchised their African American citizens through a series of tricks to suppress voter turnout. Some of these tricks—for example, the grandfather clause, which proclaimed that you could waive a literacy test if your grandfather had voted—were so blatantly unconstitutional that even the Jim Crow Supreme Court of 1913 ruled them out. Literacy tests worked until the Voting Rights

Act of 1964, and the Twenty-fourth Amendment to the Constitution outlawed the poll tax the same year.[10]

Southern African Americans began voting in robust numbers for the first time in the presidential election of 1968, and the national black voting participation rate hovered in the 50 percent range for most of the period from 1972 to 1988, falling to 43 percent in 1984.[11] Registration and turnout numbers then rose steadily from 1988, when 9.8 percent of the voting population was African American, until 2008, when that percentage went to 12.1 percent.[12]

One might speculate that Obama's victory in North Carolina and the large voter turnout increase in the South depended in part on making it easier to register and vote. For example, in North Carolina, "early voting" not only allowed people to vote from October 16 to November 1, including Saturdays, it also allowed people to register and vote at the same time during that period at "one-stop voting sites." Georgia implemented "no-excuse absentee" voting, making it a personal choice whether one would vote absentee or go to the polls.[13] Other southern states that disfranchised black voters in the 1890s now enfranchise them through early voting: Arkansas, Florida, Georgia, Louisiana, North Carolina, Tennessee, and Texas all had either early voting or no-excuse absentee voting in the 2008 election. Yet Mississippi, which also recorded a record turnout, had neither.[14]

Given the lack of historical and contextual analysis of black women's politics, some in the media found it easy to exaggerate black women's political influence in the 2008 election. For example, an inspiring photograph of a young black woman with an American flag in one hand and a button that read "I voted for Obama" ran beside Byron York's column in the conservative *Washington Examiner*. Perhaps its purpose was not to inspire but to alarm its overwhelmingly white readership and argue that black women voters wanted to increase their welfare benefits. York's column used the photograph to illustrate his argument that Obama's "sky-high ratings among African-Americans make some of his positions appear a bit more popular than they actually are."[15] Than they *actually* are? Bloggers immediately jumped on York, pointing out how his notion that black opinion "skews" polls is a bit racist.

York's column reminded me that black people were disfranchised in the South at the turn of the twentieth century because of the *high* level of their political participation, not because they were operating outside of a government of laws or wanted to overthrow the system. The problem, according to the white people, was that they were in the system and their votes made some candidates seem more popular than they "actually" were. In some southern states in the 1880s and 1890s, the black vote was the swing vote, just as it was in the last presidential election in some states. What does our lack of knowledge about black women's politics cost us? It's important for historians to provide the facts so that pundits don't make them up, which is what they are doing as they cast black women as interlopers in the electorate, energized by Oprah and determined to make Barack Obama more popular than he *actually* is.

Extracting the story of black women's politics from the larger American political history in which it is generally embedded—indeed, hidden—illuminates not only voting behavior in the 2008 presidential election, but also how minority constituencies forge tactics to turn dominant political systems to their own advantage. Moreover, understanding black women's politics underscores the need to look at black politics across the entire twentieth century, even though most (but not all) African Americans were disfranchised in the South until the mid-1960s. To find black women's politics in the twentieth century, you have to look long and you have to look low, under the radar of most political scientists, many historians, and the media. Only when you see the century-long campaign that generations of black women carried out that culminated in the 2008 election can you begin to understand democracy's agonizing march toward inclusion.

It took a century for the single most influential group of voters in the 2008 election to win their swing-vote power, and any shorter chronology of the civil rights movement occludes and distorts that political trajectory. A history of black women's politics in the first half of the twentieth century, painted in broad brush strokes, demonstrates how little black women's politics figures into traditional accounts of elections and how long it took them to gain influence in the polity. Despite the clumsiness of condensing a century of black women's politics, it is vital at this moment to launch a counternarrative to the triumphalism that the national experience with the civil rights movement of the 1950s and 1960s has inadvertently inspired. That triumphalism argues that the United States had some terrible race problems, which we quite handily fixed in the twenty-year period from 1950 to 1970. Thereafter, everyone had equal opportunity in a color-blind society. According to this interpretation, if, as late as 2008, groups voted based on identity politics, they voted for their own special interests rather than for the good of the country. We must be able to interpret the 2008 election in ways that can compete with such facile paradigms of the inherent progressivism of U.S. democracy.

Black women's politics in the twentieth century from 1900 to 1950 might be divided into four political strategies, indeed, political cultures, that dominated consecutive periods in turn. Black women moved from one constellation of strategies to another, adding new approaches to their political practices when national, state, and municipal politics changed around them. The dominant political culture of one period contributed to the next and the next. In other words, these political phases were mutually constitutive. However, in each of the four periods, one can identify a characteristic set of strategies in response to the protean nature of the politics of white supremacy:

The politics of association, 1900–1920
The politics of citizenship, 1920–30
The politics of community, 1930–40
The politics of protest, 1940–50

In the first twenty years of the century, black women sought and found the protective cover of churches and women's clubs—the *politics of association*—to work as agents of reform when black men could not. After the disfranchisement of southern black men in every former Confederate state at the turn of the twentieth century, black women stepped forward in groups to participate in government under the cloak of clients of the state. With their husbands, brothers, and sons unable to vote (for the most part) from 1900 to 1920, black women understood that their communities had to interact with white governments in practical ways. They deliberately disguised their politics within issues of family, law and order, and public health to avoid the semblance of participating in the electoral process. Through their churches and women's groups, black women across the South were community organizers in the first twenty years of the century. They lobbied city councils for playgrounds, promised to clean up neighborhoods, and founded Young Women's Christian Associations to help recent arrivals from the farm adjust to life in growing southern towns. They learned to camouflage their politics in a rhetoric of public good—for both black and white people—and to use their positions as club and church leaders to gain a modicum of power through brokering between white supremacy and black clients.[16]

Even as hard as they worked to be a part of Progressive Era reform in southern cities, many African Americans chose to move to northern cities, where black men and women hoped to find jobs, safety, and educations for their children. The Great Migration, the largest movement of a population in peacetime, resulted, by World War I, in urban black populations large enough to influence local elections. World War I hastened their political involvement. In 1917, black women took to the streets of New York City to march in sweltering July heat in silent protest against lynchings in the Midwest and South.[17] As long as they remained in the South, most African Americans had voted Republican to recognize the party of Lincoln and their enfranchisers during Reconstruction. In the North, some began to register as Democrats.

For example, 28 percent of black voters in Harlem voted Democratic in 1924.[18] With their husbands ejected from southern politics, black women used community organizing, relocation, and public protest to influence politics. If we overlook the long history of black women using those tactics in their communities, we can't understand Rosa Parks's place in it.

After women gained the right to vote in 1920, black women used the decade to practice a *politics of citizenship*. Their fight to be included in women's registration was a stealth campaign organized across the South through churches and women's clubs that left permanent political alliances among black women voters. When black women registered in the South, they opened space for black men to return to the polls in increasing numbers in the late 1920s, at least in urban areas. Their registration as Republicans in the North gave them immediate clout in elections and party positions; for example, in New Jersey, white male politicians began at once addressing their club meetings, asking for votes, and promising consideration for those votes. Their registration in the South in small numbers—often as Democrats—represented a canary in the mine that presaged the political realignment of most African Americans from the Republican Party into the Democratic Party in the 1930s.[19] For example, in Chicago, only 5 percent of the city's black voters voted Democratic in 1924, however, in 1928, 29 percent did. Women voters may have deserted the Republican Party more quickly than men did because their voting allegiance dated back only to 1920, and the Republicans did little for African Americans in those years.[20] Moreover, women's anti-lynching campaigns relocated, as Rosalyn Terborg-Penn reminds us, from the streets to the Oval Office when delegates of the National Association of Colored Women met with Republican president Warren G. Harding.[21] Black women built upon the politics of association to exercise citizenship through traditional channels of parties, precincts, and polls in the 1920s.

The frustrations that they encountered forged a politics of voting rights and inalienably connected education and politics, because literacy tests were a tool of disfranchisement. This is not to imply that black women's activism in the 1920s left some mystical memory on which students drew forty years later to register people in Mississippi. Rather, the *same* black women who jumped into electoral politics in the 1920s *became* voting-rights strategists in the 1960s. Women such as Septima Clark of South Carolina or Ella Baker of North Carolina witnessed the black women's campaign to register and vote in their states in the 1920s. Clark founded the Freedom Schools to teach adults literacy so that they could register and vote in the 1960s, and Baker founded the Student Nonviolent Coordinating Committee to go into communities and register those voters in the same decade.[22] If we omit the politics of citizenship in the 1920s, with its foundational voting-rights strategies of registration, party action, and lobbying, we never get to the Freedom Summer of 1964.

The crisis of the Great Depression brought cross-class political alliances among black women that empowered those working women who might have been less politically involved in the first thirty years of the century. This *politics of community* turned to the left as the crisis worsened. For example, of ninety-five members of the Communist Party in Virginia, North Carolina, and South Carolina in 1931, twenty-three were black women. And it wasn't just Communists who noted that black women could be counted on during strikes because they "show a fighting spirit with which the bosses must reckon." The politics of community in the 1930s meant pulling scant resources into education, for example, through adult literacy programs in which Ella Baker and Pauli Murray worked in Harlem. Septima Clark of South Carolina began to teach adult literacy there in the 1930s. Another African American political strategy of the Great Depression, "Don't Buy Where You Can't Work" campaigns, represented *gendered consumer* politics. Black neighbors began to boycott stores that refused to hire African Americans. The National Association for the Advancement of Colored People certainly helped plan and execute these boycotts, but women carried them out in their own communities. They were primarily women's boycotts that used consumption as a political weapon.[23] If we omit black women's politics of community in the 1930s—a radical left that organized working women, used education as a political tool, and executed boycotts—we can't find our way to neighborhood leaders in the civil rights movement such as Fannie Lou Hamer or Joanne Robinson in the Montgomery Bus Boycott.

As World War II mobilized black men to fight on the front lines, it inspired black women to cross the boundary into public protest on the home front. In the relative absence of men, the Double V Campaign and the March on Washington Movement depended on black women's *politics of protest*. For example, Pauli Murray, a young black woman teacher in adult education programs in New York, had been studying Gandhian techniques of nonviolence when she refused to stay seated in the back of a bus in 1940 in Petersburg, Virginia. After being arrested and convicted, she chose to go to jail rather than pay a fine, using Gandhi as her role model. Four years later, Irene Morgan refused to give up her bus seat, a refusal that the U.S. Supreme Court ratified when it found that forcing interstate passengers to abide by Virginia segregation law put an "unconstitutional burden on interstate commerce."[24]

When, as a Howard University law student, Pauli Murray led a sit-in movement in Washington, D.C., in 1943 and 1944, she said she did it for the black soldiers who could not join her. When Murray complained to Asa

Philip Randolph that she despaired of getting help from people in FDR's administration, Randolph reminded Murray that "a mass movement" didn't develop from leaders, but that "competency and conviction grow out of the movement. They are seldom brought to it."[25] Black women's politics of protest in the 1940s built the foundation of the civil rights movement ten years later. If we ignore the "stool sitting technique" that Murray practiced in 1943 at Little Palace Restaurant in D.C., we will never understand the occupation of those other stools at Woolworth's lunch counter in Greensboro in 1960.

A robust debate rages about how historians should characterize the struggle for civil rights that African Americans waged throughout the twentieth century. Some, most notably those who have focused on the 1950s and 1960s in their own work, argue that discussion of a civil rights *movement* should be limited to the decade from the mid-1950s to the mid-1960s, when black southerners marched in the streets, staged sit-ins in public accommodations, registered to vote in the Deep South, and attempted to integrate southern public schools. They argue that a "long civil rights movement" detracts from those heroic moments.[26] However, understanding black women's politics during the twentieth century demands extension of the Montgomery-to-Memphis narrative.

What's at stake for a history of black women's politics if we limit the period of the civil rights movement to the classical period of the 1950s and 1960s? If one sees the key events in the black citizenship struggle as taking place within that brief period, the fight seems shorter, and therefore easier, than it actually was. The civil rights movement becomes something that broke out, sort of like the measles, fixed the problem of racism in a decade, and then receded. If we take into account that black women fought for civil rights for the entire century, white supremacy looks tougher and more protean. If we allow that the laudable victories they achieved in the classical period of the civil rights movement represented only a part of their agenda, it becomes difficult to imagine that we are now in a "post-racial society." If we understand that all of the strategies that succeeded in the classical period had been tried in the first half of the twentieth century, the analyses of social movements that are based on studying movement tactics are on much shakier ground. If we look over the entire century, black women play a much more important role in the fight for civil rights.

The single most important reason one should characterize the civil rights movement as a long struggle is that the edifice of white supremacy was long-lived. Established in the U.S. South in the 1890s, it stood firm until the 1960s. If southern black people fought for seventy years against a white supremacist legal and social system that ruled every detail of their lives, why would one look at only the last ten years of their attack on it? Such a short view gives credit only to the action that toppled the edifice, not the seven decades of activism that undermined it.[27]

In fact, the 2008 presidential election results prove that the effects of white supremacy and disfranchisement linger still, though in decreasing measure. The cultural confusion that surrounded commentaries and analysis of black women's voting participation in 2008 resulted from truncating the long arc of African American history in the twentieth century. Our ignorance about black women's politics comes at a high cost. From 1900 to 1950, black women pioneered the politics of association, of citizenship, of community, and of protest before the period that we traditionally think of as the civil rights movement. If we include that half century in the civil rights movement, we gain new insights into the sources of social change over the American Century. Gender matters, white supremacy seems more protean, secular organizations take on more importance, the left takes a place at the table, and social-protest practices that appear to have failed leap to the forefront as necessary incrementalism. If we simply attend to the civil rights movement of the 1950s, black men in suits come out of nowhere to radicalize the nation.

If we lose the history of the long civil rights movement, black women vote for Barack Obama because he is cute, because Oprah told them to, and because they want to increase welfare. Sometimes it takes the long view to see which way the arc of justice bends.

Notes

1. Sam Roberts, "No Racial Gap Seen in '08 Vote Turnout," *New York Times*, May 1, 2009, http://www.nytimes.com; Mark Hugo Lopez and Paul Taylor, "Dissecting the 2008 Electorate: The Most Diverse in U.S. History," April 30, 2009, http://pewhispanic.org.

2. Roberts, "No Racial Gap."

3. Yvonne Scruggs-Leftwich, "Significance of Black Women's Vote Ignored," *Womensnews*, November 15, 2000.

4. Ibid.; Yvonne Scruggs-Leftwich, *Sound Bites of Protest* (Chicago: Third World Press, 2008).

5. Among the best works on black women's voting behavior are Rosalyn Terborg-Penn, *African American Women in the Struggle for the Vote, 1850–1920* (Bloomington: Indiana University Press, 1998); Cathy J. Cohen, Kathleen B. Jones, and Joan C. Tronto, eds., *Women Transforming Politics: An Alternative Reader* (New York: New York University Press, 1997); Deborah Gray White, *Too Heavy a Load:*

Black Women in Defense of Themselves (New York: Norton, 1998); Dianne M. Pinderhughes, *Race and Ethnicity in Chicago Politics: A Reexamination of Pluralist Theory* (Urbana: University of Illinois Press, 1987).

6. Mark Hugo Lopez and Paul Taylor, "Dissecting the 2008 Electorate."

7. Chris Kromm, "Election 2008: South Sets Records in Voter Turnout, Rest of Nation about the Same," http://southernstudies.org/2008/11/election-2008-south-sets-records-in.html. These figures are based on Curtis Gans's report, which counts turnout as a percentage of eligible, not registered, voters, so the figures differ from those in the *New York Times*, which were based on the Pew report.

8. "2008 Presidential General Election Data Graphs—North Carolina," http://www.uselectionatlas.org/RESULTS/datagraph.php?fips=37&year=2008&off=0&elect=0&f=0.

9. Anna Julia Cooper, *A Voice from the South* (1892; repr. New York: Oxford University Press, 1988).

10. For an overview of disfranchisement in the South, see Michael Perman, *Struggle for Mastery: Disfranchisement in the South, 1888–1908* (Chapel Hill: University of North Carolina Press, 2001).

11. Table A-1, "Reported Voting and Registration by Race, Hispanic Origin, Sex, and Age Groups: November 1964 to 2008," http://www.census.gov/hhes/www/socdemo/voting/publications/historical/index.html.

12. See Figure 2.

13. "Early Voting," http://www.ncvoterinfo.org.

14. "Absentee and Early Voting," http://www.ncsl.org/default.aspx?tabid=16604.

15. Byron York, *Washington Examiner*, April 28, 2009.

16. Glenda Elizabeth Gilmore, *Gender and Jim Crow: Women and the Politics of White Supremacy, 1896–1920* (Chapel Hill: University of North Carolina Press, 1996).

17. Adriane Lentz-Smith, *Freedom Struggles: African Americans and World War I* (Cambridge, Mass.: Harvard University Press, 2009); Nikki Brown, *Private Politics and Public Voices: Black Women's Activism from World War I to the New Deal* (Bloomington: Indiana University Press, 2006).

18. David Burner, *The Politics of Provincialism: The Democratic Party in Transition, 1918–1932* (repr. Westport, Conn.: Greenwood Press, 1981), 238–39, 241.

19. Betty Livingston Adams, "Fighting the Color Line in the 'Ideal Suburb': Working-Class Black Women and the Politics of Christian Activism in Summit, New Jersey, 1898–1945," PhD dissertation, Yale University, 2009.

20. For the development of this argument, see Glenda Elizabeth Gilmore, "False Friends and Avowed Enemies: Southern African Americans and Party Allegiances in the 1920s," in Jane Dailey, Glenda Elizabeth Gilmore, and Bryant Simon, eds., *Jumpin' Jim Crow: Southern Politics from Civil War to Civil Rights* (Princeton, N.J.: Princeton University Press, 2000): 219–38.

21. Rosalyn Terborg-Penn, "African-American Women's Networks in the Anti-Lynching Crusade," in Noralee Frankel and Nancy S. Dye, eds., *Gender, Race, Class*

and Reform in the Progressive Era (Lexington: University Press of Kentucky, 1991), 148–61.

22. On the campaign to register and vote, see Gilmore, *Gender and Jim Crow;* Katherine Mellon Charron, *Freedom's Teacher: The Life of Septima Clark* (Chapel Hill: University of North Carolina Press, 2009); Barbara Ransby, *Ella Baker and the Black Freedom Movement: A Radical Democratic Vision* (Chapel Hill: University of North Carolina Press, 2003).

23. Cheryl Lynn Greenburg, *Troubling the Waters: Black-Jewish Relations in the American Century* (Princeton, N.J.: Princeton University Press 2006), 60; Greenburg, *"Or Does It Explode?": Black Harlem in the Great Depression* (New York: Oxford University Press, 1991), 113–39; Charron, *Freedom's Teacher;* Ralph J. Bunche, "Negroes in the Depression: Ralph J. Bunche Describes a Direct-Action Approach to Jobs," in August Meier, Elliott Rudwick, and Frances L. Broderick, eds., *Black Protest Thought in the Twentieth Century,* 2nd ed. (Indianapolis, Ind.: Bobbs-Merrill, 1971).

24. Gilmore, *Defying Dixie: The Radical Roots of Civil Rights, 1919–1950* (New York: Norton, 2008), 315–29.

25. Gilmore, *Defying Dixie,* 384–93.

26. Jacquelyn Dowd Hall, "The Long Civil Rights Movement and the Political Uses of the Past," *Journal of American History* 91 (2004): 1235. For works on civil rights before the mid-1950s, see Harvard Sitkoff, *A New Deal for Blacks: The Emergence of Civil Rights as a National Issue* (New York: Oxford University Press, 1978); Steven F. Lawson, *Black Ballots: Voting Rights in the South, 1944–1969* (New York: Columbia University Press, 1976), and Lawson, *Civil Rights Crossroads: Nation, Community, and the Black Freedom Struggle* (Lexington: University of Kentucky Press, 2003); Robert Rodgers Korstad, *Civil Rights Unionism: Tobacco Workers and the Struggle for Democracy in the Mid-Twentieth-Century South* (Chapel Hill: University of North Carolina Press, 2003); Korstad and Nelson Lichtenstein, "Opportunities Found and Lost: Labor, Radicals, and the Early Civil Rights Movement," *Journal of American History* 75 (December 1988): 786–811; Robin D. G. Kelley, *Hammer and Hoe: Alabama Communists during the Great Depression* (Chapel Hill: University of North Carolina Press, 1990), and Kelley, "'We Are Not What We Seem': Rethinking Black Working Class Opposition in the Jim Crow South," *Journal of American History* 80 (June 1993): 75–112; Patricia Sullivan, *Days of Hope: Race and Democracy in the New Deal Era* (Chapel Hill: University of North Carolina Press, 1996); Lentz-Smith, *Freedom Struggles.* Arguing against a long civil rights movement are Eric Arneson, "Reconsidering the 'Long Civil Rights Movement,'" *Historically Speaking* (April 2009): 31–34; and David L. Chappell, "The Lost Decade of Civil Rights," *Historically Speaking* (April 2009): 37–41.

27. For a bibliography and an account of the establishment of white supremacy, see Gilmore, *Gender and Jim Crow.*

CHAPTER 5

The Forgotten Legacy of Shirley Chisholm
Race versus Gender in the 2008 Democratic Primaries

Tera W. Hunter

President Barack Obama and Secretary of State Hillary Clinton owe a debt to a trailblazing presidential contender.[1] In 1972, Congresswoman Shirley Chisholm became the first African American to run for president on a major party ticket. Congresswoman Chisholm knew that she had no real chance of winning, but she ran to pave the way for others and to garner attention for issues that other candidates had failed to adequately address. She was antiracist, antisexist, pro-choice, pro-labor, antiwar, fiercely independent, and, above all, principled.

Imagine a primary campaign in 2008 among the Democratic candidates in which Chisholm's legacy served as a starting point for pushing the leading contenders to address the issues that she had laid a foundation for three decades before. Instead, the primaries harkened back to centuries-old historic divisions in which then Senators Hillary Clinton's gender and Barack Obama's race were put in competition and assessed in terms of who was more oppressed. Stalwart Democrats, especially liberals and feminists, not only failed to advance the discourse, but often contributed to its retrograde qualities.

It may be premature to fully analyze the discord, so close in time as we are to the events. This chapter offers some preliminary thoughts about the divisive nature of the Democratic primary campaign along the fault lines of race and gender. It looks briefly at the misappropriation of Chisholm's legacy; critiques the race-versus-gender dichotomy that came to dominate infighting within the Democratic Party's primaries; exposes the limits of the gender-first ideology espoused by dispirited Clinton supporters as her political fortunes declined; and argues for the importance of condemning both racism and sexism while at the same time understanding how these systems of oppression are structured differently and inequitably in our political system. Finally, it looks at racial and gender trends of actual voting patterns, evident in the outcome of the election, that challenge the rush to proclaim a post-racial America by virtue of President Obama's unprecedented victory. At a historic moment in the Democratic primaries, liberals failed to learn from the intersectional analysis of racial, gender, and class oppression that Shirley Chisholm articulated throughout her political career. Instead of promoting political agendas attuned to recognizing and supporting the humanity of everyone in our electoral system, the campaigns foundered on wearisome issues.

When Chisholm ran for president, her base was primarily African Americans and white feminists at the grassroots, though she also had many committed supporters who were white men and other people of color. Many established black male leaders and white feminist leaders were either opposed or lukewarm to her campaign. Gloria Steinem, a fellow founder of the National Women's Political Caucus (NWPC), initially gave her this ambiguous endorsement: "I'm for Shirley Chisholm—but I think that George McGovern is the best of the *male* candidates."[2]

Clearly Chisholm did not enjoy the love of a universal sisterhood or the unconditional support of African Americans. Detractors told her that she was a mere symbol without much substance and that she was getting in the way of viable candidates. For some she was not black enough. For others she was too black to be taken seriously. Ironically, one of the few organizations to endorse her was the Black Panther Party, the most hyped symbol of black masculinity and radicalism of the era. Her moderate friends urged her to reject the Panthers' endorsement, but she refused. Chisholm campaigned on a shoestring budget and appeared on the ballot or was written-in in fourteen states. She brought only 28 delegates to the national convention but ended with 152, as some delegates disenchanted with events at the gathering defected to her side. Her trailblazing run ended with a unity speech in which she conceded to the victor George McGovern and vowed to help him beat his Republican opponent, Richard Nixon. Chisholm returned to the U.S. House of Representatives, where she had been elected in 1968 as the first African American woman, and served another decade before retiring.

When we celebrate Chisholm's achievements, it is important to recall that she challenged the racist attitudes and practices within the women's movement as much as she challenged sexism among African Americans and the broader society. She constantly reminded her comrades that feminism at its foundation was a fight for humanism and that women's issues could not be narrowly construed according to the dictates and the needs of white middle-class women. Eliminating the war in Vietnam and ending poverty, violence, and racism were all women's issues. She cautioned an audience of mostly white feminists in 1973 at the NWPC convention to be mindful of how race and class impacted the experiences of nonwhite and poor women: "The use of the word 'Ms.' is not a burning issue to them. They are more concerned about extension of the minimum wage . . . about welfare reform. They are not only women, but women of color and they are subject to more discrimination than whites."[3]

Clearly, race mattered to Chisholm as much as gender, since they both mattered in her life and the lives of her constituents. But unfortunately, when Chisholm's name was mentioned in the Democratic primaries in 2008, as the rhetoric of race-versus-gender heated up, her words were often misconstrued. Chisholm had said, particularly about her political career: "Of my two 'handicaps,' being female put many more obstacles in my path than being black." This is not surprising given that when she ran for office in the New York State Assembly and the U.S. Congress, her opponents were black men. In the wake of the Black Power movement, the opposition was none too kind to a black woman usurping what were considered black male prerogatives. Some Clinton supporters used the quote from Chisholm about sexism without ever noting its context or her critiques of multiple oppressions. Chisholm became the posthumous voice of a gender-first ideology that she never espoused, misrepresenting a legacy that could have advanced a more inclusive coalition and progressive agenda, which her life work had actually manifested.[4]

Rather than moving forward to build on the gains made in recognizing the complexities of the intersections of racial and gender oppression since the civil rights movement and the Second Wave feminist movement of the late twentieth century, we were jarred back to the historic quandary that first emerged when the antebellum feminist and abolitionist alliance splintered in the 1860s after slavery ended. Once the prospect for universal suffrage was no longer politically viable, abolitionists and feminists (with some in both camps) fought over the Fourteenth and Fifteenth amendments to the U.S. Constitution. The contentious questions at the center of the fight were: Who was worse off without the vote? And who should get the vote first? Leading suffragists such as Elizabeth Cady Stanton and Susan B. Anthony resorted to making racist arguments in favor of women first by arguing that white women made better citizens than black men.

During the Democratic primaries in 2008, Gloria Steinem echoed the sentiments of Stanton and Anthony by once again pitting white women against black men. In a now famous *New York Times* op-ed, Steinem endorsed

Sen. Hillary Clinton and argued that gender was the greater disadvantage in society and politics. She wrote: "Black men were given the vote a half-century before women of any race were allowed to mark a ballot."[5] What she failed to mention was the violent movement of disfranchisement that quickly followed the ratification of the Fifteenth Amendment in 1870, which proceeded to lock most black men out of the ballot box by the end of the 1890s until the Voting Rights Act was passed in 1965. Nor did she mention the refusal on the part of leading white suffragists to support black women's rights to vote when the Nineteenth Amendment was ratified in 1920.

Instead, Steinem constructed a fictional black woman figure ("Achola Obama") to measure Barack Obama's underqualifications as a prospective president and used the foil to prove that he enjoyed certain advantages as a man. Here, a black woman was pitted against a black man in yet another discursive scuffle over who goes first. Steinem failed to notice how racial privilege had benefited Clinton. "Achola Obama" would perform poorly in the polls not simply because she is a woman, but because she is a *black woman*, a category altogether different than that occupied by the former First Lady. Shirley Chisholm's campaign in 1972 and Senator Carol Moseley Braun's short-lived bid for the Democratic nomination for president in 2004 both testify to this.

Despite Steinem's claims that women are "never frontrunners," Senator Clinton initially framed her candidacy as that of an incumbent. The media depicted her as the undisputed frontrunner headed for a coronation of an inchoate family political dynasty until Obama won the Iowa Caucus in January 2008 and turned the anticipated perfunctory campaign into a real contest. Even her own staffers admitted that Clinton expected to have the nomination wrapped up by Super Tuesday.[6] The failure to prepare for the possibility of an upset left the team without a clear strategy and in dire financial straits, as it had front-loaded its spending, which forced Clinton to lend her organization millions of her own personal money to stay afloat.

Two other lines from Steinem's op-ed struck a chord and became popular refrains repeated and elaborated in print and online media by many other white feminists, including Erica Jong, Robin Morgan, Geraldine Ferraro, Frida Ghitis, and Joan Walsh.[7] As Steinem claimed: "Gender is probably the most restricting force in American life." She also stated that black men "generally have ascended to positions of power, from the military to the boardroom, before any women." These sentiments became the representative wisdom of "feminism," as alternative views from more progressive white women and from women of color rarely got mainstream media exposure.

These feminists paid no attention to the race and class privileges Clinton enjoyed while making her a universal symbol of gender discrimination. They thereby perpetuated a disregard for the relative advances that elite white women have won as a result of both the civil rights and women's movements in comparison to the gains won by African American women and men and other racial minorities. Hillary Clinton, after all, is one of the most privileged women in the world as a result of her educational, professional, and political achievements and her former status as First Lady. Gender parity has not yet been achieved in our society, but the barriers do not work against all women in the same way. Women's studies scholars have documented quite profusely for decades that while gender may be the most restricting force for some women, that is certainly not the case for all. The failure to note this in the campaign discourse also reflects broader lapses in the ways our society thinks about gender vis-à-vis race. In the backlash against affirmative action, for example, there has been a deafening silence among liberals and conservatives about the fact that the primary beneficiaries have been white women—in college admissions, corporate positions, legislative halls, and judicial chambers. The empirical evidence is overwhelming. And yet the disparagement and attacks on affirmative action have targeted blacks as if they were the only beneficiaries.[8] We have made huge strides in improving gender and race equality in this country, although both sexism and racism are alive and well, in differing, overlapping, and often contradictory ways. Both candidates faced an uphill struggle in persuading the electorate to imagine a completely new bodily figuration to place at the helm of the nation-state. Senator Clinton was without a doubt subjected to vehement misogyny. Her clothes were scrutinized, her hairstyles mocked, her laugh caricatured. One supporter of Senator John McCain asked him at a campaign stop in South Carolina: "How do we beat that bitch?" His response: "That is an excellent question." "Bitch" was also used by news journalists such as Glenn Beck on his nationally syndicated radio show; Beck at the time was also affiliated with CNN and ABC.[9]

The fact that these and other incidents happened to Clinton does not lead to a corollary that some of her supporters argued that racism is now insignificant or less tolerated than sexism. Maria Echaveste, a Clinton adviser, summed up the sentiments that she and others shared: "There's a zone of protection around Senator Obama on race where none existed on gender."[10] The most visible "zone of protection" for Obama was the armed Secret Service detail that guarded him much earlier than is normally necessary for presidential candidates, a year and a half before the general elections. Senator Dick Durbin acknowledged that the decision to give him full-time Secret Service protection "had to do with race."[11] The time-honored political tool of racial violence was an ever-present apparition hovering over his campaign.

One can enumerate many racist incidents directed at Obama that were equally offensive as the attacks on Clinton. The Internet was replete with derisive products for sale using Obama's likeness, including T-shirts with slogans such as "Welfare Recipients for Obama," "Give al-Qaeda a Chance: Vote Obama," and "Jockeys for Obama" (with a picture of Obama superimposed on a black jockey). Another T-shirt featured a KKK figure running after Obama with a noose.[12] Other less subtle names were used to describe him, including "Nigger President" by neo-Nazis and the "Mau Mau Candidate for President" by Andy Martin, executive editor of ContrarianCommentary.com. After Obama's Philadelphia speech on race, Pat Buchanan, commentator on MSNBC and CNN, described it on his blog as "the same old con, the same old shakedown that black hustlers have been running since the Kerner Commission." He followed this with a screed on how black people should be grateful for slavery. A Republican women's organization in San Bernardino, California, sent out a newsletter with a mock ten-dollar "food stamp" with drawings of Obama, a watermelon, a pitcher of Kool-Aid, a bucket of Kentucky Fried Chicken, and barbeque ribs. Lest it be mistaken that such pejoratives were limited to conservatives and extremists, the *Independent,* a reputable mainstream paper in the New York Hamptons, ran a "satirical column" in which it mimicked black English written by "Yo Mamma bin Barack." Former Nebraska senator Bob Kerrey "pretending that he was praising Obama, said he hoped Obama would play a role in a [Hillary] Clinton Administration by reaching out to Black youth and Muslims around the world."[13]

Such incidents seemed not to register for those who saw only sexism at work. Senator Clinton also suggested that she suffered more as a female candidate than Obama as a black male. Speaking to Cynthia McFadden on ABC's *Nightline* she said: "It's hard. It's hard being a woman out there. It is obviously challenging with some of the things that are said that are not even personal to me so much as they are about women ... Every so often I just wish that it were a little more even playing field ... It's hard being a woman out there."[14] The Clinton campaign, while at first reluctant to embrace gender as a mobilizing strategy, panicked in the wake of the Iowa loss and reversed course. In the debates in New Hampshire, Clinton alluded to the idea that voting for her as a woman would represent greater change—leading to the implication that voting for Obama as the first African American was less groundbreaking. As the *New York Times* reported, her campaign actively promoted this argument on the ground there at organized events.[15] She began to openly court women by asking them to help her break the glass ceiling for commander in chief, but the campaign never moved beyond either noting the potential for making history or highlighting the sexist insults launched against her. Hillary Clinton never spoke openly, critically, or engagingly about the status of women in our society, the problems of gender discrimination, and what we should do about it.

As Clinton became more forthright in claiming to be the victim of gender discrimination to advance her candidacy, Obama, meanwhile, continued to be reluctant to dwell on issues related to race and racism. The stakes were different for each of them. She was able to openly rally voters on the basis of gender, but he could not invoke race as a positive corollary for garnering votes beyond the occasional mention of the historic noteworthiness of his candidacy. He faced the challenge of calming white fears, of reassuring the populace that he was not an "angry black man" seeking racial retribution. With the middle name Hussein, as the son of a Kenyan father with a Muslim heritage, he faced the added challenge of religion serving as a proxy for race. It is true that in polite society it is no longer acceptable to use certain incendiary racial language, so religious bigotry against Islam in the age of "terrorism" often stood in its stead. As the contradictory charges of being a member of a black separatist Christian church and being a secret Muslim were hurled against him, progressive critics reproached him for not going far enough in responding beyond correcting the record. While some of his left supporters had been urging him to make more explicit his views on race and racism from the start of the campaign, there was little corresponding pressure from Clinton allies for her to address gender issues more systematically. But ultimately, the controversy over sermons by his then pastor Rev. Jeremiah Wright and his family's membership in the Trinity United Church of Christ provoked Obama to make the speech about race in Philadelphia on March 18. The dividends paid off for Obama, as it turned what could have been a fatal incident into an opportunity to make an unprecedented speech about the state of one of our society's most intractable and politically explosive historical problems.

The Obama campaign continued to pick up steam from voters despite the onslaught of negative publicity in the media post–Reverend Wright. The disenchantment among Clinton supporters about gender discrimination grew as the political fortunes of their candidate declined. They continued to paint Obama as "unqualified," invoking this and other popular anti–affirmative action canards. As Geraldine Ferraro argued: "If Obama was a white man, he would not be in this position. And if he were a woman, he would not be in this position. He happens to be very lucky to be who he is. And the country is caught up in the concept." Interestingly, Ferraro made a similar comment almost exactly twenty years before about another presidential contender: "If Jesse Jackson were not black, he wouldn't be in the race."[16] Despite Ferraro's charge that black men in America are more privileged in a political realm in which few black candidates for elective office have ever been successful at the state level (i.e., senator or governor) and none at the national level (i.e., president or vice president), Obama was not the candidate who articulated a racial advantage.

As Hillary Clinton's last hope appeared to lie in the hands of superdelegates for the Democratic Party who had the power to override the popular vote, she made her case for why they should choose her based on her "electability." She stated: "I have a much broader base to build a winning coalition on." She cited an Associated Press report to bolster her position and stated: "Sen. Obama's support among working, hard-working Americans, white Americans, is weakening again." She argued that "whites in both states [Indiana and North Carolina] who had not completed college degrees were supporting me. There is a pattern emerging here." When asked whether her remarks could be interpreted as racially divisive, she demurred: "These are the people you have to win if you're a Democrat in sufficient numbers to actually win the election. Everybody knows that."[17] These statements were not slips of the tongue, but blunt talking points pitched to superdelegates: Barack had no realistic chance of winning the general election because he is black; Clinton could win because she is white. Never mind that some political scientists, such as Larry Bartels, argue that the defection of white working-class voters from the Democrats has been much exaggerated—Clinton banked on the hope that she could appeal to them more.[18]

Many Clinton supporters continued to feel that Obama had usurped the chances of a more deserving candidate. Though he followed the rules of what would normally be trumpeted as a meritocratic system, his success in running a more astute campaign was seen as cheating, jumping ahead in line, unfairly racking up votes in primaries and caucuses in states considered to be irrelevant to the big blue state strategy of conventional political wisdom. As a white female real estate agent in Columbus, Ohio, stated succinctly: "Women felt that this was their time, and this [election] has been stolen from them."[19] Some of the most inflammatory accusations came from supporters who began to actively organize in opposition to Obama in favor of Republican senator John McCain. His selection of Governor Sarah Palin as his vice presidential running mate, initially at least, incited more promises to jump the Democratic ship. These were not necessarily all self-identified feminists, as many from this part of Clinton's constituency pledged to put aside their disappointment and support Obama if he should ultimately win the nomination. But given the muddled messages about gender inequality over the previous six months, it is not surprising that many could not get beyond deciding that the only thing that mattered was to elect a female president and seek retribution against Obama for foiling that plan. He was charged with being sexist (he called Clinton "likeable enough" in a debate), of not stopping sexism in the media or vigorously defending his opponent. These grievances generated a number of groups like Clinton Supporters Count Too, Party Unity My Ass (PUMA), and Hillary 44. Black "ghetto" metaphors and other such insults were replete on some of these groups' websites, which were always careful to indicate that they had nonwhite support, as though that was sufficient to exonerate them. As stated on the website Hillary 44: "Obama has been a lead gang-banger in the misogyny parade."[20] The myth of the black male rapist lurks barely beneath the surface of this contempt.

The gender-first ideology that drove some aggrieved Clinton constituents does not take into account that, from a moral perspective, racism and sexism are equally egregious but they have not played identical or equal roles in the structure of our political system (not to mention our economy). To paraphrase Shirley Chisholm, sexism and racism are at their roots antihumanist. They deprive us of personal dignity and the capacity to fulfill our greatest aspirations. So why stage a competition divided between two hermetically sealed columns in which some of the most ferocious crimes and misdeeds that have maimed and limited our humanity over centuries are checked off and the prize is awarded to the side that has the most marks? The sexist column and the racist column are both morally objectionable. But the political impediments standing in the way of overcoming them have not been equivalent. Two brief examples, the passage of the Nineteenth Amendment for women's suffrage and fights over proportional voting versus winner-take-all election rules, help to illustrate this.

Women did not win the right to vote until less than a century ago, long after the franchise was extended to all white men regardless of property ownership. But the struggle for white women's enfranchisement was safe from revocation once it was enshrined in the Constitution in 1920, which was not the case for black men in the 1860s or for women of color in 1920. In fact, some white suffragists used the argument that white supremacy would be buttressed by extending the vote to them. Most states, particularly western, passed women's suffrage laws before the Nineteenth Amendment was ratified, but they specifically barred Mexican American, Asian American, and Native American women from voting. Southern states waited until ratification in 1920 to extend the franchise to white women, knowing that they could keep black women out of the polls once they did so.

A controversy over election rules came up during the primaries when some Clinton supporters complained that she was losing because of the Democratic Party's proportional voting rules. But they failed to note the historical context for why those rules were implemented. They were developed as a corrective to practices in some states, like Pennsylvania, Illinois, and New Jersey, which awarded delegates based on votes in congressional districts on a winner-take-all basis, which deprived minority voters of their fair share of delegates to represent their candidates at the national convention. Jesse Jackson, Sr. had been part of a wider push for reforming the rules to make the process more democratic going back to 1972. Then, as the leader of a reform slate, he challenged the seating of the Illinois delegation led by party boss Mayor Richard J. Daley of Chicago from the floor of the convention in Miami. The Illinois delegation had ignored guidelines for proportional representation recommended by the national body, and Jackson's slate prevailed. When Jackson ran for president in 1984 and 1988, he continued to criticize the inconsistent practices that permitted some winner-take-all primaries. In the latter year, he ultimately persuaded the party to change the rules to require all states to follow proportional voting. Racial-minority disadvantage had been structured into the voting system, because they could rarely if ever win outright in racially mixed congressional districts. Under winner-take-all rules, this left them without leverage to influence the national party.

There was no similar structural bias based on sex. By 1964, women were the majority of eligible voters and have been ever since. For the first time, in 1980, women voters began to turn out more than men and in larger percentages. This ended the "traditional gender gap" in which women had voted disproportionately less than men and more often for the Republicans. The "modern gender gap" by contrast seemed to coalesce, and in it women began to vote more liberally and more Democratic than men. Feminists and women's political action groups began to use this to leverage their power within the Democratic Party, most effectively in getting Geraldine Ferraro added to the ticket in 1984 as the first woman to be nominated to run for vice president. That occurred sixteen years before an African American man would be "lucky" to get on the ticket. Changes in racial patterns in politics have been much slower. The "gender gap" turned out to be illusory in the long run, however. Though women began to vote more liberally, white women still moved to the right as their men did and voted mostly conservative.[21]

The winner-take-all rules of the Electoral College system can shape racial outcomes and perpetuate historic patterns of discrimination, as well. The indirect system of voting for president through electors was implemented at the time the U.S. Constitution was ratified in 1788, in part to mollify pro-slavery southern states. In the compromises that led to the adoption of the Constitution, the framers agreed to count three-fifths of all slaves in population totals, which would be used to determine the number of electors from each state. As law professors Akhil Amar and Vikram Amar have argued: "At the Constitutional Convention, when Pennsylvania's James Wilson proposed direct national election for the president, Virginia's James Madison countered that such a system would enable the North to outvote the South; under direct election, the South would get no credit for its half-million slaves, none of whom, of course, would be able to vote."[22] Even today, the Electoral College still has disadvantages for racial minorities. The most intransigent white voters in Republican stronghold states are located particularly in the South, making it difficult for even large black minorities to prevail under winner-take-all rules. This is similar to the challenges Latinos and Native Americans voters face in the Southwest.

The electoral system at its inception hurt women, as well, since they would be counted for purposes of figuring out population totals without giving states incentives to enfranchise them. But once women received the right to vote in 1920, this situation was mostly reversed. Racial bias lived on, however, in reinforcing the power of traditional southern (previously slave) strongholds in national elections, ensuring black subordination even after the passage of the Voting Rights Act of 1965. It is no small wonder that southerners were able to dominate the presidency for so long.

These examples of the disparate ways that gender and race have influenced our political system should not be used in the service of a sweepstakes of competing claims of oppression. There can be no winner in any such misguided rivalry, if the goal is to reach the kind of expansive political process and progressive political outcomes that Shirley Chisholm, among others, envisioned and worked toward to benefit our common humanity. Racism and sexism are equally egregious, but they have been structured distinctly, if interlocking in complicated ways, resulting in differing abilities for disadvantaged groups to move forward in multiple arenas throughout our entangled history.

Despite dire predictions during the primaries of the outcome of having a black man at the top of the Democratic ticket, Barack Obama eventually prevailed to become the nominee and the victor of the general election, shattering conventional wisdom about the character of the nation's electorate and how best to run a presidential campaign. In light of his victory, many Americans have been quick to proclaim the arrival of a "post-racial" society, arguing that by electing the first African American president the nation has now assuaged and healed its racial wounds, erasing any further need to address racial inequalities suffered by minorities. This declaration made in the shadow of the 2008 primaries, arguably one of the most racially disruptive political moments for the Democratic Party since the controversy over the seating of the Mississippi Freedom Democratic Party at the 1964 National Convention in Atlantic City, New Jersey, is far too hasty. Before we herald the end of race without eradicating centuries of racism that cannot be overcome simply with one election, it is important that we also take a look at what actual voting patterns tell us about the changing character of racial and gender politics—or the lack thereof.

The 2008 primaries exposed critical and historical fault lines on race and gender in feminist and Democratic Party politics. In the post–civil rights era, Democrats (and those leftists who may be independents) have become accustomed to pointing fingers at conservatives and the Republican Party for unsavory racial and sexual politics. Rarely has the Democratic Party been forced to look within at its own internal tensions, but those tensions exploded during the primaries and threatened to shatter presumed alliances across race, class, and gender. There has been some healing of these rifts, at least as measured by most who were able to put differences aside to carry Obama over the top. But some, mostly white women supporters of Hillary Clinton, were still angry and disillusioned by her loss. And some of them defected from the party once Clinton lost the nomination. The departure was not a total surprise, however. It is useful to go back to prior elections to discern the broader patterns behind the rightward shift.

In 2004, it was the Republican Party that had successfully used race as a wedge issue in hyping fear around terrorism and the Iraq War. President George W. Bush won reelection by gaining more support from the white electorate, 58 percent—a four-point gain from 2000. People of color, by contrast, voted overwhelmingly for the Democratic nominee, Senator John Kerry. The increase in white votes pivotal to Bush's victory came mostly from white women. While white men increased their support by one point, white women increased their support by ten points. The white wing of the potential multiracial alliance within the Democratic Party was already fragile, and white women's sharp rightward swing contributed significantly to this turn. The only Democratic presidential candidate to win the majority of white women's votes between 1971 and 1992 was Bill Clinton, and those voters reverted to Republicans after his 1996 reelection.[23]

The willingness of white female Democrats to move to the right dates back to President Richard Nixon's success in drawing them into the fold, in part, by using a racial strategy, euphemistically referred to as the "southern strategy." In the 1970s, neoconservatives began to return the lexicon of racial injury and racial injustice to pre–Civil Rights logic using the language of individualism and the advocacy of color-blind policies. Ronald Reagan carried the tradition even further, bringing along more of that constituency that Hillary Clinton invoked, "those hard working white Americans," also known as "Reagan Democrats." In 1980, Reagan kicked off his presidential run in Philadelphia, Mississippi, the infamous site where civil rights workers had been murdered in 1964, to signal his support for "states' rights." Under Reagan's leadership, conservatives became more adept at reframing racial issues from their perspective. They identified racism with color-conscious remedies designed to redress group wrongs rather than acknowledge it as structurally produced inequalities and invidious ideas or practices.

The conservative-leaning wing of the Democratic Party and its rising star, Governor Bill Clinton, took note of how the Republicans peeled off Democratic votes. He believed that he could win back the "Reagan Democrats" by offering universal programs and abandoning allegiances to race-specific reforms. When Clinton ran against President George H. W. Bush in 1992, he tried to avoid explicit appeals to the party's loyal base of black voters, showing that he was not beholden to the liberal constituents or to its conventional civil rights policies. Clinton stressed "personal responsibility," touted "family values," and promised to "end welfare as we know it." According to Andrew Hacker: "For the first time in almost half a century, the party's platform made no mention of redressing racial injustice. As a result, race never became an issue in 1992 [at the Democratic Convention]."[24] Clinton minimized his appearances before all-black audiences and made few promises to address the specific concerns of black citizens. He chastised Jesse Jackson, Sr., rebuked Sister Souljah, and raced back home to Arkansas in the middle of the campaign to witness an execution he had authorized, of a black man so mentally incompetent that he saved the dessert given to him at his last supper to eat later.

While candidate Bill Clinton capitalized on race as a wedge issue during the campaign, making it difficult for the Republicans to use it against him as they had other Democrats, once in office he governed by doing what he could to placate African Americans without alienating white constituents. He scored wider and deeper popularity among African Americans compared to any of his predecessors. Clinton's personal style and genuine comfort with dealing with black people, rooted in his youth in Arkansas and his love for elements of black culture, made him very likeable. He appointed more African Americans in the White House and in high-level government posts than any other president. Many middle-class African Americans prospered under his tenure, having higher employment, home-ownership, and business-ownership rates. African Americans were his most loyal friends at the lowest point of his presidency after being accused of having "sexual relations with that woman" Monica Lewinsky. They stood by him when others fled. Rev. Jeremiah Wright was among the clergy summoned to pray with him in the throes of the scandal.

Consistent with this pattern of resilience, black civil rights leaders, elected officials, and other elites transferred their loyalty to Bill Clinton's wife early in her campaign, assuming that the media portrayals of immanence would triumph. The weight of overwhelming black support from all quarters helped to establish Hillary Clinton's status as the frontrunner before the less well-known Obama made his mark and lit a spark with voters across diverse demographics. To move past the initial reluctance to support Obama, the black political establishment had to first relinquish the idea, taken all too literally, that Bill Clinton was the "first black president" and that his wife offered the only realistic chance to get closer to the White House once again. Few people of whatever race were fully in tune with just how much the mood of the country had shifted in the wake of the disastrous policies of President George W. Bush and how the demographic complexion of the electorate was in flux, both of which offered an opening for fresh political leadership as never before. Black Americans, by virtue of their experiences, tend to be adept at negotiating the complexities of race in society, but many underestimated the possibilities for, yes, change, as the familiar ground of race was shaken underneath everyone. Most people believed that a black man could not become president. Black elites (liberal and conservative) resisted Obama not only because of doubts that he could win and the fear of retaliation should they back the losing candidate, but also because they questioned his racial "authenticity."

Conservative pundit Debra Dickerson doubted whether Obama was really black, since his father was African-born and his mother white and he lacked U.S. slave ancestry. Cultural critic Stanley Crouch claimed Obama had not "lived the life of a black American." Former ambassador Andrew Young said Bill Clinton is "every bit as black" as Barack Obama, in a telling endorsement of loyalty that lost sight of the fact that it was Hillary who was running for office. Hillary Clinton supporter Robert Johnson tried to tar Obama as a drug user and characterized him as the Sidney Poitier character in the movie *Guess Who's Coming to Dinner?* (about a black interloper in a white world)—an odd statement coming from a black billionaire. Robert Ford, a state senator from South Carolina, argued before his state's primary that "Obama's ambition could bring all of black America down. If the Democrats lose control of Congress, we're going to go back and struggle and struggle and struggle." He said he would support either Clinton or Senator John Edwards. If not for the faith of the voters in the lily-white state of Iowa who gave Obama's campaign the breath of life, these negative predictions and derisive representations could have prevailed.[25]

Yet they did not. This does not mean we have arrived at a "post-racial" America. The politics of race were already being reconfigured in significant ways through demographic shifts in the electorate, at least since 2004. Barack Obama's organization clearly did its homework and understood what could be achieved by thinking outside the conventional political map of blue states and red states. As Bob Wing, an antiracist activist, stated presciently in 2004: "Racism is conciliated if not actively promoted by the Democratic focus on winning more white voters by moving to the right while taking voters of color for granted."[26] People of color voted overwhelmingly for Kerry, as white voters did in favor of Bush. What kind of response would this engender from political candidates in a nation moving steadily toward predominantly nonwhite population projections in the not-so-distant future? Hillary Clinton had a strong liberal record as a senator, yet she ran her campaign relying on some of the tried-and-true strategies in the playbook of the more conservative Democratic Leadership Council that had worked effectively for her husband. But nearly a decade had passed since Bill Clinton's last election. Barack Obama adopted a fifty-state strategy fighting for the South and Southwest, presumably hardcore Republican territory, and campaigning in states Democratic rivals did not count as important on the electoral map. He was thus more nimble and prepared to take advantage of the trend lines showing distinctive demographic shifts.

There is good news and bad news for the Democratic Party and feminism as a result of Obama's election. The Democratic Party tent has expanded in size, in the proportion of the electorate, and become more diverse. Obama won because of a multiracial coalition. He received more white votes than Bill Clinton, the last Democrat elected, though his Republican opponent John McCain won the white majority, 55 percent to 43 percent. The biggest shift toward the Democratic Party came from people of color and young people under thirty among all racial groups. More white men than white women voted for McCain. But the men voted Democratic by a wider margin than women, as compared to 2004. White men swung toward the Democrats by nine points more, whereas white women moved only two points (which is within the margin of error) in contrast to the huge leap they gave to Bush's reelection. The often ballyhooed "gender gap" since the 1980 election took another hit. Once again, this disputes the fallacious assumption that women qua women are automatically progressive—or, as both Steinem and Robin Morgan argued during the election, that women become the most radical group as they age. The opposite may be the case, since it is unmarried women (never-married females, who tend to be young, and divorcées of all ages) who vote more liberally. In addition, whites who voted most strongly for McCain were southerners; whites for Obama came mostly from the East. But Obama won southern states considered lost to Democrats, like Florida, North Carolina, and Virginia. The gap between black and white voter turnouts narrowed to less than 1 percent difference as blacks voted in larger numbers than the previous presidential election and a small percentage of whites stayed home. African American women turned out to vote at a slightly higher rate than other racial, ethnic, and gender groups compared to previous elections.[27]

And now that the campaigns are over, what about the charges from Clinton supporters that sexism, particularly in the media, was an overriding negative factor in her downfall? As sociologist Cynthia Fuchs Epstein stated: "It is my view that sexism, some of it still lurking in everyday life, some of it orchestrated by right-wing ideologues, was responsible for the defeat of Clinton."[28] Surely it is simplistic to reduce any political loss to one factor alone. As elaborated in this chapter, sexism and racism were both at work in the presidential candidacies—among other things. The particular charge that Clinton lost because she faced an "uneven playing field" is not persuasive.

The Project for Excellence in Journalism conducted a study based on media content during the primary season that is quite revealing. While it does not address the issue of sexism directly, it does refute the common refrain that Clinton was the victim of media bias because of her gender or for any other reason. The assertion that the media was more favorably disposed toward Obama is not sustained by the facts. The media coverage of Obama and Clinton's character, history, leadership, and appeal was "almost identical in tone" overall. Both received twice as much positive as compared to negative exposure. The positive depictions of Obama began to turn more negative in March, just before the issue of Reverend Wright arose, "shortly after Clinton criticized the media for being soft on Obama during a debate," the report states. His media coverage became increasingly negative, especially in April and May. Clinton's treatment was mostly stable, except for one notable dip, from mid-January to mid-February. Her storyline started to hit the rocks following Robert Johnson's comments and "Bill Clinton's attempt to take on a larger role in the campaign—largely as the daily attack dog," the report claimed.[29]

Both candidates' organizations were successful in controlling the positive narratives they wanted to portray of themselves. Obama effectively projected that he was the candidate of change and hope and a charismatic and powerful communicator. As the negativity mounted, he had more difficulty getting across his integrity. Clinton, by contrast, was able to communicate very well that she was prepared to lead on "day one." It was the media (more than her own campaign) that defended her as a warm and likeable person. The most negative opinion she had trouble refuting was that she represented the status quo. None of this provides a strong case for arguing that Clinton lost primarily because of sexism.

It is unfortunate that Shirley Chisholm's legacy was reduced to one dimension of her beliefs to buttress arguments that her life's work repudiated. What a missed opportunity to continue to honor her work by sustaining her commitment to enhancing our collective humanity. We have not achieved gender parity, nor have we reached full racial equality, though we have made significant advances on both. The historical barriers that have accumulated against women and racial minorities are all morally reprehensible. But gender and racial oppression have been structured differently and inequitably in our political-economic system. In failing to recognize this, certain of us will continue to be made scapegoats in the cultural wars (be they waged by liberals or conservatives), vilified at the expense of others' improvement. It does not take away from the grievances of one group to acknowledge the saliency of harm done to others. Competing for the dubious honor of the most-victimized status diminishes legitimate concerns.

It is remarkable that despite all the in-fighting within the Democratic Party, in the end, Barack Obama won resoundingly. The conflicts and the tensions that seemed so irreparable in June were worked through sufficiently by November for him to win. It is still not clear what the long-term fallout will be or how the Democrats will manage tensions that are still seething around gender and race. Neither Clinton nor Obama was responsible for inventing these schisms. They were already there, latent though they appeared to be in the Democratic Party over the past few decades. Both Clinton and Obama broke barriers that can never be erected the same way again. Clinton pushed the door ajar much further for women than Chisholm could have imagined. When Chisholm ran for president, she knew for certain she could not win. When Hillary Clinton launched her campaign, she believed the opposite to be true, and so did millions of her supporters. Chisholm would undoubtedly be proud that she had helped pave the way for the first time in U.S. history when the most viable Democratic presidential candidates were not white men. Now that the historical fault lines of race and gender have been exposed in the twenty-first century, once again, the question remains: what lessons will be learned to produce small-"d" democratic and progressive social change for all?

Notes

1. I would like to thank Nancy Hewitt, Jerma Jackson, Steven Lawson, Chana Kai Lee, Lisa Levenstein, and Richard Pierce for our many conversations during the election season that helped me to develop ideas reflected in this chapter. I appreciate their thoughtful criticism and comments on this essay, as well as those of Liette Gidlow.

2. As quoted in Shirley Chisholm, *The Good Fight* (New York: Harper and Row, 1973), 76. Emphasis in the original quote.

3. Quoted in Julie Gallagher, "Waging 'The Good Fight': The Political Career of Shirley Chisholm, 1953–1982," *The Journal of African American History* 92, no. 3 (Summer 2007): 410–11.

4. Shirley Chisholm, *Unbought and Unbossed* (Boston: Houghton Mifflin, 1970), xii. See, for example, Marilyn Fitterman, "Talking Back," press release by National Organization for Women (NOW), New York State, March 3, 2008, http://www.nownys.com, and "The Shame of the Democratic Left, Part I," http://www.hillaryis44.org/2008/11/26/the-shame-of-the-democratic-left-part-i.

5. *New York Times*, January 8, 2008. All subsequent quotes from Steinem come from this article.

6. See Michelle Cottle, "What Went Wrong?" *The New Republic,* May 16, 2008.

7. See Erica Jong, "Seeing Sexism," Huffington Post, January 10, 2008, http://www.huffingtonpost.com; Robin Morgan, "Goodbye to All That," Women's Media Center, February 2, 2008, http://www.womensmediacenter.com/; Frida Ghitis, "Sexism Not Racism Thriving: Democrats Exuberant with Congratulations," *Chicago Tribune,* February 20, 2008; Joan Walsh, "Americans More Ready for a Black President Than a Woman?" Salon, April 7, 2008, http://www.salon.com.

8. See, for example, Tim Wise, "Is Sisterhood Conditional?: White Women and the Rollback of Affirmative Action," *National Women Studies Association Journal* 10 (Autumn 1998): 1–26.

9. Marc Santora, "Pointed Question Puts McCain in a Tight Spot," *New York Times,* November 14, 2007; "CNN's, ABC's Beck on Clinton: '[S]he's the Stereotypical Bitch,'" March 15, 2007, Media Matters for America, http://mediamatters.org.

10. Echaveste comments made on PBS, "Bill Moyer's Journal," May 16, 2008.

11. "Obama Stories Prompt Racist Postings," *Chicago Sun-Times,* May 6, 2007.

12. Many of these T-shirts were sold at http://www.cafepress.com. It is difficult to now document these items, as many were taken down from the Web sites during the primaries and general election. Michael James at Dailykos.com (http://www.dailykos.com/story/2008/6/20/0338/19338/230/538782) noticed the latter one being

sold in June 2008 on the Web site Road Kill T-Shirts and wrote to the company. It claimed that it slipped through without official approval.

13. Mark Potok, "Neo-Nazis and White Supremacists Publish Ominous Threats to Obama's Life," February 22, 2008, Alternet, http://www.alternet.org/blogs/peek/77509/neo-nazis_and_white_supremacists_publish_ominous_threats_to_obama's_life; "Barack Obama Is the Mau Mau Candidate for President," March 22, 2008, http://contrariancommentary.blogspot.com/2008/03/barack-obama-is-mau-mau-candidate-for.html; Michelle DeArmond, "Inland GOP Mailing Depicts Obama's Face on Food Stamp," October 16, 2008, *The Press-Enterprise,* http://www.pe.com/localnews/inland/stories/PE_News_Local_S_buck16.3d67d4a.html; "A Brief for Whitey," March 21, 2008, http://buchanan.org/blog/pjb-a-brief-for-whitey-969; "Clinton Acolytes' Racist Attacks," *Black Star News,* December 19, 2008, http://www.blackstarnews.com.

14. "Clinton: Playing Field for Her as Candidate Not Even Because of Her Gender," February 28, 2008, http://blogs.abcnews.com/politicalpunch/2008/02/clinton-playing.html.

15. "Race and Politics," *New York Times,* January 17, 2008.

16. Jim Farber, "Geraldine Ferraro Lets Her Emotions Do the Talking," March 7, 2008, http://www.dailybreeze.com/ci_8489268. Ferraro had made a similar remark on NPR's *On Point,* hosted by Tom Ashbrook, on February 26, 2008. Quoted in Howard Kurtz, "Koch Endorses Gore; Jackson Parries Critics," *Washington Post,* April 14, 2008.

17. Kathy Kiely and Jill Lawrence, "Clinton Makes Case for Wide Appeal," *USA Today,* May 8, 2008, http://www.usatoday.com.

18. *Unequal Democracy: The Political Economy of the New Gilded Age* (New York: Russell Sage, 2009), 64–97.

19. Quoted in *New York Times,* May 19, 2008.

20. Quote originally found at www.hillaryis44.org/?p=649. Since the general election ended, many of these organizations and blogs have eliminated their earlier archived postings or restricted access to them on their Web sites.

21. Roxanne Stachowski, "What You Didn't Know about the Gender Gap in Voting," *Off Our Backs* 34 (July–August 2004): 22–23; and Daniel Wirls, "Reinterpreting the Gender Gap," *Public Opinion Quarterly* 50 (Autumn 1986): 316–30.

22. "The Electoral College Votes against Equality," http://www.law.yale.edu/news/2091.htm. Essay originally published in *Los Angeles Times,* September 8, 2004.

23. Martin Kilson, "Obama's Electoral Path to the White House (Part 1)," *Black Commentator,* October 9, 2008, http://www.blackcommentator.com; Bob Wing, "Obama, Race and the Future of U.S. Politics," Black Commentator, February 12, 2009.

24. "The Blacks and Clinton," *New York Review of Books,* January 28, 1993, 12–15.

25. Dickerson and Crouch quoted in Manning Marable, "Racializing Obama: The Enigma of Post-Black Politics and Leadership," *Souls* 11, no. 1 (January–March

2009): 1; "Andrew Young: Bill Clinton Is 'Every Bit as Black as Barack,'" *Dallas Morning News*, December 9, 2007; Katharine Q. Seelye, "BET Founder Slams Obama in South Carolina," *New York Times*, January 13, 2008; Ford quoted in Peter Wallsten, "Black Leaders Not Yet Sold on Obama," *Los Angeles Times*, January 19, 2007.

26. "The White Elephant in the Room: Race and the Election 2004," *Counterpunch*, December 3, 2004.

27. Election data from "Inside Obama's Sweeping Victory," Pew Research Center, November 5, 2008, http://pewresearch.org; Mark Hugo Lopez and Paul Taylor, "Dissecting the 2008 Electorate: Most Diverse in U.S. History," Pew Research Center, April 30, 2009, http://pewresearch.org; Wing, "Obama, Race and the Future of U.S. Politics"; Wing, "The White Elephant in the Room: Race and the Election 2004"; Steinem's quote, *New York Times*, January 8, 2008; Morgan quoted in Linda Burnham, "Obama and Clinton: The Tightrope and the Needle," Pambazuka 355 (March 20, 2008), http://pambazuka.org/en/category/comment/46807; Stachowski, "What You Didn't Know about the Gender Gap," 22.

28. "The Focus of Feminism: Challenging the Myths about the U.S. Women's Movement," *Amnis* (2008): 1 (Revue de Civilisation Contemporaine de l'Université de Bretagne Occidentale).

29. "Character and the Primaries of 2008," Project for Excellence in Journalism funded by the Pew Charitable Trusts and the Joan Shorenstein Center on the Press, Politics and Public Policy at the Kennedy School of Government at Harvard University, http://www.journalism.org/node/11266.

CHAPTER 6

Hillary Clinton's Candidacy in Historical and Global Context
Susan M. Hartmann

In an election trumpeted as marking an important break with the past, Hillary Clinton's candidacy represented both the old and the new in American politics. In an election celebrated as the moment when women broke the ultimate glass ceiling in politics, Clinton's candidacy showed how far women have come, as well as the obstacles that they continue to face. And in an election that promised a new relationship between the United States and the rest of the world, Clinton's candidacy reminds us that American women have still not caught up to the political advancement of women in other nations.

That some eighteen million voters cast their ballots for Hillary Clinton and enabled her to contend for the Democratic Party's presidential nomination right down to the bitter end of the primaries represented a historic milestone for women in American politics. Dozens of women had run in at least one presidential primary, and since 1964, several women's candidacies had been taken seriously enough to be covered in the national press. None had come close to gaining even one million votes.

Yet while Clinton's tremendous success set her apart from her predecessors, her candidacy did not represent a total break with the past. Following one's husband into political office is an old tradition in the United States. Of the first three female governors, one filled her dead husband's position, and the other two served as surrogates when their husbands could not run for reelection. Miriam A. ("Ma") Ferguson won the Texas governorship with the slogan "Two governors for the price of one," after her husband had been impeached from that office. Up through the 1960s, close to half of the women who served in Congress took their dead husbands' seats. Some of these, like Senator Margaret Chase Smith of Maine and Representative Lindy Boggs of Louisiana, carved out careers in their own right, but most served as placeholders.

Hillary Clinton's husband, of course, was very much alive—all too much alive at those times when his fuming, impolitic, and even at times racist statements damaged her candidacy. While benefitting from the opportunities to sit at the policy table during her husband's presidency and while gaining attention that came to her as First Lady, Clinton also carried the negative baggage of her husband's administration, such as the failed health care plan, the Monica Lewinsky scandal, and the midnight-hour pardons. Overall, however, Clinton gained more politically than she lost from her marriage. Although intensely hated by much of the right, Bill Clinton remained popular with Democratic constituencies; his magnetism as a campaigner, in fact, outshone that of his wife. Hillary Clinton benefited not only from her husband's name and popularity, but also from the access he afforded to policy debates and political experience, his political mentoring, his national network of potential supporters, and his access to money. Indeed, it was her connection to him that started her political career and enabled her to be a serious candidate in the first place.

The blatant sexist commentary about her candidacy also represented continuity with past political campaigns, when women were tagged with such adjectives as emotional, unattractive, scolding, and strident. More enraging to Clinton supporters than the sexism itself was the media's tolerance of—and even participation in—such talk. Coming as they did after fifty years in which women had emerged as strong, capable political leaders, the comments about her "cackling laugh," her emotionalism, her cleavage, her shrillness, and her stridency did seem much more extreme than usual—perhaps because her nomination was a real possibility.

By contrast, Republican vice presidential candidate Sarah Palin escaped much of the gender hostility that Clinton faced. There were, of course, references to Palin's clothing, makeup, and appearance generally—especially after the press reported how much money had been spent on such items; and some critics questioned the ability of a woman with five children under age twenty-one to be both a good mother and an effective vice president. Overall, however, Palin encountered less sexism, perhaps because critics found other aspects of her candidacy, such as her unpreparedness, to highlight. Among many Republicans, her strong right-wing credentials, importantly including opposition to much of the feminist agenda, seemed to render her immune to gender hostility.

"Iron my shirts!" and similar taunts hurled at Clinton reflected persisting attitudes that pollsters found among some 5 to 10 percent of respondents who said they would not vote for a woman for president under any circumstances. To start out with even a five-point deficit poses a steep obstacle for any candidate, but, in addition, pollsters found that much larger percentages of respondents did not think that the nation was ready for a female president or believed that people they knew would not vote for a woman. Future polls may show a decrease in such attitudes, because Clinton's near success and Palin's vice-presidential nomination helped to normalize the idea of women as candidates for the highest offices.

Marking a departure from the past, Clinton was not only the first female candidate who possessed a burning desire for the power of the presidency and the disposition for hard-nosed political warfare, but also the first who had a real chance to win. Her predecessors ran to make particular statements or to position themselves for other offices. The first major party candidate, Senator Margaret Chase Smith, put her hat in the Republican ring in 1964 "to break the barrier against women being seriously considered for the presidency," but she withdrew after coming in fifth in the first primary race. In 1972, New York Congresswoman Shirley Chisholm became the first woman to run for the Democratic Party nomination and the first African American to run for the presidency in either major party. She ran not with the expectation of winning, but to establish her right as an African American woman to do so. Chisholm explained, "The mere fact that a black woman dared to run for president *seriously*, not expecting to win but sincerely trying to, is what it was all about. 'It can be done'; that was what I was trying to say." Patsy Mink, Democratic representative from Hawaii, filed in the Oregon primary in 1972 to focus attention on the Vietnam war. Abortion opponent Ellen McCormack ran in eighteen Democratic Party primaries in 1976 to gain publicity for the pro-life position. And Elizabeth Dole, who like Clinton benefited from her marriage to a leading politician and had her own executive and government experience, as well, tested the Republican political waters in 1999, according to some in order to position herself for a vice presidential nomination.[1]

Women's increasing political ambitions reflected the rise of a new women's movement that took institutional form with the 1966 founding of the National Organization for Women (NOW), whose purpose was "to bring women into full participation in the mainstream of American society." Five years later, feminists created the National Women's Political Caucus, a bipartisan organization dedicated specifically to electing women to office and increasing their influence in party affairs. Greater material support for female candidates came with the founding of EMILY's List in 1985. This political action committee collected and distributed funds to candidates well in advance of their primaries. In 1992 it provided $6.2 million to women's campaigns, and in 2000 it raised $20 million to support female candidates and mobilize women voters. Because EMILY's List funded only pro-choice Democratic women, conservative women founded in 1992 their own political action committee, the Susan B. Anthony List, to fund pro-life candidates.[2]

Although Hillary Clinton's achievement owed much to the late-twentieth-century women's movement, she did *not* attempt to appeal to women with a feminist agenda, a distancing from feminism that separated her from many previous presidential contenders. The very first female candidates, Victoria Woodhull in 1872 and Belva Lockwood in 1884 and 1888, both ran on the Equal Rights Party ticket. Democrat Patricia Schroeder, representative from Colorado, explored a presidential bid in 1988 to get feminist issues and antimilitarism into the national debate. Indeed, nearly all of the Democrats who have run in the last four decades addressed feminist issues. By contrast, Clinton neither ran as a feminist nor highlighted women's issues. In fact, despite endorsements from NOW, the National Women's Political Caucus, and EMILY's List, many feminists rejected her candidacy. They decried her acquiescence in the dismantling of the New Deal welfare state, when Bill Clinton signed the bill abolishing Aid to Families with Dependent Children, her votes for the Iraq war, and her apparent flexibility on abortion rights. Obama's parallel tendency to soft-pedal racial issues—aside from one major speech on race—reflected the perceived need on the part of both aspirants to submerge the aspects of their identities that had defeated candidates like themselves for so long. Both had to prove that they would represent the entire population and not favor those who shared their gender or racial identity, a standard that white men never had to meet.

Clinton had to negotiate what is perhaps the biggest challenge to Democratic women running for president—appealing to the party's constituencies of liberals and feminists on issues of peace and social welfare and at the same time cultivating an image of toughness needed to pass the so-called commander-in-chief test. While generally distancing herself from feminism, and though taking somewhat more liberal positions on domestic issues than Obama, Clinton stressed her ability to be a strong and firm leader on foreign and military policy. Yet it is clear that many Democrats—and many feminists—voted for Obama because of his early and consistent opposition to the Iraq war and his promise of flexibility and restraint in foreign policy. Especially after 9/11, it is doubtful that a female candidate could have taken a stance comparable to Obama's and still have been considered strong enough on national security, which suggests that an easier path for the next female presidential contender may lead from a governor's office.

Moreover, despite Clinton's greater hawkishness on national security issues, respondents to public opinion polls rated Obama higher on the ability to serve as commander in chief.

Clinton did overcome the major roadblock for women to high political office—Chisholm, Schroeder, and Dole all deplored their difficulty in raising money. The Dole campaign's financial struggles were so great that table centerpieces were being auctioned off for five dollars at campaign events. Clinton, by contrast, had a national campaign structure, a network of powerful supporters, and loads of money. And while she left the ring with a large debt, she was the first woman to have the material resources necessary to win the election.

The degree to which her sex contributed to Clinton's defeat will never be conclusively determined, in part because so many considerations beyond gender play a part in determining how people will vote. Certainly sexism—and racism, though in more subtle forms—were ever-present in the primaries, and the commander-in-chief dilemma did and continues to burden women. Clinton did best in regions traditionally not hospitable to female politicians, states that have the lowest percentages of women in office; and she bettered her opponent among white, male, less-educated voters. This may be a cause for optimism about the possibility of overcoming gender barriers to political office. A darker possibility is that those white, male, working-class voters supported Clinton primarily because the alternative was an African American.

Two powerful elements combined with Clinton's gender to deny her the nomination. The first was the Clinton campaign's deficit in strategy and organization when compared to her opponent's attention to caucus states and his massive mobilization of grass- and net-roots supporters. Secondly, Obama appealed to voters as a transformative candidate, one who in the eyes of so many Democrats was right on the Iraq war, one who spoke to an intense desire for a new kind of politics, and one who answered a profound longing for racial reconciliation.

Considering Clinton's presidential campaign in an international context sheds further light on its outcome and on the possibilities for female candidates in the future. Since the 1960s, more than fifty women have served as heads of states around the world. Like Clinton, many of these presidents and prime ministers had vital family connections—their fathers in the cases of Indira Ghandi in India and Benazir Bhutto in Pakistan, for example, and their husbands in such cases as Corazon Aquino in the Philippines and Cristina Kirchner in Argentina.[3]

Perhaps most important in accounting for women's absence from the highest office in the United States is its presidential system. Most of the women around the globe who became heads of state on their own, not benefiting from family connections, did so in parliamentary systems. Thus, for example, Golda Meier in Israel, Margaret Thatcher in the United Kingdom, Gro Brundtland in Norway, and Angela Merkel in Germany did not face a national electorate; rather they rose to their positions as prime minister on the basis of their political skills and experience. Even when women ascended to power through family connections, parliamentary systems made those connections more potent.

Most of the female heads of state around the world avoided what past female candidates in the United States have named their biggest obstacle—raising huge sums of money. Women like Thatcher and Merkel rose to power in systems where the emphasis was on the party platform and on candidates' contributions to the party more than on the individual contender and the cult of personality. Finally, women in other countries avoided lengthy campaigns and a media that often focuses on personal traits and endless repetition of candidates' misstatements, appearance, manner of laughing, and flag pins or their absence—all designed to inflame passions and gain an audience rather than to help the public understand where candidates stand on substantive issues.

Calculations about the future of women in high office must take account of the pipeline, which in many other countries produces a larger pool of potential female candidates. In the United States, the conduit that leads from the governor's mansion to the White House has grown in the past decade, yet between 2001 and 2009, only fifteen women served as governor. In Congress, the launching pad so far for most female presidential candidates, including Hillary Clinton, women's numbers have been inching up so slowly that in 2009, women held just 16.8 percent of the seats (seventeen in the Senate and seventy-three in the House). Further down the pipeline, in state legislatures, the percentage of women stuck stubbornly around 22 for a decade before reaching 24.3 in 2009. Comparable numbers of Democratic and Republican women have served as governors in recent years, but in both houses of Congress, female Democrats have far outnumbered Republicans, while in state legislatures women hold significantly higher percentages of Democratic seats than they do of Republican seats.[4] Overall, the portion of women in the pipeline for higher office is very small in contrast to that of men, but within that pool, Democratic women have an advantage.

By contrast, larger proportions of women around the world are entering the political pipeline through quota systems. These procedures set either a minimum level of representation for women among the candidates standing for office, or, in a more gender-neutral way, a maximum for both sexes.

Some forty countries have legal requirements for quotas in elections to national legislatures, while political parties in more than fifty others, including most of Europe, have voluntarily adopted some form of quota system. Such requirements have boosted women's representation in parliaments around the world, with women's members at nearly half, for example, in Rwanda and Sweden, and above 30 percent in such countries as Norway, Argentina, Costa Rica, Germany, New Zealand, and Nepal.[5] Ranking about seventieth in the percentage of women in its national legislature, the United States lags behind much of the world in opportunities for women to enter pipelines to the highest office.

If profound changes in the electoral structure of the United States would help female candidates to overcome gender-based obstacles, what else do the primary campaigns of 2008 suggest about women's future prospects for winning the White House? Like any male aspirant, the first woman to achieve the presidency will possess a burning passion for wielding power, the confidence that she can actually win, and access to enormous amounts of money and political connections. The successful woman will have a more solid and lengthy political résumé than Obama had and at the same time will have avoided taking positions on controversial issues. If she runs on the Democratic ticket, to a greater extent than any male candidate she will project both an image of toughness in foreign and military policy and sensitivity to the needs of the disadvantaged. She will have a harder time than male opponents in establishing her independence from any political liabilities her spouse may bring to her quest; and unlike men who have won the White House, if she has children, they will have neared or reached adulthood. Hillary Clinton surmounted most, though not all, of these historical obstacles facing female candidates. In the end, she could not control the stroke of history that produced a competitor who combined brilliant strategy with a charismatic personality and an ability to speak to deeply felt desires for a new brand of politics.

Notes

1. For historical information on women's presidential candidacies, see Jo Freeman, *We Will Be Heard: Women's Struggles for Political Power in the United States* (New York: Rowman and Littlefield, 2008), 85–110; and Ruth B. Mandel, "She's the Candidate! A Woman for President," in Barbara Kellerman and Deborah L. Rhode, eds., *Women and Leadership: The State of Play and Strategies for Change* (San Francisco: Jossey-Bass, 2007).

2. For a brief survey of women's roles in politics since 1945, see Susan M. Hartmann, "Gender and the Transformation of Politics," in Mark C. Carnes, ed., *The*

Columbia History of Post–World War II America (New York: Columbia University Press, 2007).

3. For women's political participation and leadership around the globe, see Pamela Paxton and Melanie M. Hughes, *Women, Politics, and Power: A Global Perspective* (Los Angeles: Pine Forge Press, 2007).

4. Current and historical statistics for women in public office can be found at the Web site of the Center for American Women and Politics, Rutgers University, http://www.cawp.rutgers.edu.

5. Drude Dahlerup, *Women, Quotas and Politics* (London: Routledge, 2006), 18–21.

CHAPTER 7

Defining a Maverick
Putting Palin in the Context of Western Women's Political History

Melanie Gustafson

Republican presidential candidate John McCain spoke with great grace when he conceded the election to the Democratic candidate Barack Obama on the evening of November 4, 2008.[1] He readily acknowledged that, though he had been bested, this was a "historic election" that left "no reason" for "any American to fail to cherish their citizenship in this, the greatest nation on Earth." After thanking his wife, who was on his left, and other family members for all their support, Senator McCain turned to his running mate, standing to his right. "I am also . . . very thankful to Governor Sarah Palin, one of the best campaigners I have ever seen." As the crowd cheered, "Sarah! Sarah!" he called Governor Palin "an impressive new voice in our party for reform and the principles that have always been our greatest strength" and predicted that Americans "can all look forward with great interest to her future service to Alaska, the Republican Party and our country." Senator McCain did not, however, give Governor Palin the opportunity to speak. Instead, he continued his concession speech by giving thanks to other members of his team and invoking both the past and the future. "Americans never quit. We never surrender. We never hide from history, we make history."[2]

As the audience applauded and cheered, Sarah Palin, the very person who made history in his campaign, stood by smiling, with great emotion in her face, silent or silenced by a campaign team that had chosen her in August but given little or no thought to how Palin should run as a woman despite having the reference of Hillary Clinton's just-failed campaign, data from three decades of both successful and unsuccessful high-stakes political campaigns by other women, and more than a century of women's political history to learn from. The McCain team may have chosen Palin to win the votes of women, and those of conservatives, but they failed to understand or deal directly with the problem people have with associating "woman" with "political." As the former governor of Vermont Madeleine Kunin wrote in 1994, "The female politician is unexpected; her presence provokes a brief digression during which the public wanders off into internal musing about how this woman is like a man and yet not like a man." If Kunin's insight still holds for 2008, and I think it does, then at the same time that Sarah Palin had to run her race, she also had to do what all other political women have had to do—establish and prove that she has a legitimate claim to political power. This was necessary because of the public's ignorance about women's political past and its demand for a priori proof (despite the numbers of women currently holding office) that women can be politicians. One tool that campaigns can use to overcome these sorts of challenges is political storytelling in which they insert their unfamiliar or unconventional candidates into familiar American stories of personal persistence, democratic triumph, and victory against adversity.[3]

While most Americans may have been initially confused by the selection of a woman running mate whom Ellen Goodman called as "unfamiliar as the tundra," Palin's compelling personal story was meant to make her more understandable and acceptable. Personal stories have always been an essential part of political culture, but a weakening of party loyalty in recent years has increased their power. Sharon Begley has argued that personal stories, "whether captured in snapshots (Jack Kennedy, PT boat captain; Teddy Roosevelt, Rough Rider) or in a biography spanning decades (Bill Clinton, 'The Man From Hope,' per the 1992 video), and whether fully accurate or not," define candidates. According to Michael Beschloss, the "feeling that we need to know who these people are has become so enormous that a good part of Sarah Palin's appeal is her life history, the choices she made, things that let voters form a bond with her."[4]

The initial reports about Sarah Palin crafted a story about her rise from the Wasilla town council to the governorship of Alaska and concentrated on this Republican woman phenom's good-government, tax-cutting administration, as well as on her conservative practices and ideals. Because time was so short between when she was placed on the ticket and election day, her personal story needed to be supplemented with a stock story. Stock stories, explains literary scholar Janice Hubbard Harris, help people "understand and make decisions" quickly by reinforcing already accepted "reigning narratives." In political culture, stock stories come into play when a serious issue is involved and time is a concern. Sarah Palin's stock story emphasized the theme of women's advancement. In her August 29 speech in Dayton, Ohio, where she was announced as McCain's running mate, Palin stated: "I can't begin this great effort without honoring the achievement of Geraldine Ferraro in 1984 and, of course, Hillary Clinton, who showed determination in her presidential campaign. It was rightly noted in Denver this week that Hillary left 18 million cracks in the highest, hardest glass ceiling in America. But it turns out the women of America aren't finished yet, and we can shatter that glass ceiling once and for all." In her September 3 nomination speech at the Republican National Convention, broadcast to close to forty million television viewers, Palin again tipped her hat to the progress of American women, coupling that message with an homage to her parents. "My mom and dad both worked at the elementary school in our small town. And among the many things I owe them is a simple lesson that I've learned, that this is America, and every woman can walk through every door of opportunity."[5]

The significant postconvention bounce in the polls for Palin was negatively affected by, among other things, a widespread debate that developed about Palin's feminism and a few questions that were raised about John McCain's seemingly subservient relationship with the woman he called the "most marvelous running mate in the history of this nation." Talk-show host Laura Ingraham claimed Palin represented a "new feminism," the cultural critic Camille Paglia wrote that Palin embodied "a brand new style of muscular American feminism," and Michele Combs published a statement on the Christian Coalition of America website claiming that Susan B. Anthony, "the original feminist," would be proud of Palin. Katha Pollitt, on the other hand, claimed Palin helped clarify that "feminism doesn't mean voting for 'the woman' just because she's female," while Gloria Steinem said, to paraphrase, feminism is not about getting one position for one woman but is about making life more fair for all women. Palin responded "I do" to television anchor Katie Couric's question about whether or not she considered herself a feminist, but when she answered the same question from NBC's Brian Williams she said, "I'm not gonna label myself anything . . . and I think that's what annoys a lot of Americans, especially in a political campaign, is to start trying to label different parts of America different, different backgrounds, different . . . I'm not going to put a label on myself." John McCain may have tried to bring an end to the debate about Palin's feminism with his late-October statement that she "is a direct counterpoint to the liberal feminist agenda for America." Or he might have been addressing a related issue that appeared just after the national convention when the press learned plans were being laid for McCain and Palin to campaign in tandem on the *Straight Talk Express*. The *New York Times*'s Frank Rich wrote in response to this decision that McCain's "conspicuous subservience to his younger running mate's hard-right ideology and his dependence on her electioneering energy raise the question of who has the power in this relationship and who is in charge." In the end, the stock story of women's advancement stalled over the contested term "feminist" and the seemingly uncontested idea of proper gender power relationships in the partisan sphere. It probably also did not help that pollsters had started predicting that, despite the hopes of the Republican Party, the soccer-mom supporters of Hillary Rodham Clinton were not going to cross the partisan playing field for this self-described "hockey mom."[6]

At the same time, Palin's personal story began to look like one of "America's trashiest daytime soaps" as reporters began filing stories not only about her sketchy educational background, book-banning efforts as mayor, and ideas about creationism and global warming, but also a "Troopergate" investigation that included accusations that her sister's ex-husband Tasered his stepson and rumors about her own and her seventeen-year-old unmarried daughter's pregnancies. Very quickly, "a race that began as *The West Wing*," wrote British journalist Jonathan Freedland, turned into one that looked "alarmingly like *Desperate Housewives*." What Sarah Palin and her campaign team urgently needed was a counterstory to convince American voters to support the McCain–Palin ticket. According to Harris, a counterstory told well can create a bond between influential listeners (voters) and the teller. Its power is not in its refutation of a stock story, but in its ability to "quicken and enlarge consciences" by bringing into the discussion "new information, a different perspective, an unsettling angle." Two points about counterstories are instructive when one looks at the McCain–Palin ticket during the 2008 campaign. First is the fact that political culture does not encourage counterstories. Second, counterstories are usually told by outsiders whose stock stories don't fit comfortably into dominant overarching narratives. These points help explain why, after the rise and fall of the first-woman stock story, time was wasted on fitting Palin into the stock story of her running mate and why, instead, consideration should have been given to finding a way to connect Palin's story to a larger history of American women that could then be incorporated into the national narrative of American democracy, because that narrative—the story that we tell ourselves about who we are as a nation and a people—still has meaning to many voters.[7]

McCain's stock story centered on three things: his captivity narrative, his "maverick" moniker, and his self-identification as a "Teddy Roosevelt Republican." McCain's captivity narrative, which he began to relate to the media in May 1973, soon after his release by the North Vietnamese, evolved with different tellings but always included tropes that have been central to captivity narratives since Mary Rowlandson, who penned one of the most historically important narratives, wrote about her three-month captivity during King Philip's War in 1676. The captors are "uncivilized"; McCain's North Vietnamese captors are "gooks" and one is a "psychotic torturer," while the Christian writer Rowlandson called her Indian captors "heathens." The story of survival involves "removes" and "redemption," where the captive's increasing isolation from "civilization" awakens or intensifies a commitment to transcendent ideals; McCain related that the "guidance and wisdom" he prayed for during his captivity led him to "the conclusion that one of the most important things in life—along with a man's family—is to make some contribution to his country."[8]

McCain's redeemed-captive image was buttressed by his equally compelling representation as a maverick, which signaled to voters that he was a man who would act independently and against conventions when needed. The figure of the maverick emerged out of America's frontier mythology, which is an important element in the larger political and popular narrative of American democracy. Historically, the term *maverick* comes from the actions of Samuel Maverick of Texas, whose failure to brand his cattle in the mid-nineteenth century led to problems on the range and a new addition to the lexicon; *maverick* came to mean someone who does not abide by the rules, uses unconventional practices, or holds unconventional and most likely controversial beliefs.

In politics, *maverick* is often used synonymously with *reformer,* one of the most malleable political words of the last century. In calling himself a Teddy Roosevelt Republican, McCain invokes Theodore Roosevelt, "the Rough Rider" of the Spanish–American War, the genuine but cautious reforming president of the United States, and the thoroughly educated easterner who spent part of each year during the 1880s in the Badlands of North Dakota. Those western sojourns were critical to the development of Roosevelt's character; late in life he said that he would never have become president had he not experienced the West. Roosevelt's words echo those of the late-nineteenth-century historian Frederick Jackson Turner, who argued that America's energy and strength, and its sense of freedom and democracy, are formed at its frontiers. It was these tropes—the "limitless possibilities of the American dream, the expansion of American values, the national effort to tame faraway places, the promise of a bounty just over the horizon, and the essential virtue of the American people who explore and settle these frontiers"—that made McCain's stock story compelling and coherent to many voters.[9]

It is not hard to see why the Republicans thought that Sarah Palin of Alaska would be an energizing force on a ticket that was emphasizing the stock story of a strenuous life of redemption and reformism. Throughout the campaign, Palin used the word *maverick* effortlessly and frequently, including no fewer than six times in the vice-presidential debate alone. In her September 3 nomination speech, Palin placed herself on the frontier by calling herself "a gal who knows the North Slope of Alaska," and she identified with the reform tradition in American politics by explaining that she went into politics to "challenge the status quo, to serve the common good, and to leave this nation better than we found it." She was a maverick, a reformer, she indicated, who understood that "sudden and relentless reform never sits well with entrenched interests and power brokers. That's why true reform is so hard to achieve."

While the campaign team may have hoped that by invoking Theodore Roosevelt the political discussion would coalesce around a positive tradition of reforming Republicans, the press and public had another idea about how to use this image. Stories about "Teddy Roosevelt in a skirt" began to appear, and reporters and bloggers began to publish lists of the reasons why Palin, not McCain, was more like Roosevelt—and they didn't discuss reform credentials. Instead, they described how both Palin and Roosevelt were young politicians when they hit the national stage; she was forty-four and Roosevelt was just forty-one when they became vice-presidential candidates. They told how both had about two years under their belts as governors and both took on political corruption while in that office. Rounding out the lists were facts about their large families and shared interest in hunting large animals. The public discussion of similarities quickly wore thin as Sarah Palin demonstrated that she is no Theodore Roosevelt. She lacks a grounding in history, languages, world affairs, and even the basics of the U.S. Constitution, whereas Roosevelt was the author of twenty-six books and thousands of magazine articles and speeches that display his deep knowledge of science and nature, history and literature, and global politics.

Sarah Palin also showed she is no Ronald Reagan, the other western Republican politician to whom she was compared. After listening to her convention speech, Michael Reagan was quoted as saying, "Welcome back, Dad, even if you're wearing a dress and bearing children this time around." Like the identification with Roosevelt, the connection to Reagan rings true in some instances. Both had a career in front of the camera. Both played up their ordinary backgrounds peppered with, for Reagan, the spice of Hollywood, and for Palin, the wonder of beauty contests and hunting trips. Both were attacked for their lack of experience, but both drew enormous praise for their convention speeches. But after her "attack dog" convention speech, Palin never again showed the speaking genius that made Reagan so successful. Palin seemed comfortable with herself, but her inability to answer pointed questions in television interviews with Charlie Gibson and Katie Couric proved troubling. It was probably a great relief to many Americans when these past Republican presidents were allowed to get back into their masculine clothing, but it was probably an even greater relief when McCain began to assert an independent presence on the campaign trail and Palin was metaphorically kept under house arrest.

There was no way the public was going to accept Sarah Palin as a reincarnation of or even the legitimate heir to the legacies of Theodore Roosevelt or Ronald Reagan. More importantly, the campaign wasted time trying to get voters to accept the transmission of McCain's stock story to Palin. It could not work, because McCain's story is fitted out for a man. Despite the fact that many women and men have embraced a common narrative about America's great democratic experiment manifestly performed on the world stage, and despite the fact that women and men have shared in their personal and public lives past and present, the response of the public to women in politics is different from their response to men, because men's and women's political histories have been different. Those running the Republican campaign seemed not to grasp the important fact of these different political histories or the fact that, because of this, they took on an additional, two-part task when they placed Palin on the ticket: to introduce a counterstory that would allow the public to engage in a different and more intelligent discourse about women and the need to embed that counterstory into the larger political narrative.

Sarah Palin is an Alaskan Republican woman, and her counterstory is located in the West of the American imagination. It was in the West that American women first won the right to vote, held significant political offices, and championed a sense of political inclusion and even, at times, gender equality. The first territories and states to give women the right to vote were in the West. Wyoming led the way, followed by Utah, Idaho, and Colorado. Alaska joined the list in 1912. The first woman mayor was elected in frontier Kansas in 1887. Colorado elected the first women as state representatives in 1894. The first state woman senator took her seat in Utah in 1896. Jeannette Rankin, a Republican from Montana, became the first woman in the U.S. House of Representatives in 1917 and then was elected again in 1941.

Sarah Palin might also have invoked the history of women in her party. Three women attended the founding meeting of the Republican Party in Ripon, Wisconsin, still considered a frontier town in 1854, and Republican women were active in every campaign thereafter. Republican Party activist

Anna Dickinson traveled the country and became one of the best-known, and highest-paid, partisan lecturers of the 1860s. Republican women created their first national partisan organization, the Woman's National Republican Association, in 1888 and expanded their presence both in the party and at the polls when women won the constitutional right to vote in 1920.

Bringing this history into play by telling a counterstory of western women's triumphs would have provided an opening for a vibrant discussion about the long history of women's efforts to legitimize their exercise of political power. Reaching into history would have connected Palin's historic run to Belva Lockwood's 1884 run for the presidency. Lockwood was a "Beltway insider" who worked as a lawyer in Washington, D.C., but her candidacy came about because a California woman, Marietta Stow, decided it was time for a woman to run for president. During Lockwood's campaign, partisan men dressed themselves and their opponents in women's clothing to use gender confusion as a political tool, but Lockwood's biographer argues that the candidate herself was treated with respect. Respect was often missing in the discussion of Palin's candidacy.

Connecting the celebration of women's achievements to the ridicule that successful women have faced would have deepened and made more poignant Palin's personal story. Palin could have drawn on the story of Susanna Madora Salter's historic 1887 victory as the Prohibition–Republican candidate for mayor of Argonia, Kansas. Unlike Lockwood, Salter was nominated as a joke, but the twenty-seven-year-old took her job seriously once she was elected. She took her family seriously, too; the second of her nine children was born while she was mayor. Salter's election was not without its detractors, and one of them sent her a card with a drawing of a pair of men's pants and the following verse:

> When a woman leaves her natural sphere,
> And without her sex's modesty or fear
> Assays the part of man,
> She, in her weak attempts to rule,
> But makes herself a mark for ridicule,
> A laughing-stock and sham.
> Article of greatest use is to her then
> Something worn distinctively by men—
> A pair of pants will do.
> Thus she will plainly demonstrate
> That Nature made a great mistake
> In sexing such a shrew.

It is a long time between 1887 and 2008, and many readers might agree with Christine Stansell's 2007 assessment that "women politicians are too numerous, and a few are too powerful, to be invisible or dispensable. They are no longer weird and exotic. Their sheer variety . . . refutes the old stereotypes." Maybe so, but that does not mean that the two things that Erika Falk argues hurt women candidates the most—being ignored and being stereotyped—no longer need to be addressed. Only when Palin and other women politicians embrace stories that have meaning to them and figure out how to tell counterstories that connect them to voters will they be able to challenge stereotypes built out of ignorance and silencing. It won't be easy, because, as Janice Harris explains, as "poignant counterstories get told, advocates of the stock stories are incited to competition." However, women's history is there to be used, and a revised historical narrative about American democracy will do wonders for American political discourse.[10]

Perhaps Sarah Palin recognizes this potential. After her 2008 loss, Palin threw out the traditional political playbook and feminism was again part of her political vocabulary. At a May 2010 gathering of the Susan B. Anthony List, Palin said she was a "frontier feminist" and positioned herself as part of a "new conservative feminist movement" in America. This movement, she stated, had been "influenced by the pioneering spirit of our foremothers . . . tough, independent pioneering mothers, whose work was as valuable as any man's on the frontier." She concluded that as "an Alaskan woman I'm proud to consider myself a frontier feminist like those early pioneering women of the West."[11] On August 20, 2010, in anticipation of the ninetieth anniversary of the Nineteenth Amendment, Palin began her Facebook post endorsing seven women candidates by discussing "the depth of gratitude we owe to those brave feminist foremothers" and concluded by quoting Abigail Adams to support a call to action. "So, ladies, let's lead," Palin wrote, "Let's get things done."[12] Palin has given contradictory messages about her own political plans, but her actions and words have made clear that she expects women to run and win political office, and she will be part of that effort. Kay S. Hymowitz argues that "by leading a wave of new conservative women into the fray," Palin "has changed feminism forever. In fact, this new generation of conservative politicas—having caught, skinned, and gutted liberal feminism as if it were one of Palin's Alaskan salmon—is transforming the very meaning of the women's movement."[13] And this transformation has the power to rewrite history, which, as we know, is constantly under revision. How Palin's own historical candidacy and her subsequent actions will contribute to the rewriting of women's political history is uncertain, but the facts make clear that, whatever the fate of Western women politicians on the national stage, women's history will be part of the public discussion that informs political strategy and all that follows from it.

NOTES

Dedicated to Katherine Jensen, 1946–2010.

   1. I would like to thank Liette Gidlow, David Scrase, Mary Lou Kete, Lisa Schnell, and Ron Formisano for their supportive and helpful comments on this chapter.

   2. *New York Times,* November 5, 2008.

   3. Madeleine Kunin, *Living a Political Life* (New York: Knopf, 1994), 205.

   4. Sharon Begley, "Heard Any Good Stories Lately?" *Newsweek,* September 13, 2008. Beschloss is quoted in Begley.

   5. Janice Hubbard Harris, *Edwardian Stories of Divorce* (New Brunswick, N.J.: Rutgers University Press, 1996), 60; "Alaskan Is McCain's Choice," *New York Times,* August 29, 2008; "Palin's Speech at the Republican National Convention," *New York Times,* September 3, 2008.

   6. Richard Sisk, "John McCain and Sarah Palin Campaign for Swing Voters in Midwest," *New York Daily News,* September 5, 2008; Laura Ingraham quoted in Robin Abcarain, "Sarah Palin's 'New Feminism' Is Hailed," *Los Angeles Times,* September 4, 2008; Camille Paglia, "Fresh Blood for the Vampire," http://www.salon.com, September 10, 2008; Michele Combs, Christian Coalition of America website at www.cc.org, created on September 9, 2008. See also Rebecca Traister, "Zombie Feminists of the RNC," http://www.salon.com, September 11, 2008; Katha Pollitt, "Sayonara, Sarah," *The Nation,* November 24, 2008, 11; Gloria Steinem, "Palin: Wrong Woman, Wrong Message," *Los Angeles Times,* September 4, 2008; "One-on-One with Sarah Palin," *CBS Evening News,* September 24, 2008; "Brian Williams Interviews Sarah Palin," *NBC Nightly News,* October 23, 2008; Lois Romano, "Ideology Aside, This Has Been the Year of the Woman," *Washington Post,* October 24, 2008; Frank Rich, "The Palin–Whatshisname Ticket," *New York Times,* September 14, 2008.

   7. Jonathan Freedland, "Who Knows if Palin Will Bring Victory or Defeat? But the Culture Wars Are Back," *The Guardian (UK),* September 3, 2008; Harris, *Edwardian Stories of Divorce,* 66.

   8. *U.S. News & World Report,* May 14, 1973; Mary Rowlandson, *The Soveraignty & Goodness of God, Together with the Faithfulness of His Promises Displayed; Being a Narrative of the Captivity and Restauration of Mrs. Mary Rowlandson, Commended by her to all that Desire to Know the Lord's Doings to, and Dealings with Her. Especially to her Dear Children and Relations,* 1682.

   9. The quote is from John Tirman, "The Future of the American Frontier," *American Scholar* (Winter 2009). On the November 14, 2004, broadcast of NBC's *Meet the Press,* Democratic strategist James Carville stated: "By and large, our message has been we can manage problems, while the Republicans, although they will say we can

solve problems, they produce a narrative. We produce a litany. They say, 'I'm going to protect you from the terrorists in Tehran and the homos in Hollywood.' We say, 'We're for clean air, better schools, more health care.' And so there's a Republican narrative, a story, and there's a Democratic litany." Evidence that some Republicans had been discussing a narrative strategy came with the September 2008 comments of Peggy Noonan, who, not realizing that a studio microphone was capturing her words, stated in reference to the announcement about Palin: "The most qualified? No. I would think they went for this, excuse me, political bullshit about narratives. . . . Every time the Republicans do that, because that's not where they live and it's not what they're good at, they blow it." Noonan attempted to clarify her remarks in the *Wall Street Journal* of September 3, 2008. Compare these comments to her December 15, 2000, *Wall Street Journal* article "Return to Normalcy," in which she wrote about George Bush: "Now that he's on stage—a large, grand stage—he needs a greater narrative and a bolder sense of drama."

10. Christine Stansell, "Madame Candidate," *The New Republic Online*, April 5, 2007; Harris, *Edwardian Stories of Divorce,* 4.

11. Sarah Palin, Speech to the Susan B. Anthony List, May 14, 2010.

12. Sarah Palin, "Proud to Support More Women Leaders on the 90th Anniversary of Women's Suffrage," http://www.facebook.com, August 20, 2010.

13. Kay S. Hymowitz, "Sarah Palin and the Battle for Feminism," CITY Journal (Winter 2011), http://www.city-journal.org.

CHAPTER 8

Populist Currents in the 2008 Presidential Campaign

Ronald P. Formisano

> "Populism is everywhere in American politics, but nowhere in particular."
> —Alan Ware

The 2008 presidential campaign, notably the primary contests for the Democratic presidential nomination, attracted unprecedented attention to issues of race and gender because of the candidacies of Senators Hillary Clinton and Barack Obama. At the same time, from the early stages of the nominating process for both the Democratic and Republican parties, to the months following the nominations of Obama and Senator John McCain, populist appeals shaped the campaign strategies of both parties' candidates.

Populism as style and rhetoric has long dominated American political campaigns. Its roots reach back deeply into the nation's history to the American Revolution and the early days of the Republic. In the colonial struggle for independence from Britain, as well as in the making of the national constitution, American political leaders invoked "the people's sovereignty" as the theoretical basis of their rebellion and subsequent nation-building.[1]

Although "the people" might be sovereign, the Founding generation of gentlemen tended to be exclusive rather than inclusive in their often vague definitions of just who constituted the people. In the early years of the republic, Virginia gentlemen, for example, were not above "swilling the planters with bumbo" on election days, but they tended to disdain courting voters. In the post-Constitution states, which resembled aristocratic republics more than "democracies," candidates "stood" for office rather than "ran," while their political allies exerted "influence" on their behalf.

But by the 1820s, aspirants for office not only couched their appeals to and for "the people," but also styled themselves as truer representatives of ordinary folk than their opponents. Andrew Jackson, the first president not from Virginia or named Adams, won election in 1828 in large part because of his popularity as a military hero, but also because he seized the populist mantle of the "common [white] man." Even so conservative a political leader as Senator Daniel Webster declared, in his famous 1830 debate with South Carolina's Robert Y. Hayne over the nature of the Union, that it was "the People's Constitution, the People's government, made for the People by the People; *and answerable to the People.*"

In 1840, General William Henry Harrison, a sometime Indian fighter, parlayed his military reputation and alleged log cabin roots into a winning presidential campaign for the Whig Party. Harrison indeed had won battles against Indian and British foes, but he had been born on a Virginia plantation, a son of a signer of the Declaration of Independence. Nevertheless, the Whigs' "Hard Cider and Log Cabin" campaign of 1840 became a historic marker of the triumph of populist posturing in elections.

To be sure, authentic *populist movements* arising from the grassroots and claiming to represent the people also have played a prominent role in American political history. They have ranged from armed agrarian insurgencies in the late eighteenth century to social movements and third parties in the nineteenth and twentieth centuries that also employed a populist rhetoric and style. Populist social movements and parties, too, have been both progressive and reactionary, and often have mixed contradictory impulses from opposite sides of the political spectrum.[2] The focus here, however, will be on the rhetorical and symbolic populism expressed by various candidates during the presidential campaign of 2008. In any year, a latent populist mentality forms part of the bedrock of American politics, but in 2008, lingering culture wars and a staggering economy repeatedly intensified populist appeals in the presidential campaign.

A populist strategy aims to align candidates with ordinary people who lack power or are being oppressed by undemocratic elites who wield excessive power. The essence of populist language is to set up an *us* who claim to speak for the people against a *them* of elites or a powerful few who have taken over or corrupted the political system and rigged it to benefit themselves. These few have assumed various incarnations throughout our history, including "aristocrats," "the money power," "the Slave Power," "capitalists," "robber barons," "malefactors of great wealth," and "economic royalists." Economic populism has usually struggled against cabals of the wealthy and powerful who not only oppressed but looked with contempt upon ordinary people. A Kansas Populist of the 1890s characterized them as "the aristocrats, the plutocrats, and all the other rats."

More recently, especially since the rise of anticommunism in the 1950s and the culture wars growing out of the 1960s, an invigorated cultural populism has targeted an additional set of elites that are alleged to violate traditional "values" of morality, family, and religion. These cultural elites wield power in big cities, universities, and Hollywood and look down upon ordinary, "everyday" Americans who live in small towns or rural areas. Cultural populists' enemies tend to have un-American "values," foreign tastes, and especially put themselves on the wrong side of divisive issues that offend religious fundamentalists: reproductive rights for women, gay marriage, prayer in schools, public religious displays, and opposition to censorship. Cultural populism enjoys fervent enthusiasm among many average Americans, especially the religious right, but its propagation has also been well funded by wealthy conservatives and aggressive business networks intent on cutting taxes, deregulating the economy, and wresting other economic advantages from conservative legislators and presidents.

Attacking one's opponents as un-American, or unmanly, or too learned and intellectual is nothing new in the nation's political history. Anti-intellectualism, especially, is embedded deep in popular culture. But since the 1950s, an anti-intellectual cultural idiom has held a prominent place in our political campaigns.[3]

Historian Michael Kazin has argued that up until World War II, populist rhetoric had been employed generally by political leaders seeking progressive reform or social justice, or challenging the status quo on behalf of the dispossessed. The latter, however, did not usually include racial minorities. Kazin and other scholars have shown that for the last several decades, populist rhetoric, especially that focusing on cultural issues, has been appropriated by conservative champions of corporations, free-market ideologues, the religious/fundamentalist right, and the white backlash against the civil rights movement. "It was a remarkable shift. The vocabulary of grassroots rebellion was now used to reverse social and cultural change, rather than to promote it." And, in the words of Thomas Frank, "[c]ultural anger is marshaled to achieve economic ends."[4]

Progressive economic populist appeals, however, have hardly disappeared. Rather, during a political era of conservative ascendancy they have coexisted while lagging behind a cultural populism that also manages to graft onto itself a faux economic populism. Both progressive and reactionary populist rhetoric and symbolism figured prominently in 2008, and, despite the rather negative view of populism generally that prevails among some thoughtful observers, they continue to be woven into the fabric of American political culture.[5]

The 2008 presidential campaign unfolded in circumstances that encouraged candidates to channel frequent expressions of populist anger directed at both economic and cultural elites. Popular frustration and indeed outrage drew heavily on powerful currents of discontent: a seemingly endless unpopular war, an economy shedding jobs, mounting foreclosures, and declining home ownership. Economic insecurity rose, feeding an overwhelming conviction among citizens that the country was headed in the wrong direction. Indeed, by early October 2008, a Gallup poll found that only 9 percent of Americans were satisfied with the direction of the country, the lowest margin since 1979 (12 percent).

In the early stages of the campaign going back to 2007, when both major parties fielded several candidates vying for the nomination, populist candidates appeared across the political spectrum, from John Edwards and Dennis Kucinich on the left to Ron Paul and Mike Huckabee on the right. Just the name "Mike Huckabee from Arkansas" has a populist ring to it, even without a nickname such as that acquired in the 1890s by the prairie Populist orator known as "Sockless Jerry" Simpson. Jeremiah Simpson won that sobriquet campaigning against a well-dressed Republican politico known as "Prince Hal" Halowell. Simpson pointed out that all princes wore "silk socks" but he, Jeremiah Simpson, wore no socks at all.

A populist message is still conveyed by casual clothing when candidates mingle among voters at factories, community centers, clubs, or local halls. The venue and the clothing are meant to convey connection to average people. Though not necessarily sockless, they appear in shirtsleeves or open collar, or wearing a sweater, windbreaker, or zippered jacket—the latter often bearing the logo of the crowd's association.

In 2000 and 2004, George W. Bush, a graduate of elite schools from a privileged background, effectively presented himself as an ordinary guy and set up a Potemkin-like ranch in Texas for "brush-cutting" (sold as soon as he left office). It is well documented that in 2000, the press corps much preferred Bush and his easygoing style to, in their eyes, the uptight, professional style of Al Gore. "W" was the "guy" they—and many ordinary Americans—would have preferred to sit down with and hoist a brew. Subsequently he became the president who addressed a tuxedo-clad gathering of corporate tycoons by saying that he was happy to be there with "the haves and the have-mores." But Bush's success in conveying a "regular guy" persona—in contrast to the nerdy, policy-wonk images of his opponents Gore and John Kerry (2004)—weighed on the minds of the candidates and consultants of both parties who sought to succeed him.

Accordingly, in 2007–8, populist candidates flourished among the several hopefuls fielded by both major parties. On the Republican side, Congressman Ron Paul, the country doctor from Texas, offered a mix of progressive and mostly reactionary populism. Mike Huckabee appealed far more than Paul to religious Republicans, but with a smile and a dash of economic populism. The former Arkansas governor also had a much bigger impact on the Republican primaries than Paul, undercutting former Massachusetts governor Mitt Romney's formidable candidacy by winning Iowa and drawing evangelical voters away from Romney in other states. He also pleased his religious base by professing his nonbelief in evolution, following in the footsteps of that late-nineteenth- and early-twentieth-century populist Democrat William Jennings Bryan. Like Bryan, too, Huckabee articulated a sharp economic populism, criticizing corporations, calling for changes in U.S. trade policies, charging that Wall Street held too much power over the nation's economy.

Most of the Republican candidates, with the exception of John McCain, took a hard stand on illegal immigration and expressed a widespread populist impulse among Republicans to control our borders and not to provide blanket amnesty to undocumented immigrants. This posture, of course, taps into a long standing nativist strain in American society, though it also draws upon legitimate resentment of job losses, lowered wages, cut benefits, and economic exploitation by the likes of Wal-Mart and Swift Meat Packing.

On the other side of the political spectrum could be found the most unmixed example of a progressive populist, Congressman Dennis Kucinich of Ohio. From his life story, to his standing up to the banks and power companies as mayor of Cleveland, to his exile and vindication in the 1990s, Kucinich fit the profile of a people's champion. Though dismissed by many pundits as one of the "vanity" candidates, Kucinich championed a long list of progressive causes.

The mainstream Democrat most often associated with populism was former vice presidential candidate John Edwards. Edwards, in case the reader has not heard, is the son of a mill worker and the first in his family to go to college. A writer in the progressive *Nation* magazine described Edwards as "Populism's Candidate" because Edwards had cast himself as a fighter against corporate power on behalf of those who have lost jobs as manufacturing has fled the country. After the defeat of the Democratic ticket in 2004, Edwards worked conspicuously to fight poverty and announced his candidacy for 2008 in New Orleans's Katrina-ravaged Lower Ninth Ward.

Edwards designed his populist campaign to appeal to the Democratic base in the primaries. Some critics regarded it as insincere and pointed to the "three H's" as contradicting his professions: his $400 haircut, his home of 28,000 square feet in Chapel Hill, and the hedge fund where he worked after 2004 that invested in companies that foreclosed on mortgages held by victims of Hurricane Katrina. Critics also suggested that perhaps a multimillionaire lawyer was not the best spokesman for the poor. On that point, given the role of money in our politics, if the well-off cannot speak for the poor and disadvantaged, who will?

Less well covered than Mr. Edwards's wealth and hair but also standing in marked contrast to his populist campaign was his procorporate record as senator from 1998 to 2004, when he voted for free trade deals opposed by labor unions, including normalizing trade relations with China. In 2007–8, Edwards said that he regretted many of these votes and, like his vote authorizing President Bush's Iraq war, they were mistakes.

None of this is unusual in American politics. Witness the transformed, trans-America Mr. Romney on the Republican side, who in Massachusetts had won election as governor as a cultural liberal and efficiency-oriented business Republican, but who flipped wholesale to hard-rock conservatism for the Republican primaries. Similarly, Edwards embraced a populist platform as a strategy to win the Democratic nomination. His problem, however, surfaced in one of the final three-way Democratic debates among him and Senators Hillary Clinton and Barack Obama. Just after an exchange in which his rivals had pointed to the historic nature of each of their candidacies, Edwards ruefully commented to the effect that, well, I'm the white guy.

Edwards left the race on January 30, 2008, and from February to early June, Senators Clinton and Obama infused their campaigns with earthy populism as they competed to win over the working-class and economically distressed voters who presumably had supported Edwards. During the rivals' drawn-out and grueling tong war for the nomination, Obama had already established a lead in elected delegates that he never relinquished. But the continuing closeness of their race intensified the struggle as well as their populist campaigning, as did the fact that a potentially decisive number of uncommitted superdelegates intently followed the proceedings. Clinton stayed in the race hoping to convince those delegates that she was the more electable in a general election, even if Obama managed to win more primary and caucus delegates.

The fierce competition and the passionate followings of each candidate also stimulated a remarkable outpouring of enthusiastic participation as the supporters of each campaigned and voted in primaries in unprecedented numbers. The policy differences that separated Clinton and Obama were never great, but each embodied a dramatic contrast to the occupant of the White House, and their followers invested each senator, quite reasonably, with hopes for dramatic changes in policy from the Bush administration. Thus the Democratic primaries of 2008 themselves generated impressive displays of grassroots populist engagement by new voters and previously unengaged Democrats and independents who embraced Clinton or Obama with an enthusiasm not remotely comparable to that elicited by Al Gore or John Kerry eight and four years earlier.

Apart from the competition for Edwards voters, the troubled economy and the unpopularity of most Bush administration policies ensured that the Democrats would continue to deliver messages of economic populism. By February, news reports of the two campaigns regularly emphasized the Democrats' adoption of "Populist Postures." "Clinton and Obama Attack Big Business," ran one headline. The report asserted that Senators Clinton and Obama "intensified their populist appeals . . . responding to widespread economic anxiety and pushing the Democratic Party further from the business-friendly posture once championed by Bill Clinton."

With polls showing that two-thirds of Americans favored some sort of intervention in the economy, both candidates criticized oil-company profits and "special interests" and promised more infrastructure spending and the creation of "green" jobs. As the Wall Street financial crisis began to take hold, Clinton hammered away at hedge-fund managers, drug-company subsidies, and the "two oil men in the White House," while Obama said that with Bush–Cheney the wealthy had "made out like bandits." He also called for ending tax breaks to corporations that move jobs to foreign countries and denounced trade agreements laden with "perks for big corporations but absolutely no protections for American workers."

Conservative observers such as the London-based *Economist* lamented the criticism the Democrats directed at free trade, but a memo leaked from the Obama campaign in March embarrassed the Illinois senator while comforting free traders. A senior member of the Obama campaign apparently had told Canadian officials that the candidate's criticism of NAFTA was "political posturing."

Presumptive Republican nominee John McCain, however, criticized both Democrats' attacks on free trade as preaching "the false virtues of economic isolationism." McCain had secured the Republican nomination as early as March 3 with big wins over his remaining challenger Huckabee in primaries in Ohio, Texas, Vermont, and Rhode Island. Up to that point, his campaign had shown little interest in developing populist themes. When he began to outline his economic proposals in earnest in April, more than one observer described them as "traditional GOP tax-cutting with a dash of populism sprinkled on top." The "dash" consisted of acknowledging the "economic pain" many Americans were experiencing and denouncing corporate malfeasance and "extravagant salaries and severance deals for CEOs."[6]

That same month, the temperature of populist heat in the Democratic contest shot up because of an unguarded statement by Obama that his opponents jumped on to charge that he was out of touch with ordinary people. This was the first of several events that would cause spikes in the populist content of the campaigns.

On Sunday, April 6, at a private fund-raiser in San Francisco, Obama (unaware of being recorded by a Huffington Post blogger) responded to a question about working-class people in small towns and rural areas voting for conservatives. He answered that economic hardship made them "bitter" and so they "cling to their guns and religion." Despite his remarks containing what some commentators acknowledged as considerable truth—one quipped that a candidate's "gaffe" now consisted of saying something that was true—this incident damaged Obama. And it gave his opponents the opportunity to brand him as an "elitist" and to tout their own populist bonding with ordinary folk.

"Elitist, out of touch, and frankly patronizing," said Clinton as her campaign distributed "I'm Not Bitter" stickers and buttons. McCain joined in the critique and shortly after launched his call for a summertime gas tax holiday, removing the 18.4 cent-per-gallon federal tax from Memorial Day to Labor Day. When Obama along with most economists rejected the idea as a gimmick that would do nothing to dampen gas prices, McCain and Clinton kept brandishing the tax holiday, though there was no chance Congress would enact it. Clinton upped the ante by adding that the oil companies should be forced to pay the difference with a windfall profits tax, another unlikely outcome.

To highlight her differences with Obama, Clinton now told her audiences of how her father had taken her hunting and taught her to shoot. Most memorably, in the town of Crown Point, a Chicago suburb in Indiana, at Bronko's Restaurant and Lounge, the media recorded her downing a shot of whisky and a beer, just like one of the guys. (One "geographic irony": the NAFTA-bashing Clinton's whisky was Crown Royal, made across the border in Manitoba, Canada.) By early May, Clinton had transformed herself from a corporate lawyer into Mother Jones.

"Hillary Rodham Clinton began the campaign in pearls, assembling a team of fundraisers that included luminaries from New York's financial services sector." Now she was waging it "in pickup trucks, Dairy Queens and fire stations, taking a 2-by-4 to 'Wall Street money brokers' and vowing to break up oil-rich OPEC."[7]

Obama fought back, first by apologizing for poorly chosen words with his "bitter" remarks, and with speeches that were "unabashed populism," but stumbled again by looking to find the common touch in a bowling alley. Besides wearing a tie, he posted a miserable score (37) while sending several balls awkwardly off the alley into the "gutter." Clinton immediately called for an end to "gutter politics" and offered to settle the nomination with a bowling match—signaling that *she,* unlike Obama, was a regular guy and no nerdy elitist. While Obama was still reeling from the "bitter" fallout, however, Clinton, too, suffered self-inflicted damage when she was found to have exaggerated the dangers of a 1996 visit to wartime Bosnia, boasting, falsely, that she had landed at an airport there in danger of sniper fire.

Both print and electronic media covering the primaries intensified the rivals' battle to wear the populist mantle by relentlessly addressing the question of how white working-class Democrats were voting in the primaries—most of them for Clinton. Although blacks, the young, and the college educated cast ballots reliably for Obama, women, the elderly, and whites, especially males without college education, leaned heavily to Clinton. Pundits on cable news programs focused relentlessly on identifying disaffected white working-class voters as *the* key swing vote, in the Democratic primaries and in the general election to come. The media's obsession with the white working class—they hardly ever mentioned an upper class—allowed wealthy commentators on cable networks to engage in their own form of populist pandering running parallel to that of the candidates.

White working-class voters' favoring of Clinton in Democratic primaries continued to be a central theme of media coverage as she defeated Obama in Ohio and Pennsylvania and racked up huge margins in West Virginia and Kentucky. But Obama's lead in delegates remained steady, and in mid-May John Edwards, who had based his campaign on populist appeals to the working class and poor, endorsed Obama. On June 3, finally, despite Clinton's much-trumpeted hold on white working-class voters, and what one critical reporter called her "paste-on populism," Obama clinched the nomination by reaching the needed number of delegates—augmented by a rush of superdelegates after the final decisive primaries.[8]

Now the question would be whether McCain or Obama could stake a stronger claim to being a people's candidate.

During the summer months, no new populist themes overtly entered the campaign. McCain's campaign became less populist in style because he did less "town meeting" events as his advisors started cutting down on his unscripted exchanges with voters as well as reporters. This resulted in part from McCain's staff deciding that the "liberal media" had turned against a candidate they had previously admired and were now out to play "gotcha" with him. In late July, however, they managed to put Obama on the defensive after he toured the Middle East and Europe and spoke, as in the United States, to huge admiring throngs. On July 30 the Republicans began running TV and Internet spots comparing Obama to "celebrities" like Paris Hilton, all show and no substance, not a "man of the people," just popular.

Although Obama's advisors worried that the "celebrity" attack was damaging, they were ultimately unwilling to give up the crowds who clamored to see Obama speak. This resulted from the Obama organization pursuing a kind of *"technological populism."* At every rally, the audience was asked to pull out their cell phones and to call or text friends and neighbors to support Obama. The campaign also signed up hundreds and thousands of volunteers or donors on the spot. This "techno populism" had begun months before and continued on into the fall. It climaxed during the Democratic nominating convention in Denver in August when extra cell towers were brought to Ivesco Field to handle the outpouring of calls and texting.

Another kind of populism—symbolic—formed the setting for Obama's acceptance speech before a throng of some eighty thousand. He spoke from a stage with a backdrop of a neoclassical temple facade, four huge Doric columns and ten substantial pilasters connected by a frieze and arranged in a curving arc. One architectural critic saw the setting as conveying stability, martial strength, and deep historical continuity, as well as "populism and public participation—the highest-minded ideals of democratic government."[9]

Up until the nominating conventions, themes of economic populism had been most prominent. Amid worries about job losses, mortgage foreclosures, and shaky financial institutions, the cultural populism evident in both Clinton and McCain's efforts to brand Obama as an intellectual elitist had not taken on the status of a full-blown culture war. That changed dramatically with McCain's startling choice of Alaska governor Sarah Palin as his running mate. With Palin's acceptance speech of September 3 to the Republican convention, the culture wars and right-wing populism as embodied by Palin suddenly took center stage in the campaign.

McCain's inner circle of advisers picked Palin precisely because of her conservative populist appeal to the Republican "base" that Karl Rove had mustered for George W. Bush in 2000 and 2004. Although previously unknown to the nation, Palin had been governor of Alaska for two years and before that mayor of a town with a population smaller, said one wag, than that of the bleachers in Fenway Park. But Palin effectively presented herself as an "everyday American," a small-town girl, a hockey mom, a mother of five including an infant with Down syndrome, an NRA member and moose hunter, and opponent of abortion even in cases of rape and incest. She claimed to be, like her newfound mentor John McCain, a "maverick" reformer.

Her speech signaled her role in the campaign: to energize the evangelical right and to attack Washington, the media, and cultural "elites," and to link Obama to them (eventually she would try to link Obama to terrorists). Her denigration of Obama as a "community organizer" subtly referenced the 1960s in the way Republicans habitually had used that decade's upheavals. Indeed, her spunky defiance of the media elite recalled the 1964 Goldwater convention and radical-right Republican delegates screaming invectives and shaking their fists at television newsmen.

One of Palin's harshest critics called her speech, crafted weeks before by a Bush speechwriter, "a political masterpiece, one of the most ingenious pieces of electoral theater this country has ever seen." And Palin's delivery was bravura. With smiles, winks, nods, and cheerful smirks, she played the crowd like the beauty contestant she once was. In the following weeks, her appearances on the campaign trail indeed energized the base as thousands turned out to see this new celebrity, a counternarrative and countersymbol to Obama. Palin skillfully worked the "us versus them" rhetoric and associated herself with "Joe Sixpack," working-class [white] folk, and especially, in her pandering to rural, small-town Americans, "the real America."

On the ticket "to be something," Palin embraced her role with a vengeance, brushing off criticism of her lack of readiness for office and lack of knowledge of public affairs by retreating into a populist mantle of the virtues of the ordinary and average. Palin's masquerade of false populism distracted attention from her extreme policy positions, but after the McCain–Palin ticket received a bump in the polls from her meteoric debut on the national scene, Palin mania steadily eroded.

The Republican base remained excited about Palin, flocking to rallies where she was present (but not to those featuring only McCain). One Republican columnist declared that, like Reagan and Goldwater, "she embodies the values of the American West." Conservative William Kristol, never one to conceal his own erudition and one of Palin's recent tutors in current affairs, offered a populist defense of Palin by claiming that most of the recent blunders and delusions of American public policy have been made "by highly educated and sophisticated elites."[10] Meanwhile, however, several prominent Republicans and conservative columnists (Kathleen Parker and George Will, among others) defected from the Palin bandwagon. Independents and moderates took a second look at her readiness for national office.

By October 9–12, a majority of those polled by Pew Research thought her unqualified for office (52 percent *after* her debate with Democratic vice presidential candidate Joe Biden). Her populist aura diminished, too, following revelations of a designer-clothes shopping spree minimally set at $150,000.

The last major effort of the McCain campaign to make a populist connection with ordinary Americans came on October 15 during the third and final presidential debate. It arose almost by accident when Obama, campaigning in an Ohio suburb, was asked by a local resident about his tax plan. The citizen, Samuel Wurzelbacher, said that he was planning on buying a business with an income of over $250,000 and believed Obama's tax proposals would affect him adversely. Obama answered by pointing out how small businesses would benefit as well as incur taxes with his plan, and finished by saying that fiscal policy should benefit everyone ultimately, including those on the bottom, "you know, spread the wealth around." During the debate three days later, McCain brought up "Joe the Plumber" repeatedly, accusing Obama of wanting to raise taxes on ordinary people and "spread the wealth around."

This populist gambit attracted the usual media frenzy but ran out of steam even more quickly than Palin populism. Joe the Plumber's name was not Joe, nor did he have the resources to buy a business, nor was he a licensed plumber, and he had problems with unpaid taxes. McCain's use of "Joe" sputtered to embarrassment on the morning of October 30 when he called for Wurzelbacher to come forward at a rally and "the plumber" failed to appear. The "spread the wealth" charges against Obama continued, however, escalating to "socialism." Some media commentators saw the charge as not simply ludicrous but a sign of desperation.

Obama meanwhile steadily counterattacked by claiming that 98 percent of small businesses and anyone else who made less than $250,000 a year would have their taxes reduced. McCain's tax plan, he claimed, favored corporations, not workers, and McCain would give more tax breaks to corporations that "shipped American jobs overseas."

In early October at a Pew Forum discussion in Washington on the role of "the culture war" in the campaign, several of the panelists agreed with the proposition that "economic populism almost never triumphs. It's easier to resent intellectual arrogance than economic success."[11] But in this election, the inexorable downward slide of the economy made economic populism the trump card, and the Obama campaign's relentless association of Senator McCain with Bush administration economic policy took its toll.

So, too, did mistakes by McCain. In September, as the financial crisis worsened, McCain assured voters that "the fundamentals of our economy are strong." The Democrats pounced on this statement and kept hammering away on themes of economic populism. Surprisingly, as the crisis deepened, Obama crafted an image of steadiness while McCain appeared rudderless, veering in too many directions.

In the final weeks before the election the culture war ignited by Palin faded, and McCain–Palin attacks on Obama as a "socialist" or "palling around with terrorists" rang hollow, arousing only the Republican base. Obama's decisive victory in the popular vote (66,882,230–58,343,671) put him 7 percentage points ahead of McCain (53% to 46%). But the spread among the real plumbers—not the unlicensed tax dodger named Samuel—was even greater. Among families with income of less than $50,000 a year, Obama beat McCain by 60 percent to 38 percent. Blue-collar cities throughout the country, like Democratic vice presidential candidate Joe Biden's hometown of Scranton, Pennsylvania, voted for Obama.

This should have come as no surprise, but for the media obsession with the conservative "values" of the white working class.[12] The notion that this group has become more conservative and is moved inordinately by moral issues has been sharply challenged by Princeton political scientist Larry M. Bartels. His research shows that low-income whites "have actually become more *Democratic* in their presidential voting over the past half-century, partially countering Republican gains among more affluent voters." Even more against conventional wisdom, Bartels finds that low-income white voters "continue to attach less weight to social issues than to economic issues." Further, his analysis suggests that economic issues remain central in presidential elections, "*especially* among 'the people on the losing end' of the free-market system."[13]

In 2008, economic populism trumped cultural populism within a deteriorating economy and a weakening of religious zealotry. In 2004, gay marriage referenda in thirteen states had brought out the Republicans' fundamentalist base. But popular attitudes to mixing religion and politics showed signs of declining. In 1996, 54 percent of those polled believed it proper for churches to engage in politics (43 percent opposed). After slight declines to majorities of 51 percent in 2000 and 2004, by 2008 a small majority of 52 percent now believed that churches should keep out of politics, with 45 percent still approving.

Economic populism alone did not determine the outcome of the 2008 election, but it pervaded other framing elements of the November vote, particularly the retrospective perception that the Bush economic policies had failed and that McCain was associated with them and Obama was not. Most voters were not "better off" in 2008 than they had been in 2004, and they knew it. The unpopular war in Iraq, a worsening of the U.S.–Allied war in Afghanistan, scandal in the Justice Department, the administration's handling of Katrina, and much more influenced the outcome. Further, it needs to be noted that Barack Obama, willing to pound away at oil-company profits, at tax breaks for corporations and the wealthy, at corporations that ship jobs overseas, at unfair labor laws, and more, is no thoroughgoing economic populist.

Like Clinton during her primary run, Obama throughout the campaign enjoyed support from financiers and Wall Street. Speculation arose early in the campaign that if Obama were elected president, his Supreme Court appointments, like those of Bill Clinton, were unlikely to be economic populists.[14] Political analysts often commented on Obama's restrained brand of economic populist rhetoric, even during September. He himself said on one occasion that his populism was aimed less at frustration with big business than at dysfunctional government. "When you hear me talk about people versus the powerful," he told a *Washington Post* reporter in August, "my populism is built most powerfully around the sense that government is nonresponsive to these folks. They're probably less angry at Wall Street for making money and angrier at Washington for not just setting up some basic rules of the road." Why, then, he was asked, single out oil companies for a windfall-profits tax? Because, he said, the companies' "outsized profits" had no relation to their investments or production costs. Just after at a town meeting, however, he responded to the same question differently: "Does it make more sense for the oil companies to pay for it [the tax], or does it make more sense for the struggling waitress who is barely getting by to pay for it?" "And the answer is, I'm going to fight for the waitress, not because I hate the oil companies but because I think it's more fair."[15]

The rhetoric of economic populism flourished as job losses mounted and Americans' retirement accounts dwindled. And a good deal of sincerity infused Senator Obama's calls for fairness. But just as Obama needed to avoid sounding like "an angry black man," so, too, he could not adopt the populist style of a Dennis Kucinich or even of the 2000 Al Gore.

At times, as in his rejection of a summer gas-tax holiday, Obama's populism consisted of a Harvard Law School populism that rejected simplistic solutions and, as in his historic speech on race, treated voters as adults. Barack Hussein Obama sprang from an economic and cultural background a world apart from the blueblood, old-money origins of Franklin Delano Roosevelt. But when the aristocratic FDR denounced the "economic royalists" in the throes of the Great Depression, no one confused him with the demagogue Huey Long. During Obama's dramatic presidential campaign, he not only projected, but, according to all inside accounts of his decision making at critical moments, *maintained* a cool detachment. Though not of the gentry bred, Obama's sangfroid might have drawn the admiration of that Upper Hudson River Valley patrician with the cigarette holder and his jaunty upper-class breezy confidence.

The 2008 victory of a candidate of education and intellect, after a campaign in which the opposition targeted those qualities as "elitist" and antipopulist, represents something of an anomaly. Although the pattern is not airtight, candidates painted as overeducated and out of touch with ordinary Americans more frequently have lost presidential elections. The branding of Adlai Stevenson as an "egghead" comes to mind, along with the depictions of Michael Dukakis, Al Gore, and John Kerry as technocrats or bookish intellects without the common touch. Dukakis's appeal to "competence over ideology" notably failed to play in Peoria.

The anti-intellectual strain of American populism began conspicuously in 1828 with the victory of "unlettered" Andrew Jackson over the learned and intelligent incumbent president John Quincy Adams. Jackson postured as the fierce enemy of elites and a champion of the people. His supporters trumpeted his popularity as a military leader, which, as Daniel Walker Howe recently pointed out, constituted an ancient but not necessarily democratic political appeal. The contest, said the Jacksonians, was "Between J. Q. Adams who can write / And Andy Jackson who can fight." Jackson's well-organized campaign of emerging politicos relentlessly mocked Adams's intellect and his experience as a diplomat, establishing "a pattern in American politics, warning aspiring politicians to conceal their intellect rather than proclaim it."[16]

In 2008, Senator Obama not only deflected attacks on his intellect and "elitism," but also tilted in his favor the populist economic impulses energizing the electorate. Yet if well-tempered populism can be highly effective as a campaign strategy, it can also be a hindrance to governing and crafting policy. Populist appeals of any kind inevitably raise expectations for results, and disillusionment with or withdrawal from politics on the part of segments of the citizenry have been the flip side of promises to give government "back to the people" or to transcend "politics as usual."

Increasingly in American political life, popular expectations ranging from deliverance to doom have focused on the presidency. But this is hardly a new development. Bruce Ackerman, in *The Failure of the Founding Fathers,* described the rise of the "plebiscitarian presidency" coming into being as early as the 1800 election of Thomas Jefferson. According to Ackerman, the president came to represent the "Voice of the People" and became a tribunal chief executive not anticipated or wanted by the makers of the 1787 constitution, leading to institutional confrontations that periodically have threatened to upset the constitutional balance of power.[17] While I disagree with Ackerman's location of this development in the early republic, the term "plebiscitarian presidency" well describes both the accretion of power to the presidency and the populist expectations that have gravitated to it since at least the mid-twentieth century.

But powerful as the presidency has become, those expectations are often unrealistic. Many citizens, holding a wide variety of policy preferences, get caught up in believing that simply with the election of the right individual as president, the right liberal or conservative, a new era will begin. Thus the president's every move and utterance is scrutinized, magnified, and broadcast across the land—and a president's power is enormous and a few words may indeed have enormous consequences. But there is often a disconnect between populist promises and expectations generated by candidates' obligatory democratic rhetoric suffusing campaigns and the structures of governance standing apart from the presidency.

Take the issue of "partisan gridlock in Washington" as addressed by candidates from the early primary season through the 2008 election. Most candidates, including Mitt Romney, John McCain, and Obama, promised to "fix Washington," or "reach across the aisles," or bring a new spirit of conciliation to governing. Certainly a new administration can bring to bear in its dealings with the opposition a fresh tone of civility and willingness to negotiate. But both candidates and media coverage routinely ignore the structural changes in Congress, for example, that have increased hyper-partisanship.

In the 1970s, Democratic reformers in the House enacted new rules that undermined two-party negotiation as well as seniority and shifted the emphasis to party loyalty. Thus if committee chairs want to stay in power, they need to toe the party line. As seniority declined, party discipline flourished. When Republicans took over Congress in 1994, they made further rules changes and enforced party discipline with a vengeance. Meanwhile, personal friendships among legislators have declined as they return to their districts more frequently. Television coverage prompts congressional orators to declaim in a more confrontational partisan vein, and outside pressure groups and lobbyists often work against compromise. Beyond these Beltway-based causes of rigid partisanship, the rise of overtly partisan media on television, radio, and the Internet have promoted ideological division in the electorate and representatives. Even the so-called mainstream media tend to undermine bipartisanship by their preference for covering or even encouraging conflict.[18]

Not least of the structural inducements to partisan militancy springs from gerrymandered safe seats for House incumbents with district lines drawn that defy geography, common sense, and community and that elect Republicans or Democrats by large margins. All of Congress's history shows that representatives from districts that are competitive are the most willing to compromise.

Populist expectations are embedded in our political culture. The theory of the people's sovereignty and democratic rhetoric constantly proclaim that the "the people's will" shall or should prevail. These bedrock assumptions will continue to shape political campaigns. And certainly the tension between the ideal of "rule by the people" and the reality of rule by elected and unelected elites is likely to continue.

NOTES

1. Edmund S. Morgan, *Inventing the People: The Rise of Popular Sovereignty in England and America* (New York: Norton, 1988); Christian G. Fritz, *American Sovereigns: The People and America's Constitutional Tradition Before the Civil War* (New York: Cambridge University Press, 2008).

2. On the former, Ronald P. Formisano, *For the People: American Populist Movements from the Revolution to the 1850s* (Chapel Hill: University of North Carolina Press, 2008); for third parties and populist appeals, Mark Voss-Hubbard, "The 'Third Party Tradition' Reconsidered: Third Parties and American Public Life, 1830–1900," *Journal of American History* 86 (June 1999): 121–50.

3. Richard Hofstadter, *Anti-Intellectualism in American Life* (New York: Knopf, 1963). "Again and again, but particularly in recent years, it has been noticed that intellect in America is resented as a kind of excellence, as a claim to distinction, as a challenge to egalitarianism, as a quality which almost certainly deprives a man or woman of the common touch," p. 51.

4. Michael Kazin, *The Populist Persuasion: An American History* (Ithaca, N.Y.: Cornell University Press, 1998, rev. ed.; orig. pub. 1995), 4; Thomas Frank, *What's the Matter with Kansas?: How Conservatives Won the Heart of America* (New York: Metropolitan, 2004), 5.

5. John Lukacs, *Democracy and Populism: Fear and Hatred* (New Haven, Conn.: Yale University Press, 2005).

6. Quotations from Peter Gries, "McCain Fleshes Out His Economic Plan," *Christian Science Monitor* (April 28, 2008): 2, and Michael Cooper, "McCain Outlines Broad Proposals for U.S. Economy," *New York Times*, April 16, 2008.

7. Glenn Thrush, "Her Populist Push: Hillary Takes Aim at Gas Prices; Targets Wall St. on the Economy," *Newsday* (May 6, 2008).

8. Quotation from Joe Klein, "The Game Changer," *NewsBank* (May 19, 2008).

9. Christopher Hawthorne, "Critic's Notebook: Obama Pledges Greek; The Athenian Backdrop for His Acceptance Speech Is Rife with Symbolism," *Los Angeles Times*, August 30, 2008. Of course other symbolism was at play: the stadium setting

echoed John F. Kennedy's 1960 convention acceptance speech at the Los Angeles Memorial Coliseum, and Obama's acceptance came on the anniversary of Martin Luther King Jr.'s 1963 "I have a Dream" speech.

10. Michael Gerson, "Starbucks Does Not Equal Savvy," *Newsweek* (September 29, 2008): 34; William Kristol, "Here the People Rule," *New York Times*, October 20, 2008.

11. Eleanor Clift, "Palin Reignites the Culture War—Palin, Obama and the Culture War," *Newsweek Web Exclusive* October 3, 2008, http://www.newsbank.com.

12. The other major reason for surprise was the expected "Bradley effect" that failed to materialize, that is, that white voters express more willingness to vote for an African American when polled but vote otherwise when in the privacy of the polling booth.

13. Larry M. Bartels, *Unequal Democracy: The Political Economy of the New Gilded Age* (Princeton, N.J.: Princeton University Press, 2008), 3–4, 66.

14. Jeffrey Rosen, "Supreme Court Inc.," *New York Times Sunday Magazine* (March 16, 2008): 66, 68.

15. Ruth Marcus, "Pivoting to Populism," *Washington Post*, August 7, 2008, regional edition; also, Eleanor Clift, "The Elusive White Male Vote—Clift: Edwards, Obama and Working Class White Men," *Newsweek* (May 16, 2008); Nelson D. Schwartz and Steve Lohr, "Looking for Swing Votes in the Boardroom," *New York Times*, August 17, 2008; Jeff Zeleny, "Obama Looks to Shift Focus of Campaign to Economy," *New York Times*, September 17, 2008; Patrick Healy, "In a Time of Crisis, Is Obama Too Cool?" *New York Times*, September 26, 2008.

16. Daniel Walker Howe, *What Hath God Wrought: The Transformation of America, 1815–1848* (New York: Oxford University Press, 2007), quotation 279, 282; Lynn Hudson Parsons, *The Birth of Modern Politics: Andrew Jackson, John Quincy Adams, and the Election of 1828* (New York: Oxford University Press, 2009), xvii. "John Quincy Adams's resume may indeed have been impressive, but his defeat . . . was a signal that in the future such resumes might not be sufficient and indeed might be handicaps. In the same way, his powers of intellect, conceded by friend and foe alike, and which had served him so well as a diplomat, were dismissed as irrelevant to the presidency," *ibid*.

17. Bruce Ackerman, *The Failure of the Founding Fathers: Jefferson, Marshall, and the Rise of Presidential Democracy* (Cambridge, Mass.: Belknap Press of University of Harvard Press, 2005), 5–6.

18. Ronald Brownstein, *The Second Civil War: How Extreme Partisanship Has Paralyzed Washington and Polarized America* (New York: Penguin, 2007).

PART III
Legacies
Democracy Undermined?
Feminism Redefined?

CHAPTER 9

Obama 2.0
Farewell to the Federal Campaign Finance System and the Secret Ballot?

Paula Baker

The massive cost of the presidential campaign and the way that candidates raised such astonishing amounts are among the less-celebrated "firsts" recorded in the 2008 elections. It was the most expensive presidential campaign ever: together, candidates John McCain and Barack Obama spent more than $1 billion. Include all of the candidates who fell away before the conventions and the figure rises to $2.4 billion. Everyone helped, but Obama's campaign really propelled the great leap forward. He was the first candidate to finance his own general-election race since the system came online in 1974, therefore bypassing both the $84 million in federal funds and the restrictions that taking those funds imposes. Free to raise as much as possible, the Obama campaign brought in more than $750 million—more than the 2004 Kerry and Bush campaigns combined; more than triple the 2004 Bush campaign, the previous champ; and $400 million more than McCain's campaign, even after including the Republican National Committee's help. The Obama organization was so flush that it was able to buy time from the major networks for a half-hour infomercial that ran right before the general election (delaying a World Series game, an incidental reminder that baseball is no longer the national pastime), expand the reach of its ads to include Xbox games, pay campaign workers' salaries and health benefits through the end of December, and allow workers to keep their laptops.

Another record breaker recorded by the Obama campaign was how much of the money came via the Internet. According to the campaign, about three million donors clicked on the "donate now" button, both when the news was good and especially when the opposition seemed to be gaining. Having clicked once, donors were never alone again. They could count on e-mail and text messages urging them to do more to participate in the cause by giving again. The button continued to beckon and the e-mails and texts persisted even after Obama's victory, with the contributions and proceeds from the purchases of Obama-logoed T-shirts, posters, fleece scarves, and other gear directed to the Democratic National Committee. The reports of so many donors and success in raising money in small sums were enough to make traditional watchdogs roll over. Obama's campaign had made an "extraordinary breakthrough in small donor fundraising on the Internet," according to Fred Wertheimer, president and CEO of Democracy 21 and former president of Common Cause, two organizations long identified with campaign finance reform aimed at eliminating the influence of money on politics. No matter how staggering the sums spent and raised, Wertheimer saw "the pathway to the future" in the Obama campaign's success in Internet fund-raising.[1]

The 2008 fund-raising feats, especially those of the Obama campaign, are certainly firsts. But are they "historic"—do they suggest breaks with past patterns and put us on "the pathway to the future"? As money kept flowing to Obama's campaign, it was hard to escape the conclusion that the future will not look anything like the existing system of public financing for presidential campaigns. What candidate with even a shred of a chance of winning would again take public funds and risk being outspent by as much as four to one in swing states, as McCain was? But I'm at least as impressed with the continuities with past patterns as with most of the apparent changes. First, the next time we enjoy another round of campaign finance reform, it will be underpinned by partisan considerations, like all others in the past. Second, while the Obama campaign raised the bar on fund-raising and spending, that bar had been steadily rising, and the freakish circumstances of 2008 compelled massive fund-raising and spending. Third, the mix of small and large donations was not very different from that of campaigns past, especially those candidates who came to embody a cause. Finally, while I consider Internet fund-raising as an update to direct mail—a technological refinement of earlier techniques aimed at raising small contributions—the Internet makes possible what I consider a worrisome result: the demise of the secret ballot, at least for those moved to contribute to a campaign. *That* could be historic, and not in a good way.

The place to begin is with the taxpayer-funded campaign system. Created in 1971, amended in 1974, and refined and litigated ever since, the Federal Election Campaign Act (FECA) replaced the ineffectual Federal Corrupt Practices Act passed in the 1920s. Like the earlier swipe at regulating money in politics, the FECA promised to purify politics by requiring candidates to disclose the sources of their funds, preventing corporations, unions, and other large organizations from making direct contributions, and limiting how much campaigns could raise and spend. There were important innovations: the FECA created the Federal Elections Commission (FEC), introducing an enforcement mechanism that previous legislation lacked, and provided public funds, generated in part by taxpayers directing a dollar of their taxes to the program by checking a box on their returns.

The FECA was not the product of scandal. It predated the revelations of the 1972 Nixon campaign's shakedowns of corporations. Instead, like earlier efforts to control the impact of money on politics, it was the result of the steady work of policy wonks concerned about campaign spending and contributions and of a political coalition featuring independent Republicans and Democrats that pushed legislation that eventually attracted wide support. So it was in 1883 and 1907, when reform-minded ("mugwump" or "progressive") Republicans and Democrats spearheaded civil-service reform and the Tillman Act, which banned corporate contributions. However stirring the good-government rhetoric, the laws aimed to combat the regular Republicans' advantages in raising funds. So it was with the Corrupt Practices Acts of the 1910s and 1920s, with their ludicrously low spending limits for congressional campaigns. Republicans shot back with attempts to stop the flow of money from organized labor in the late 1930s. Democrats and independent Republicans, as political scientist Raymond La Raja has argued, prefer rules that maximize the freedom of groups outside of the parties (labor unions are the archetype) to raise and spend while limiting the Republican Party's advantages in collecting funds by and for the use of centralized party organizations. Each party plays to its strength and looks to trip up the other.[2]

The partisan pushing and shoving continued in the more recent rounds of campaign finance reform. The FECA and its 1974 post-Watergate amendments limited what candidates could contribute to their own campaigns (a provision found unconstitutional) and how much candidates could spend (ditto, unless candidates accepted public funds). They required disclosure of contributions over $100 (later raised to $200), capped individual contributions to campaigns to $1,000 and political action committee contributions to $5,000, discouraged large contributions to the political parties, and set up a compliance system monitored by the FEC. Such rules favored the Democratic decentralized way of doing things, while Republicans took advantage of revisions in the late 1970s that loosened the contribution and spending rules covering the parties to strengthen its organization and fund-raising capacity.

These revisions also opened the "soft money" loophole, allowing state parties to collect funds targeted to get-out-the-vote activities. Donors were disclosed to the FEC but were not bound to federal contribution limits. "Soft money" became a mainstay of Democratic Party budgets. Growing concerns about "soft money" (often mistakenly called "unregulated"), the power of political action committees, and, by the late 1990s, the spending of new "527" organizations (a nickname that refers to the section of the federal tax code that covers tax-exempt political groups) produced the Bipartisan Campaign Reform Act (BCRA, or McCain-Feingold) in 2002. The BCRA's increased contribution limits—currently $2,300 to candidates in both primary and general elections—nodded in the direction of the Republican Party, which had a smoothly running system for generating donations under the federal cap. Parties, however, lost many of the fund-raising advantages gained in the late 1970s (a plus for the Democrats), while new rules controlled PAC spending. 527s continued to occupy a regulatory limbo, and with other "soft money" roads blocked, attracted the mega-contributions in 2004.

Reform has changed how candidates, parties, and outside organizations raise and spend funds, but it hasn't succeeded in controlling costs. Totals for all candidates that used to be in the millions ($228.9 in 1996 and $649.5 in 2000) leapt into the billions ($1.01 in 2004 and more than double that in 2008). Spending has been trending up, and for good reason. Campaigns cost money. It's expensive to raise money, especially in small sums; it costs money to hire staff, craft a message, communicate with voters across media platforms, organize volunteers, and travel. It still costs more to promote Pepsi for a year than to elect a president. Perhaps there is a point of spending overkill. Like many in Ohio in 2008, where the campaign on the airwaves lasted nearly two years, I can imagine a safe cutoff well below the sums dumped on politics-weary Buckeyes. But no campaign with money in the bank (except Senator John Kerry's in 2004) wants to risk not conducting that final ad blitz and losing. The old advertiser's saw about how "half of advertising money is wasted, but we don't know which half" works for political campaigns, too.

Because of campaign costs and regulations that directed when candidates who took federal money could spend it, candidates who had a chance to win began to reject taxpayer subsidies for primary campaigns. Senator Robert Dole's 1996 campaign was the dismal cautionary tale. It had burned through all but about $2 million of its spending allotment fending off primary challengers five months before the Republican convention, after which it could tap general election funds. The Dole campaign went silent, while incumbent president Bill Clinton, without a primary challenger, took the opening to spend the $19 million stashed away. So in 2000, candidate George W. Bush wagered correctly that he could raise more than the federal limit and opted out of the public funding system for the primaries. In 2004, his campaign was joined by those of Governor Howard Dean and Senator John Kerry.

In the 2008 primary season, no one with ambitions of winning accepted taxpayer funds and their restrictions.

The 2008 money race was more intense than usual, because for the first time since 1952, neither party ran an incumbent or a presumptive nominee. Political reporters measured the candidates' credibility through polling, but also through their quarterly FEC reports. Suitably big dollar figures and numbers of donors indicated which candidates had caught on with whom, and which candidates had the chance to catch on once more voters were paying attention. Money in the bank in early 2007 had practical as well as symbolic importance, since many states, including ones with expensive media markets, had pushed forward the dates of their primary elections. If a candidate—say, Senator Hillary Clinton—could build on her early fund-raising advantage and build a substantial financial lead, the nomination contest might have been over in February.

But it wasn't. The real surprise was Senator Obama's ability to match or exceed, depending on the calculation, Clinton's take in the first quarterly report. Clinton brought in $26 million, a sum that included funds left over from her senate campaign, while Obama totaled $25 million in new contributions. The Obama campaign's first-quarter fund-raising success was not a fluke: by the end of 2007, it had collected more than $103.8 million, lagging only slightly behind Clinton's receipts. Even better, from the point of view of the Obama campaign, only one-third of his contributors had given $2,300, the federal maximum, while half of Clinton's contributors were maxed out. The Obama campaign could return to these donors, the most likely to give, again.[3]

That it did, over and over, a routine made cheap and easy by the Internet. Since early in the twentieth century, the parties and candidates have borrowed the newest technologies to locate and dun likely donors, especially those of relatively modest means who might replace the steady support the armies of public employees provided in the nineteenth century. The problem was that small-donor programs (the original ones adapted the models of World War I bond and Community Chest drives) usually barely repaid the investment. Direct mail, a tool used by marketers, found its way into politics in the 1960s. The Barry Goldwater 1964 campaign made good use of it, but the method came into its own with Morris Dees. Dees had made his fortune in direct-mail sales and thereafter devoted himself to liberal causes, especially civil rights, cofounding the Southern Poverty Law Center in 1971. He designed a wildly effective direct-mail fund-raising campaign for Senator George McGovern's 1972 campaign. With big donors providing the seed money in the form of contributions or loans, Dees constructed a high-quality mailing list using the names McGovern had stockpiled, along with membership lists of anti–Vietnam War and other groups that might be sympathetic to McGovern. The campaign raised $30 million, with only slightly more than 25 percent coming in contributions of more than $100. The campaign kept in touch with those who gave, encouraging them to join such things as the "McGovern Presidential Club," with a coupon book serving as a reminder to write another check. Some found it "slick and offensive," like a bank savings-plan promotion, to be urged to "'budget' myself like a Christmas Club to have you as our President," wondering if a president or "an electric fry pan or a clock" would be the bonus. But it worked. At least six hundred thousand people contributed, sending money even when polling made it clear that the campaign was doomed.[4]

An effective direct-mail program requires targeted lists, which are costly to rent or purchase, and even then a good deal of money spent on staff, postage, and materials heads straight to the recipient's trash. By contrast, former California governor Jerry Brown's toll-free number, repeated incessantly in his 1992 presidential campaign, needed only to pay for the line and the operators standing by. Donors (subject to Brown's own $100 limit) selected themselves, eliminating duplication, waste, and large up-front costs. Joe Trippi, a Democratic campaign operative, noticed the simple elegance of the Brown fund-raising operation, one that allowed the campaign to keep going on small contributions while candidates shouldering larger fixed costs dropped away. He built on the idea when he managed Governor Howard Dean's 2004 presidential campaign. Dean's early opposition to the war in Iraq separated him from most of the rest of the field, while his fund-raising success—even leading the field of better-known and more connected rivals—gave his candidacy credibility and buzz. By 2004, all candidates had Web sites, of course, but none was as extensive as what Trippi had designed for Dean, and none matched the interactive features that connected donors, many of whom became volunteers, with the campaign and with one another.[5]

In the end, Dean's candidacy looked more like that of other cause candidates who attracted small contributions. Goldwater, Alabama governor George Wallace, McGovern, television commentator Pat Buchanan in 1992, and Congressman Ron Paul in 2008 all inspired excitement and intense loyalty in their varied constituencies. Their supporters were stirred to give even small amounts to candidates who seemed to speak a populist truth to power. Obama's campaign shared some features of earlier cause candidates. A new face in politics, an inspirational speaker, an opponent of the Iraq war, a young man, and an African American, Obama promised to be a break from the stale cultural battles and compromises, a promise that attracted many who found Clinton to be the embodiment of a worn-out political formula. For those who considered their opposition to the war in Iraq as the make-or-break issue, Obama was the best candidate who also had a chance to win in the general election.

Obama's technologically sophisticated campaign built on the Dean model and expanded it to incorporate innovations in social media. An Obama supporter could spend a good amount of time on my.barackobama.com, not only doing the standard stuff—learning about what the candidate was doing and saying and perhaps reading an issue paper. They could also give advice, encourage other supporters, and compare notes about what they were doing for their candidate. Many tech-savvy Obama supporters created their own videos—priceless politically because they were (or seemed) authentic, not the product of an ad agency. Most of all, they gave money, prompted by messages from the campaign and from their online peers.[6]

But the campaign was also different from cause candidacies of the past in its financing. Yes, the campaign attracted a record number of small donors. It also drew in a record number of large donors, as we might expect in a campaign that, well, brought in record numbers, period. More important, the percentage of donors who gave less than $200—the figure under the BCRA that triggers disclosure—was in line with that of previous campaigns. George Bush and John Kerry received 25 and 20 percent respectively of their contributions from donors who gave $200 or less. According to political scientist Michael Malbin, who aggregated the contributions of individuals whose under-$200 contributions eventually added up to an amount above it, 27 percent of contributions to Obama fit the conventional (under $200) definition of "small." Those giving the largest sums—those in the $4,600 range and bundlers of same—were those who have been steady supporters of Democratic nominees. They were the men and women in financial services and investment banking, the technology industry, entertainment, and law firms. But there were also middle- and upper-middle-class people who, out of their disgust for the Bush administration or their hope for an Obama presidency, gave repeatedly.[7]

Obama's success with both small and large donors allowed him to reject the support of the federal taxpayer-funded system. "The public financing of presidential elections as it exists today is broken," Obama said, "and we face opponents who've become masters at gaming this broken system." The explanation is peculiar, since the 527 groups and cash they raised were a good deal more heavily stacked on the Democratic than the Republican side in both 2004 and 2008. That said, if candidates opt out, then the system is, by definition, broken. Special circumstances—a charismatic candidate, an unusually long and closely contested primary season, and what now seems by contrast a relatively flush economy—made Obama's fund-raising take perhaps the exception rather than the rule from here out.[8]

Still, with the ease of Internet giving and the relatively widespread sense that giving to campaigns is an important form of political participation, we can expect the pattern of an ever-larger group of donors to continue. There may not be enough small donors to fund a successful campaign on their own, nor might we want presidents chosen exclusively from the famous or charismatic who'd likely be most successful at it. Absent a long, competitive primary season, candidate fund-raising in 2012 might not climb to the heights of 2008. Presidential candidates, however, likely will take McCain's experience to heart and bypass public funding if they sense the opportunity to do better without it.

Candidates' campaign organizations and party committees are not alone in raising and spending money on political races. PACs and 527 groups have run ads and provided campaign labor; an even wider array of organizations has produced "issue" ads. The Supreme Court's recent decision in *Citizens United* overturned decisions dating from the 1990s and 1940s that prevented corporations and unions from tapping their general treasuries for political contributions and expenditures. Unions have seized on the new rules. Dedicating $10 million (largely soft money) to ads against Louisiana senator Blanche Lincoln in a Democratic primary, the American Federation of State, County and Municipal Employees and the AFL-CIO hoped to punish an enemy. When Lincoln won anyway, an unnamed White House official remarked the unions had flushed their members' "money down the toilet on a pointless exercise." Will corporations go on a political spending spree? If for-profit corporations' slowness in launching PACs is a guide (they did not extensively use the device, invented by the AFL-CIO in the 1940s, until the 1970s), we should expect to see them use the opportunities opened by the decision slowly and carefully. They have stockholders who might object, customers who might be insulted, and strategies in place for reaching politicians. Target discovered the pitfalls of political contributions when the corporation's gift to MN Forward, a group interested in candidates of both parties who might improve Minnesota's business climate, created enough controversy to force an apology. (This even though the company had a solid reputation for support of gay rights and for treating its employees fairly and had in the past directed most of its PAC funds to Democrats.) Still, unions and ideological nonprofits are likely to continue to test the new rules and push the limits of the older ones. Before the *Citizens United* decision, nonprofits designated as 501(c)(4) groups in the tax code could engage in political activity and did not have to disclose their donors. In 2010, Crossroads GPS used this provision to raise enough money and run enough ads to make some observers—even President Obama—imply or believe that they were seeing the impact of a flood of new money freed by *Citizens United*. They were not, and Democrats as well as Republicans will no doubt explore the possibilities of such organizations.[9]

Political scientists and election-law experts can worry about that. Meanwhile, for the curious and scholarly, left out there are the millions of names. One can go to the Huffington Post, OpenSecrets, CampaignMoney, or elsewhere on the Web—all with nicer features than the FEC site—and poke around. The Huffington Post maps contributors; CampaignMoney will give a history of an individual's contributions. One can search employers or industries, although the contributors may have been vague about both. The data these sites provide include only contributions at and above $200. Sums smaller than that are not subject to disclosure to the FEC.

Around Christmas of 2007, I was puzzled to find a list of donors who had contributed to the primary presidential campaigns in the newspaper of my father's hometown. What was strange was reading the names of people who had given under $200. I remembered reading lists of contributors—generally in the $1,000 to $20,000 range—in newspapers in the 1930s, when how the rich or famous were spending their political money was news. But in 2007, didn't $200 trigger disclosure? And who would care about who gave $150 to a campaign? The reporter apparently had not gone to any of the sites mentioned here, which download and make more accessible FEC data above the disclosure line.

Instead, the reporter must have plugged local zip codes into the FEC's search engine. Sure enough, there were the microdonations along with larger ones, found by searches by name, employer, city, or zip code.

For a political geek, it's hours of fun. Supplemented by the magic of Google, the site can tell us more than we need to know. I sorted those who described themselves as "not employed" by the size of campaign contributions. Who without employment could give the maximum amount to a campaign? Those I found were employed, usually as consultants, or were retired, generally from law firms or financial services. Which "students" could max out? Some still in elementary school. Who gave too much, and had to backtrack (or have their additional contributions redesignated)? Were there many party switchers—people who supported Republicans in the past but now supported Democrats?

Then there are the small—very small—contributions. With these donations, found by searching on names, city, or zip code, Obama and Paul's appeal to people of modest means is clear. We can also track the greater success Clinton had with small donors in the late primaries. We can discover what the Obama campaign already knows about what events or appeals inspired small donors, or, absent a team of research assistants and more versatile software than I own, learn this only for selected cities. By cross-checking names with Facebook accounts, we can find out about an individual's participation in the campaign beyond making a small donation. We can learn in some cases about employers and participation in community activities.

We can unearth an astonishing level of detail about individual donors even if it is in a format inconvenient for political scientists accustomed to working with large datasets and random samples. For a historian like me, who once worked with nineteenth-century records, matching names across the bits of information tossed up in a Google search seemed easy and much more complete than relying on what people in the past decided to save. I once worked with late-nineteenth-century "canvass books"—lists of voters, with names, occupations, location, party, how the man would vote in the next election, and other relevant information (such as whether a voter needed a ride to the polls, was a veteran, or needed to be paid to vote). These were books prepared by the political parties in competitive states in the days before polling so party leaders could assess their chances and direct their resources wisely. I was interested in what shaped party loyalty, so I matched a large sample of the names with census records, church records, club memberships, tax records—anything that had names. Some of the problems of Web searches existed with matching these records. Was the Delos Mattice in the polling book the same person as the D. Mattice in the Reformed Church? Web searches tended to generate too much information, but they did so quickly (no digging around to find church membership rolls) and without the ambiguities of nineteenth-century handwriting and incomplete records.

Those visited by the canvass taker had no expectation of privacy in their political choices. Most states did not adopt the secret ballot until the early twentieth century. Before that, men went to the polls, pausing outside to pick up a bundle of paper tied together from a ticket peddler. States did not yet print ballots; the parties did, and they also handled distribution. The ballots might be distinguished by color, so it was clear whether a voter picked up a Democratic or Republican bundle. In full sight of whoever was milling around—and election days drew crowds—the voter deposited his tickets, sometimes to cheers or jeers. If the canvass taker misspelled a name in the canvass book, it was unlikely that he got party affiliation wrong. Local people who made politics their business knew the political affiliations of their neighbors.

Perhaps that is also true of someone who gave $5 to the Obama campaign: perhaps such people plastered their cars with stickers and turned their front yards into obstacle courses of signs. Or perhaps not: many who gave, especially those who gave small amounts, probably have no idea that their political contributions are public, even in an inconvenient format. The rhetoric surrounding the adoption of the secret ballot involved the sanctity of individual political choice. No one should feel pressure, from employers, the community, or a party, in making political decisions. Campaign workers should be kept a safe distance away from the polls, and the individual voter should be able to enter a neutral site (not a home or a store or saloon), pull the curtain, and exercise his or her choice using a state-printed ballot. The secret ballot was part of Progressive era reforms that celebrated the individual, rational, informed voter, in contrast to voters who were in thrall to partisan loyalties. It is one of the Progressive-era political ideas with the greatest staying power: voting for the person or the policies, not the party.

Historians over the years have found a lot to criticize in Progressive reform, but the secret ballot is rarely included among the list of blind spots, unexamined assumptions, and class, race, and gender biases scholars have criticized. The secret ballot is an indication of democratic elections, according to nongovernmental organizations that monitor elections. It seems unlikely that Americans favor abandoning it. Yet technology brings two Progressive-era assumptions—disclosure as cornerstone of a campaign financing system free from corrupt special interests and the secret ballot—into conflict.[10] Twenty-first-century innovations that allow campaigns to raise small donations cheaply on the Internet—political participation that campaign finance reformers favor—and anyone's ability to search the records moves us back to the days of public voting. Since disclosure is the one point of agreement between Democrats and Republicans on campaign finance reform, it is likely to remain a key feature of whatever revisions are made to the laws in the future. Fear of money given in secret will trump the secret ballot.

Notes

1. Wertheimer quoted in *Minneapolis–St. Paul Star-Tribune*, November 2, 2008.
2. Raymond L. La Raja, *Small Change: Money, Political Parties, and Campaign Finance Reform* (Ann Arbor, Mich., 2008).
3. Data on campaign receipts and spending are drawn from the Federal Election Commission year-end reports. On the proportion of maxed-out givers, see Campaign Finance Institute, "Newly Released 2007 Reports Give Clues to Candidates' Financial Strengths and Vulnerabilities Going into Super Tuesday," press release, February 1, 2008, www.cfinst.org/pr/prRelease.aspx?ReleaseID=177.
4. Herbert E. Alexander, *Financing Politics: Money, Elections and Political Reform*, second ed., (Washington D.C., 1980), 60; and Mrs. Robert A. Gross to George McGovern, April 5, 1971, Box 299, George McGovern Papers, Princeton University.

5. Noam Scheiber, "Joe Trippi Reinvents Campaigning," *The New Republic,* January 30, 2004.

6. Accusations on various Web sites flew about the presence of "sock puppets" (posters on Internet forums who pretended to be someone else) or "straw man sock puppets" (people who pretended to hold an opinion for mischievous purposes) poisoning opponents' and other websites. Campaigns accused each other of encouraging staffers to post on the opposition's website or on political sites without disclosing their relationship to a campaign or of pretending to be, for example, an evangelical who voted for Bush in 2004 but who was rejecting the Republican Party in 2008. The Internet opens a whole new field for old-fashioned campaign dirty tricks.

7. Michael Malbin, "Reality Check: Obama Received about the Same Percentage from Small Donors as Bush in 2004," press release, November 24, 2008, http://www.cfinst.org/Press/PReleases/08-11-24/Realty_Check_-_Obama_Small_Donors.aspx. The paper has inspired a good deal of debate. One critic, Bob Bauer, legal counsel for the Obama campaign, disputes some of Malbin's definitions and conclusions, for example. See "Obama Fundraising and the 'Small Donor': Strange Views from the Campaign Finance Institute," www.moresoftmoneyhardlaw.com/updates/other_related_legal_developments.html?AID-1378. For a breakdown on the Obama campaign's bundlers, see "Bundlers," http://www.opensecrets.org/pres08/bundlers.php?id=N00009638, and the Web site White House for Sale, on bundlers, http://www.whitehouseforsale.org/candidate.cfm?CandidateID=C0009. Bundlers, or individuals who use their contacts to collect large donations, thereby saving the candidates' campaign the trouble, are subject only to voluntary disclosure by the candidates. Excluding the most recent figures, Obama's campaign received 47 percent of its funds from large ($1,000–$2,300) contributions, in contrast to Bush and McCain (both at 60 percent) and Kerry (56 percent).

8. *New York Times,* June 20, 2008.

9. Suzy Khimm, "The Citizens United Effect," *Mother Jones,* June 7, 2010; Ben Smith, "White House Official: 'Organized Labor Just Flushed $10 million Down the Toilet,'" Politico, June 8, 2010; Brody Mullins and Ann Zimmerman, "Target Discovers Downside of Political Contributions," *Wall Street Journal,* August 3, 2010; Neal St. Anthony, "Target Spreads the Wealth," *Minneapolis Star-Tribune,* August 3, 2010; Campaign Finance Institute, "Election-Related Spending by Political Committees and Non-Profits up 40% in 2010," press release, October 8, 2010; "Remarks by the President at a Rally for Maryland Governor Martin O'Malley," Bowie State University, Bowie, Maryland, October 7, 2010; and Michael Luo, "Effort for Liberal Balance to G.O.P. Groups Begins," *New York Times,* November 23, 2010.

10. The conflict has been highlighted in a map created by those who opposed California's Proposition 8, which banned same-sex marriage. The result was a "mash-up" that brought together Google maps and California's rather stringent but easily accessible campaign-finance records. For a discussion of some of the issues involved in the creation of and easy access to the map, see *New York Times,* February 7, 2009.

CHAPTER 10

Political Feminism and the Problem of Sarah Palin

Catherine E. Rymph

As recently as August 2008, how many would have anticipated that by the end of the year, many Americans would be referring to a woman as current standard-bearer of the Republican Party? Sarah Palin's status as a leading contender for the 2012 Republican nomination seems remarkable, given common (if exaggerated) perceptions of the Republican Party as an anti-woman bastion of white male supremacy. That there are women—and men—in the Republican Party who were genuinely energized in 2008 by a tough female candidate unapologetic about her political ambitions suggests that the position of women in the party and in American politics has shifted in the decades since Second Wave feminists sought to transform the role of women in our society.

Leading up to the 1972 elections, Betty Friedan predicted that 100 women would win congressional seats that year and that in 1976 a woman would run for president. Despite Shirley Chisholm's symbolic presidential run in 1972, and the election of a few more women to the House four years later (to raise the number to 16), Friedan's forecast proved overly optimistic, to say the least. But her prediction reflected the goals of the emerging political feminism: that more women be elected to public office and serve as leaders in the political parties, and that feminist issues be advanced through the political system. Political feminists clearly understood these goals to be connected. Getting more women elected was a feminist goal in and of itself, because it would mean opening seats of political power to women (not to mention expanding to them yet another traditionally male career option); but electing women also was understood to be a step toward enacting legislation in line with feminist thinking—electing more women would mean electing more feminists. A certain amount of the debate about Sarah Palin indirectly centered on the question of whether or not her candidacy was in line with those goals. Was her historic run to be celebrated as a milestone for women—or not?

Her status as a Republican was not necessarily a problem when looked at historically. Political feminists in the 1970s were found in both political parties, and the most prominent organization of political feminism at that time—the National Women's Political Caucus—was a bipartisan organization. The idea was to advance both Democratic and Republican women and nurture a feminist movement with adherents on both sides of the political aisle. For the most part, this vision failed. Since roughly 1974, Democratic women have far outnumbered their Republican counterparts in the House, and the same has been true in the Senate since 1992. Democrats today dominate among women in both houses of Congress and hold slightly more governorships. And while the ranks of Republican women elected include pro-choice moderates like Susan Collins and Olympia Snowe, most Republican women don't describe themselves as feminists.

It wasn't always that way. Republicans made up a greater number of the women serving in the Congress in the 1940s and were about evenly matched with Democrats in the 1950s and 1960s. One of their number, Senator Margaret Chase Smith of Maine, even made a brief bid for the presidency in 1964, becoming the first woman in a major party to officially do so. Furthermore, as recently as 1976, women who proudly and openly identified as feminists enjoyed influence and leadership positions within the Republican Party. Their numbers included Audrey Rowe-Colom, who headed the National Women's Political Caucus; Congresswoman Margaret Heckler of Massachusetts; Jill Ruckelshaus, who worked in the Nixon White House; and "Feminist Betty," the wife of President Gerald Ford. (The Catholic Heckler opposed abortion, but this position did not prevent her from identifying as a feminist.)

Although their pearls and their hairdos made them seem stodgy to plenty of women's-rights advocates at the time, Republican feminists accepted many of the insights and objectives of the women's movement that enjoyed wide support in the 1970s. Importantly, Republican feminists urged their party to embrace a women's-rights agenda that included support not only for the Equal Rights Amendment (which the Republican Party platform had first endorsed in 1940, four years before the Democrats, and which was now awaiting ratification by the states), but also for reproductive rights, affirmative action, federally funded child care, reform of discriminations in the tax code, and job training for "displaced homemakers." They also wanted to see more women serving in leadership positions within the party and elected on the Republican ticket.

In 1974, Richard Nixon resigned in disgrace over the Watergate scandal. The party was demoralized and unpopular. Something needed to be done to revitalize the organization and rehabilitate its image. In a gesture intended to indicate a break with the past and move toward reform, Gerald Ford, who succeeded Nixon to become president, named Mary Louise Smith of Iowa to be the first female chair of the Republican National Committee. Smith, an experienced grassroots party organizer, was also a member of the National Women's Political Caucus and an active supporter of the ERA and reproductive rights. The selection not only of a woman, but of one of the party's "most ardent feminists," to be RNC chair, was widely seen as a savvy choice; the GOP needed to show the country that it was looking to the future and still relevant at a time when a mere 18 percent of Americans identified as Republican.[1]

The political climate of the mid-1970s certainly had its parallels in 2008. That year, Americans rejected the GOP, due, in no small part, to what was widely perceived as the incompetence of two-term Republican president George W. Bush, whose favorable ratings sunk to 27 percent in July.[2] In both the post-Watergate years and in 2008, the Republican Party experienced low approval and low voter identification and was in danger of suffering large political losses. It was at these crisis moments that the party selected "female firsts" (Smith in 1974 and Palin in 2008); crisis bred opportunity. Given women's traditional political marginalization, a high-profile female nomination can symbolize change. It is hardly surprising that a party would choose to break new ground for reasons that were, to a considerable degree, pragmatic. But the differences in those pragmatic calculations are significant. Smith was selected RNC chair because Republican leaders believed American voters in the mid-1970s might embrace a party that placed a feminist in a position of leadership and power. Despite Palin's self-identification as a feminist, one would be hard-pressed to argue that this was part of John McCain's calculus in 2008. (It was, more likely, Palin's potential appeal to conservatives and independents that was attractive.)

In the mid-1970s, Smith and other Republican feminists continued to maintain that feminism was compatible with Republican traditions. Yet they had to confront the fact that not all Republicans—and not all Republican women—agreed with them. A battle over feminism, as well as a battle over Republican womanhood, was occurring in the party. By the late 1970s, it was becoming more and more difficult to argue that "Republican feminist" was a viable political category as organized opposition to the ERA and to feminism became firmly associated with the GOP. This link was attributable in large part to the effective activism of Republican antifeminist Phyllis

Schlafly. Mary Louise Smith did her best to counter the view that "Republican feminist" was a contradiction in terms. She insisted, "Phyllis Schlafly is not a role model for Republican women. While it's true that some of us may be homemakers, or law students, or Midwesterners, or articulate, or even blond and bouffant, for most the resemblance ends there."[3] Smith and others continued to argue that feminism and Republicanism were compatible, yet Schlafly's female followers were now coming to define what it meant to be a Republican woman.

Schlafly, a longtime Republican activist, had, to use a term from our current political lexicon, "gone maverick" after a falling-out with the party leadership in 1967. By the mid-1970s, she had developed a devoted following of women opposed to the new women's movement. Schlafly described feminists as bitter women who "hated men, marriage and children" and who sought political solutions to their personal problems. She mocked feminists for what she saw as their silly desire to "conceal their marital status" by insisting on being called "Ms."[4]

Schlafly's energies were particularly directed toward opposing the ERA, which she argued would harm American women by eliminating privileges such as the right to be supported by a husband and the right not to be drafted into the military. She complained about feminists "strident[ly] advocating the rights of women to be treated on an equal basis with men in all walks of life." What of the women, she asked, who didn't want to compete with men as equals?[5] Schlafly mobilized a mass organization of women—mostly full-time homemakers from conservative religious backgrounds—to ultimately stop ratification of the ERA.

To Gloria Steinem, Sarah Palin was "Phyllis Schlafly, only younger."[6] (In the blogosphere, Palin has been referred to as "Phyllis Schlafly with Better Make-up.")[7] Certainly, Palin shares traits in common with Schlafly. Both are Republicans, are conservative, have large families, oppose reproductive rights, are religious, and are accomplished, ambitious women. Schlafly was not opposed to women running for political office (she had done so herself in the past and did enthusiastically endorse Palin in 2008). But in comparing Palin to Schlafly, it is worth taking Palin's own claims to be a feminist more seriously than many of her critics have done. Whatever one thinks of Palin's understanding of feminism, it is noteworthy that she chose to embrace the term, given that only about 25 percent of American women today do so.

During the campaign—especially in the early weeks—there was much chatter about whether Sarah Palin was a feminist and whether her nomination should be seen as a step forward for women. Palin and her supporters claimed that her nomination struck a blow for women's equality. A gloating

Rush Limbaugh declared her the "new face of feminism."[8] Camille Paglia called her a "powerful new feminist force."[9] Palin herself identified as a pro-life feminist. The *New York Times* reported that she preferred to be called "Ms." She credited Title IX—that great feminist achievement of the 1970s—with having empowered women of her generation with a sense of equality. And when asked by Katie Couric if she was a feminist, Palin answered in the affirmative, citing her upbringing, in which she was expected to do everything her brothers did—chopping wood, hunting, and fishing to provide for the family.

Opponents rightly noted that her record and the positions of the McCain ticket belied any claim that Palin would be an advocate for women's rights. Palin—a symbol for many women of the very real struggle to balance work and childrearing—didn't seem to offer many concrete solutions to working mothers. Indeed, the 2008 Republican Party platform opposed reproductive rights, made no mention of equal pay for equal work, and offered little to families hoping for better access to quality child care and universal preschool education. Yet Palin's identification as a feminist is nonetheless a noteworthy indicator of how the feminist movement of the last forty years has affected even women of deeply conservative backgrounds like Palin. Sarah Palin in 2008 is not Phyllis Schlafly in the 1970s. The conservative, religiously devout Palin did not malign career women the way Schlafly had. Palin herself is a working mother with a demanding job and young children. Indeed, that became—perhaps counterintuitively—part of her appeal. Whereas Schlafly in the 1970s argued that feminists were pathetic, bitter women who were simply mad that God made them women instead of men, Palin comfortably and proudly insisted in 2008 that women could do anything men can do.

Schlafly claimed that the ERA would free husbands from responsibility to support their wives, requiring women to work outside the home and put their children in day care. At a time when only 39 percent of women with children under the age of six worked outside the home, this inaccurate yet frightening scenario resonated deeply with the conservative religious homemakers who were Schlafly's constituency. Thirty years later, when that figure had climbed to nearly 64 percent, many of Palin's conservative female supporters were themselves struggling with demands of work, child care, and family.[10] While those supporters may not have placed their ongoing struggles as women (to balance work and family, for example, or to earn a living wage) in the context of a feminist movement and may indeed have rejected government solutions to those problems, they did respond powerfully to a woman who seemed to embody those struggles and who presented herself as a tough woman, the equal of any man.

Antifeminists in the 1970s who aligned with Phyllis Schlafly feared the disruptions that an ERA might bring. Many of the changes they feared, however, occurred even without the ERA, partly through legislation and the courts; partly because more career opportunities became available to women; and partly as a result of economic changes that made two incomes more necessary for more families. Sarah Palin and the women who so strongly identified with her are among the results of those changes.

Due to the rise of the New Right (with the help of Phyllis Schlafly and her supporters) and the declining influence of moderates like Mary Louise Smith and her allies, the Republican Party in 1980 nominated Ronald Reagan to be president on a platform that rejected particular positions supported by Republican feminists, including the ERA and abortion rights. This marked a defeat for Republican feminists in particular; it also marked the end of the vision of a feminist movement with supporters in both parties, as feminism once and for all became firmly associated with the Democrats. For Democratic women, the nomination of Ronald Reagan in 1980 and the final defeat of the ERA in 1982 left them reeling—but also strategizing. In the 1980 elections, Reagan had not done as well with women voters as with men. And leading up to the 1984 campaign, polls suggested that only 38 percent of women approved of the job Reagan was doing. Since Reagan (and the Republican Party platform in 1980) opposed important feminist issues, feminists believed that the party would continue to lose support among women if it did not change its positions. In 1984, for some supporters of Democratic presidential candidate Walter Mondale, the gender gap led to a belief that a woman on the Democratic ticket could pull enough support away from the Republicans to bring Mondale victory. They worked behind the scenes to create a widespread demand to place a woman on the ticket.

Advocates of a female nominee settled on Geraldine Ferraro of New York, who had been elected to the House in 1978. As a three-term congresswoman who was not part of the House leadership, Ferraro was arguably less experienced than Governor Palin in 2008. Yet in 1984 there were no Democratic women serving in the Senate or as governors (the usual places parties look for vice presidential candidates). Although Ferraro was clearly selected because she was a woman, the Mondale/Ferraro campaign went on to do little to directly appeal to women voters in the fall. Ferraro was the first woman nominated for vice president by a major party. Having her on the ticket was supposed to be enough to inspire women to vote in election-changing numbers help make history. Gender was the main consideration in Ferraro's selection, and it backfired. Reagan, who was reelected in a landslide, actually increased his support among women voters by ten points over

1980. Ferraro later recalled that stay-at-home mothers and older women particularly rejected her, believing they saw in the many achievements of the vice presidential nominee a symbolic rejection of the lives they had led.

Both Ferraro and Palin injected their running mates' campaigns with an initial burst of excitement. Both gave stirring acceptance speeches widely considered to be the highlight of their conventions, and both Mondale and McCain received a bump of about fifteen points in the polls after picking female running mates. But those bumps would be short-lived. It is a longstanding pattern in women's political history that before significant numbers of women break into particular levels of elected office, they are likely to be picked to run in elections that the party expects to lose anyway. The nominations of Ferraro and Palin generated interest and enthusiasm for otherwise flagging campaigns, but each came to be liabilities (for a variety of reasons) and each was blamed, at least partly, for her ticket's defeat.

During the 2008 campaign, Palin was often compared to Ferraro and Schlafly, and occasionally to the lesser-known Smith. Although all three offer instructive historical context for understanding the emergence of Sarah Palin, in the immediate terms of the 2008 election, the most direct reference was, of course, Hillary Rodham Clinton. John McCain's choice of a female running mate initially appeared to be a cynical play for disgruntled Clinton supporters who, frustrated that their candidate had not won the Democratic primary, would theoretically vote in significant numbers for McCain out of hunger to see a woman on the ticket (albeit as number two). And faced with this possible storyline, Clinton supporters called foul. "Does McCain really think we are that stupid?" was the frequent complaint. The significant differences between Clinton and Palin were frequently enumerated: Clinton's experience as an attorney, her time as First Lady, and her eight years in the Senate far exceeded Palin's experience with the Wasilla City Council and her two years as Alaska governor; Clinton had traveled extensively abroad, met with dozens of foreign leaders, and served on the Senate Foreign Relations Committee, while Palin's foreign-policy experience seemed—by her own admission—to rest on her position as governor of a state with geographical proximity to Russia. Clinton possessed deep and broad knowledge of issues and was an articulate—if wonkish—speaker and debater, whereas Palin's knowledge on most issues seemed woefully thin. Despite her rousing stump speeches, Palin appeared out of her league in the few interviews she gave.

The most significant complaint, though, about any suggestion that Palin was to be seen somehow as the equivalent of Hillary Clinton concerned the issues. Clinton had been fighting for the rights of women, children, and families for more than three decades, whereas Sarah Palin's positions and record on women's issues were either nonexistent or in opposition to the positions of organized feminists. McCain, in this analysis, was making a similar mistake to Mondale's in 1984—assuming that women would blindly vote according to gender regardless of the positions of the candidate in question. Yet wooing Clinton voters was not the real reason he chose Palin. She was picked, it seems, largely to shore up the conservative base (which had been wary of McCain) and to reinforce McCain's "maverick" and reformist credentials (to help him with independents).

A more relevant parallel with Hillary Clinton concerns the ways their campaigns exposed the place of sexism in American political discourse. An arsenal of sexist language and imagery is available in our society to demean and disparage women we don't agree with, including political women. Critics of Clinton and Palin often had legitimate reasons for their own opposition—because they disagreed with the candidate ideologically, or because they felt she would do a poor job. But too often in voicing their intense opposition, they turned to the debased discourse of sexism. Many ostensibly neutral journalists did so, as well. Both candidates were presented in sexualized ways—Clinton was a castrating bitch ex-wife, while Palin was a "MILF" (presumably more flattering, but equally degrading). Rush Limbaugh, in his declaration that Sarah Palin represented the "new face of feminism," pointedly juxtaposed a particularly cruel close-up of Clinton's wrinkles—some kind of puffy-faced bad-hair-day outtake—with a flattering photo of the more glamorous (and younger) Palin, whom he declared to be "hot."[11]

In the primary campaign, those who viciously attacked Hillary Clinton in sexist terms often denied that their remarks were sexist because Hillary really was "a bitch" (so it was fair to call her that). In the general election, Palin's opponents who mocked her hair, who obsessed about her clothes and her past as a beauty pageant contestant, who attacked her parenting choices and her ability as a mother of young children to serve didn't see their comments as sexist because Palin wasn't a feminist, was poorly qualified, and was running on the Republican ticket and so deserved what she got. It seems Americans of all stripes can tolerate and even embrace sexism when it is used as a weapon against women with whom they disagree or whom they see as representing the wrong picture of womanhood.

That Clinton and Palin were so often compared accentuates the fact that each was running not only for office, but also, to some degree, for Symbol of American Womanhood. The absence of women at the highest levels of American government (either as president or a heartbeat away) seems to render the prospect of a woman being elevated there to a kind of zero-sum game. An opponent of Clinton might think: "I'm all for a woman in the

White House, but please don't let it be *that* one." Or a passionate Palin critic might feel that "if that woman wins, women like me lose." Indicative is a Pew Research Center poll conducted in June revealing that only 20 percent of Republicans would support a candidate who was the mother of school-age children.[12] Yet once Palin received the nomination, most Republicans were able to overlook her status as an ambitious working mother because she seemed to be "like them" (not like a generic liberal career woman, presumed to be selfish in her ambitions and only a halfhearted parent). Because we have not had a woman as president or vice president, the imperative that a woman in the running for that job "be like me" or "represent the version of womanhood that I endorse" is much more intense than it is for women running for other offices. Female candidates for Congress and at the state level appear to have received much less of this kind of commentary in 2008 than did Clinton and Palin.

The emergence of Sarah Palin also indicates that American women—even conservative women—do hunger to see other women in positions of leadership. This doesn't mean they would vote for someone "just because she is a woman," but if she shares their positions they can be powerfully energized. Palin was never going to attract many committed Democrats and liberals. But for other women—Republicans and many independents—she was appealing as an accomplished woman who could understand their lives. She had kids, she worked, she shopped at Wal-Mart, she was tough, and thus she could relate to ordinary women. Her hairdresser, Jessica Steele, recalled a supportive Palin advising her, after the birth of Steele's third child, "not to make excuses for why I am not a stay-at-home mom or have my kids at the shop."[13] Palin could also serve as a model of female empowerment and accomplishment. As one twenty-one-year-old Wellesley student put it, "I mean, how cool to have a young woman on the ticket who's doing exactly what I want to do when I grow up."[14] This enthusiasm was difficult for many liberals and feminists to understand. But a considerable part of what appealed to Palin's supporters was that their candidate was all of these things—accomplished, a role model, able to relate to ordinary women—yet was not a liberal. Americans, including Republicans, seem to have accepted—and in some cases even grown to appreciate—transformations propelled by the women's movement, while remaining wary of or hostile to liberal feminism itself.

If Palin's nomination was not an effort by the party to reclaim the Republican feminism of the 1970s, then, in the end what does Palin's historic run mean for political feminism? During the 2008 primary campaign season, approximately 17.5 million voted for Clinton, who won Democratic primaries or caucuses in twenty-two states. About 58 million voted for the

McCain–Palin ticket in the general election, and the ticket won twenty-two states. Although some who supported Clinton in the primaries did vote for McCain in November, for the most part these numbers do not represent the same individuals. This means that in 2008, roughly 70 million people voted for a woman to be either president or vice president, nearly twice as many as the 37.5 million who voted for Mondale/Ferraro in 1984. It means millions of Democrats and Republicans, liberals and conservatives voted for a woman for president or vice president in 2008. And millions of young women had the opportunity to be inspired by the example of women they saw as representing their views and their values running for high office. This is a significant threshold and suggests that, from now on, women will run in the primaries of both parties. To see women running for president was at least one of the dreams of both Democratic and Republican feminists in the 1970s, although Sarah Palin might not have been the kind of candidate they would have hoped for. Women may not necessarily receive their party's nomination, or be elected, or run without a certain level of sexist attention, at least for now. But they will run, and run seriously. That their numbers will include Republicans as well as Democrats will be one of Palin's legacies.

Notes

1. Catherine E. Rymph, *Republican Women: Feminism and Conservatism from Suffrage through the Rise of the New Right* (Chapel Hill: University of North Carolina Press, 2006), 204.
2. Fox News poll, July 2008, http://www.foxnews.com/projects/pdf/FoxPoll.pdf.
3. Rymph, *Republican Women*, 225.
4. Phyllis Schlafly, *The Power of the Positive Woman* (New Rochelle, N,Y,: Jove, 1977).
5. Phyllis Schlafly, "The Right to Be a Woman," *Phyllis Schlafly Report*, November 1972.
6. Gloria Steinem, "Sarah Palin: Wrong Woman, Wrong Message," *Los Angeles Times*, September 4, 2008.
7. "Sarah Palin: Phyllis Schlafly with Better Makeup?," September 16, 2008, http://momocrats.typepad.com.
8. "The New Face of Feminism," August 29, 2008, http://www.rushlimbaugh.com.
9. Camille Paglia, "Fresh Blood for the Vampire," Salon, September 10, 2008, http://www.salon.com.
10. U.S. Department of Labor, Bureau of Labor Statistics, "Labor Force Participation Rate of Women by Age of Youngest Child, March 1975–2007."

11. http://www.rushlimbaugh.com/home/daily/site_082908/content/01125108.guest.html. Limbaugh has since taken this post off his Web site.

12. Julia Baird, "From Seneca Falls to . . . Sarah Palin?" *Newsweek*, September 22, 2008.

13. Jan Hoffman, "The Upshot on Palin and her Updo," *New York Times*, September 12, 2008.

14. Amanda M. Fairbanks, "Young, Republican, and Inspired by Palin," *New York Times*, October 29, 2008.

CONCLUSION

The Difference that "Difference" Makes

Elisabeth Israels Perry

"Do I think a woman'll ever be President? How do I know?" exclaimed Dr. Malvina Wormser, one of Sinclair Lewis's more sympathetic feminist characters in his 1933 novel *Ann Vickers*. If only I'd been as evasive when students and colleagues asked me that question. Instead, starting around the mid-1990s, I'd answer: "2008."

Here's how I arrived at that date. The night Bill Clinton won the presidency in 1992, he and his running mate, Al Gore, came out on a stage in Little Rock, Arkansas, and promised us a government that would "look like America." These words thrilled me. After previous presidential elections, I used to clip press photos of new governmental appointees, tape them onto my office door, and scrawl underneath, "Does this look like America?" And of course, it never did. Most of the images (and sometimes all) were of a homogeneous set of white middle-aged men.

The Clinton administration kept its promise pretty well. Feminists were especially pleased by Janet Reno's appointment as attorney general, a so-called "hard" cabinet post that no woman had ever held. Clinton broke other new ground when he named two African American women to "softer" posts, Hazel O'Leary to Energy in his first term and Alexis Herman to Labor in his second. He named Donna Shalala head of Health and Human Services and Madeleine Albright ambassador to the United Nations, and when in his second term he made Albright his secretary of state, she became the first woman to hold that post. Other cabinet appointments, such as those of Ron Brown (Commerce) and Federico Fabian Peña (Transportation), broke racial and ethnic barriers. Feminists cheered when Clinton appointed Ruth Bader Ginsburg, a lawyer and judge with a long-standing commitment to gender equity, to the U.S. Supreme Court.

These appointments, I thought, would help Americans get used to seeing women and people of color in high places and to accept their exercise of authority as a matter of course. I expected Clinton to be reelected in 1996 and his vice president Al Gore to succeed him in 2000. Gore, I fantasized further, would diversify government even more, and after his two terms Americans would be ready for a woman to be president.

Then all my calculations went awry. Clinton was impeached, an event that, though it ended without his removal from office, discredited his presidency. In 2000, instead of Al Gore we got George W. Bush, and in 2004, thanks (in part) to the horrific events of 9/11 and the subsequent anxieties over terrorism and war, we got him again. Bush deserves credit for increasing the number of women and minorities in high-profile positions, most notably when he appointed two African Americans as secretaries of state, first General Colin Powell and then Condoleezza Rice. Women and members of racial and ethnic minorities occupied other cabinet seats (Gale Norton, Margaret Spellings, Ellen Chao, Ann Veneman, Alberto Gonzalez, Rod Paige, and Carlos Gutierrez). At the same time, the numbers of women in higher office were also rising, albeit slowly. The percentage of women in Congress increased to 16.8 percent of the full body, and more women were winning statewide executive posts, including governorships.[1] Thus I still believed that a woman might actually reach the White House in 2008.

During this entire fifteen-year period, I never imagined an African American getting there first. Colin Powell's name kept coming up on the Republican side, but he had refused to run. Barack Obama was on the Democratic horizon, but mostly as a "too-soon-to-tell" political novice. Then Hillary Rodham Clinton began to emerge as the Democratic Party frontrunner. Could she be the first female president I had predicted for 2008? Perhaps, but her candidacy worried me. Despite their rocky marital history, she and her husband were still "a couple," and too many ordinary Americans could not bear the idea of Bill back in the White House, even (or especially) as "First Gentleman." Her supporters countered that she shouldn't be penalized for his behavior, and I agreed. But, as Kathryn Sklar observes in Chapter 1 of this anthology, many people considered Hillary merely a surrogate for Bill, and as Susan Hartmann suggests in Chapter 6, Bill could never qualify as the husband "beyond reproach" that a successful female presidential candidate requires. No other woman prominent in politics had Hillary's name recognition or national political experience, however. And so she ran, and ran well, looking more and more "presidential" (or, as Sklar suggests, "passing the masculinity test") as the campaign wore on. But in the end, despite his slim national experience, Obama proved the more inspiring, or, as Hartmann suggests, "transformative" candidate.

Where do I stand now on a woman becoming president? Taking my cue from the fictional Dr. Wormser, from now on I plan to say, "How do I know?" At the same time, I would assert that the 2008 election campaign changed American presidential campaigns for good. The nation watched in fascination as Barack Obama, an African American man, ran against a strong female contender, Hillary Clinton, in the primary of a major political party. They watched with equal fascination as a female vice-presidential candidate, Sarah Palin, received the lion's share of media attention in the months after the other major party's convention. They then saw Obama carry his party to a stunning victory and install the first African American family in the White House. Meanwhile, Palin, who despite her impulsive resignation from the governorship of Alaska and the sharp critiques of her public performances, remains a compelling media attraction and a future contender for high office. More important, she is an inspirational figure for millions of people, especially women, who share her ideological views. The United States has never seen a presidential campaign like that of 2008. Can the nation return to the status quo ante? To my mind, a future presidential race consisting of four male Americans of European origins will be hard for major political parties to justify or put across. In short, the election of Barack Obama has made an eventual woman president more likely than ever.

The Political Interdependence of Women and African Americans

Although during the 2008 campaign the media often portrayed the primary contest between Clinton and Obama as a zero-sum game, in which a Clinton victory signified a loss for "blacks" and an Obama victory a loss for "women," the chapters in this book suggest that the quest of women and minorities for meaningful political representation has been more complementary than competitive. Melanie Gustafson and Catherine Rymph show how the experiences of American women in politics in the past paved the way for the historic candidacies of Hillary Clinton and Sarah Palin. Glenda Gilmore argues that black women provided the "swing" votes in many elections and that black women's activism in the "long civil rights movement" facilitated Obama's victory. In this conclusion, I reinforce these points by arguing that women's gradual gains in achieving higher office over the course of the twentieth century allowed Americans to become accustomed to seeing "different" kinds of people exercising power and that these gains helped the nation as a whole accept an African American president in 2008.

The struggles of American women of all races and of African Americans in particular for political rights have been interdependent for almost two centuries. A dual system of laws and customs prevented both groups from exercising their full citizenship rights. To undo that system, activists first had to win the amendment or repeal of those laws that kept them from performing certain tasks, such as holding a particular office or serving in an official capacity in a court of law. Winning legal changes took decades, but these changes in themselves were never enough to accomplish all that was needed. The social mores and beliefs that undergirded the laws remained in place. While most Americans today would think of an ideology of separate spheres as outmoded, for example, many still resist the idea of women exercising authority outside of the home. Similarly, even those European Americans who say they abhor an ideology of white supremacy might still be unable to accept a black person in a position of superiority.

A comparison of how women and African Americans changed people's attitudes on these ideological points shows the close links between the two groups' journeys toward political representation. It also shows that, although African American males were the first to receive political rights, they were also the first to lose them, and as they receded into the political background, women—both white and black—began moving into the foreground. By making gradual but increasingly visible claims to public authority, these women facilitated the leap forward that African Americans made after the Voting Rights Act passed in 1965 and that women of all races made through the women's movements of the 1960s and 1970s.

As Sklar notes in her chapter, the political fates of women of all races and African Americans became linked in the early 1800s, when women abolitionists recognized disturbing similarities between conditions for slaves and constraints in their own lives. That link was partially broken after the Civil War, when the fourteenth and fifteenth amendments to the U.S. Constitution, which were ratified in 1868 and 1870, accorded political rights to former male slaves but not to women. Bitter over the prospect of black men exercising political power while white women remained disfranchised, some prominent white woman suffragists, led by former abolitionists Elizabeth Cady Stanton and Susan B. Anthony, refused to support the amendments. In the belief that only black male enfranchisement could be achieved at that moment in history, but not the enfranchisement of both African Americans and women of any race, black women abolitionists and some white women abolitionists continued to support the amendments. They also kept up their work for woman suffrage but focused on a state-by-state approach to winning the vote rather than on amending the U.S. Constitution.

In the end, the level of political power black men achieved through the Reconstruction amendments was disappointing. In the late 1800s, only two African Americans ever reached the U.S. Senate: Hiram Revels, appointed by the North Carolina legislature in 1870 but serving only a year before accepting a college presidency, and Blanche K. Bruce, who won election from Mississippi and served a full term from 1875 to 1881 but was not reelected. In 1868, John Willis Menard of Louisiana won a place in the House of Representatives, but an election dispute prevented him from being seated. Between 1870 and the 1890s, only twenty men, all from the South and all representing districts with black majorities, won House seats. Other high posts awarded to black men included ambassadorships, one to Haiti, the other to Liberia. After being elected to the Louisiana State Senate, Pinckney Benton Stewart Pinchback, a businessman, journalist, and politician, rose to the lieutenant governorship of the state and then in 1872 served as governor for five weeks; he later won election to the U.S. House of Representatives and a year later to the U.S. Senate, but he was never seated because of charges of election "irregularities."

Below these top officeholders, as historian Eric Foner has shown, almost two thousand black men held public posts at federal, state, and local levels in the Reconstruction South. Forty black men held posts in customs houses, and many more held other federal patronage positions, such as postmaster, deputy U.S. marshal, treasury agent, and clerk. Foner asserts that, contrary to derisive statements that white supremacists often made about these officeholders, many of them were educated, accomplished, and broadly acquainted with public affairs.[2] They worked hard to achieve better conditions for southern blacks, such as equal treatment on public transportation and in public accommodations. White supremacists worked just as hard to thwart them, threatening black officials and their families with violence, sometimes driving them from their homes and resorting even to murder. Virulent opposition against their exercise of authority drove many black officials to give up their offices and turn to other pursuits; some died in penury, unable to practice their professions or get jobs.

By the end of the century, coalitions of Democrats and conservative Republicans had re-imposed white rule and disfranchised the black populations of the South. The U.S. Supreme Court decision in *Plessy v. Ferguson* (1896) legalized "separate but equal" conditions for black people, thereby assuring that African Americans would not be treated as full American citizens. By 1901, no African Americans were left in Congress. A few local black officeholders held on, but, unless aided by sympathetic white Democrats or Republicans, with dwindling authority.

The political interests of white woman suffragists and African Americans, which had diverged so painfully in the late 1860s, began to reconverge in the Progressive Era, when both black and white women political activists took up civil rights causes. In the 1880s and 1890s, middle-class black women educators and social workers formed associations to improve living and working conditions for African Americans, focusing especially on those who had migrated out of southern agricultural areas in order to find employment in industrial cities. Josephine St. Pierre Ruffin, Victoria Earle Matthews, Mary Church Terrell, Fannie Barrier Williams, Ida B. Wells, Margaret Murray Washington, Lugenia Hope, and Anna Julia Cooper were among the most prominent leaders in this effort. By 1900, their organizations had adopted political agendas calling for the restoration of civil rights for people of color, federal anti-lynching bills, and votes for women.

White middle-class women also advocated civil rights causes through organizations such as the most popular woman's group of the late nineteenth century, the Woman's Christian Temperance Union (WCTU). Working for government controls over the consumption of alcoholic beverages, this organization became deeply involved in partisan politics, allying itself with political parties that promised to put prohibition planks into their platforms. While most of the organizations founded by white women set up separate branches for "colored" members, some women's organizations founded in the early 1900s were interracial. Mary White Ovington, a white social settlement worker and descendant of abolitionists, was a leader in the movement to found the National Association for the Advancement of Colored People (NAACP). Other white settlement workers, such as Jane Addams, Florence Kelley, and Lillian Wald, all early NAACP founders, were active in campaigns to improve race relations. Women activists got involved in party politics, as well. Addams, Kelley, and Wald were all outspoken leaders in Theodore Roosevelt's Progressive Party campaign of 1912. After women in Illinois won partial suffrage in 1913, African American women in the racially segregated Second Ward of Chicago were able to influence the election of Chicago's first black alderman, Oscar De Priest.

Despite the beginnings of a convergence between the interests of white women activists and African Americans around the turn of the twentieth century, points of deep conflict remained. Most white women temperance and suffrage activists rejected the idea of federal intervention to solve the many challenges black Americans faced, from discrimination in education, jobs, housing, and public accommodations to beatings and lynchings. Nor did they welcome blacks as equal members of their organizations. Concerned not to alienate white southern supporters, the WCTU, the Young Women's Christian Association, and the National American Woman Suffrage Association not only maintained separate branches for blacks but avoided taking controversial stands on racial issues. Moreover, the leadership of the Progressive Party, which had attracted the participation of many women social reformers, disappointed many of them by deciding against seating southern African American delegates in a vain attempt to win support from southern Republicans. As the twentieth century advanced, some of these conflicts abated. The development of interracial organizations, spearheaded in great measure by black and white women active in social issues through their churches, and inspired by the Commission on Interracial Cooperation (CIC), which had been established to address racial tensions in southern cities after World War I, began bringing the interests of black and white Americans closer together.[3]

During and after World War I (1914–18), increasing numbers of southern black families moved to the North. Through the black majorities they formed in northern and midwestern cities, black officeholding reemerged. Oscar De Priest was elected to Congress in 1928, the first black congressman since 1901 and the only one until his defeat by another African American, Arthur Mitchell, in 1934. After replacing Mitchell in 1942, William L. Dawson also served alone until Adam Clayton Powell Jr. of New York joined him in 1945.

In proportion to their numbers in the population, before the recent era African Americans had achieved only negligible representation in public office. After the passage of national woman suffrage in 1920, the political progress of women, who of course represented over half the general population, was at first not much better. Entrenched cultural biases against women's leadership in the public sphere proved to be powerful obstacles.

Efforts to counter these biases took many decades. First, women had to rid the laws of the gender-specific terminology that defined qualifications for certain public roles or the award of licenses to practice certain professions. Since the legal profession offered the most common route to political office, women's exclusion from state bars as practicing attorneys as well as from prestigious law schools also hindered their political progress. Challenges to those exclusions began as early as the 1870s and succeeded first for unmarried women. Still, some major law schools and bar associations, the source of networks important for lawyers to advance in public life, refused to admit women until the second half of the twentieth century.

In addition to facing restrictions on practicing law, even after they had won the vote women in about half the states were also excluded from courtrooms as jurors. Opponents of women jurors argued that women's "delicate" natures could not withstand the lurid details of crimes, that their monthly cycles would make them periodically unfit to make rational judgments, and that their family responsibilities precluded their being sequestered. Restrictions on women jurors gradually gave way, but only after civic activists waged state-by-state campaigns to eliminate them. The opposition of some women to jury service, on the basis that it conflicted with their family duties, made the task of reform especially difficult, as activists had to persuade not only men, but also women that jury service and respect for women's citizenship went together. By the late 1930s, activists had persuaded most states to qualify women for jury service, but most of those states made such service elective only. This meant that women had to sign up deliberately to serve or, if called, could receive an automatic exemption just for being female. Efforts in the 1940s and 1950s to make women's jury service equal to that of men failed repeatedly. Finally, in 1975, in a case unconnected to the campaigns for women's mandatory service, the U.S. Supreme Court ruled that since juries had to represent a fair cross section of the community they had to include women on the same terms as men.[4]

Similar difficulties faced African American men in their quest for jury service. Just as they had received their political rights before women, through the 1875 Civil Rights Act they were also eligible to serve on juries before most women. But, as in politics, black jurors faced systematic exclusion. When black defendants appealed negative decisions made by all-white juries, the courts ruled inconsistently, sometimes saying that such juries violated the Equal Protection Clause of the Fourteenth Amendment and other times that their decisions did not necessarily imply the occurrence of discrimination. In 1883, the U.S. Supreme Court declared the 1875 Civil Rights Act unconstitutional, thereby all but ending the requirement to put any black men on juries, especially in the South. Protests against this exclusion revived in the 1930s, particularly around the famous case of the "Scottsboro Boys," nine young African American men accused of rape by two white women. Civil rights activists had to protest further cases before racial discrimination in jury selection was finally ruled illegal in 1986. That did not end the practice, however. Although charges of discrimination are hard to prove, critics still claim that attorneys use racial criteria in challenging particular jurors.

Despite the resistance to women's exercise of authority in the public sphere, in the early decades after woman suffrage, a few white women began to achieve public office. As they learned how to run political campaigns, they gradually worked their way up in political-party hierarchies. By earning advanced degrees in fields that led toward public office, such as law, economics, and public administration, over time they proved their worth to the male political leaders who still monopolized the power to nominate them for office.

Some ran for office supported by networks of women's voluntary associations, like suffrage and other reform organizations; others received nominations from political party leaders to succeed husbands who had died in office. Jeannette Rankin, a Montana suffragist, a pacifist, and the first woman to serve in the U.S. House of Representatives, is an example of the first type. Elected in 1917, she lost her party's nomination for a seat in the Senate but in 1940 rejoined Congress, where she gained wide notoriety for her solitary vote opposing the U.S. declaration of war against Japan after Pearl Harbor. Supported by women's consumer groups and women Democratic Party activists, Frances Perkins became the first woman to serve in a presidential cabinet when President Franklin D. Roosevelt appointed her secretary of labor in 1933. Representative of the second type of early woman officeholder, Nellie Tayloe Ross succeeded her late husband as governor of Wyoming in 1925 and later received the political appointment as director of the U.S. Mint; Edith Nourse Rogers succeeded her husband in Congress in 1925 and went on to represent Massachusetts for thirty-five years; Hattie Wyatt Caraway of Arkansas succeeded her husband in the U.S. Senate in 1931 and then won two more elections. A few women with famous politician fathers also had moderately successful political careers. Among them were Ruth Hanna McCormick, the daughter of Ohio politician Mark Hanna and wife of a former U.S. Senator, who won election to Congress in 1929 but served only one term, and Ruth Bryan Owen, daughter of orator and politician William Jennings Bryan, who in 1933 became the nation's first female ambassador. During the New Deal, President Roosevelt's wife, Eleanor, promoted the appointment of women in key administrative positions, including her longtime friend, African American educator Mary McLeod Bethune.

A mid-twentieth-century effort to improve minority political party representation on local governing bodies illustrates how the interests of women and African Americans were becoming even more interconnected in that time period. The effort involved getting cities to change their voting methods to "proportional representation," a method that gives voters representation on governing bodies in proportion to the votes their candidates receive. "PR," as this method is called, contrasted with the "winner-take-all" principle, which awards sole victory to the one person who wins a numerical majority of an election district's votes. Winner-take-all elections, proponents of PR claimed, disfranchise minority parties, keeping out candidates who might have a considerable following among voters but not quite enough to win. PR, they argued, would guarantee minority-party candidates seats in proportion to the number of votes they received, regardless of whether they win a majority.

Between 1915 and 1948, twenty-two American cities adopted PR. And indeed, in those cities, more political independents, members of racial and ethnic minorities, and women won seats on local city councils. But the reform was short-lived. Voters did not like the complexity of PR voting methods, which required the ranking of candidates and time-consuming counting measures. They also objected to some of the results of PR, such as the election of radicals (i.e., Socialists or Communists) and (in some cities) African Americans. Opponents of PR took advantage of these objections and persuaded all but one city—Cambridge, Massachusetts—to restore traditional winner-take-all voting methods.[5]

Even with the failure of PR, women's representation in higher office continued to climb. In the early 1940s, fewer than a dozen women were serving in Congress and women filled only 144 seats in state legislatures. The number rose slowly to twenty in the early 1960s, dropped down later in the decade, and then climbed back up by the end of the 1970s. Moreover, some female members of Congress had high national profiles: Democrats Bella Abzug, Shirley Chisholm, Elizabeth Holtzman, Barbara Jordan, Pat Schroeder, and Geraldine Ferraro, among others, were frequently in the news for their stands on feminist issues, race relations, and President Richard Nixon's "Watergate" scandal and subsequent impeachment trial. As Tera Hunter writes in Chapter 5, Chisholm was the first African American woman to hold a seat in Congress and Jordan was the first African American woman from the South to serve. Their milestone elections received tremendous attention from the press. Moreover, Chisholm's decision to run for president and Jordan's eloquent speeches defending the Nixon impeachment and her later keynote address to the Democratic National Convention were major news events of the early 1970s.[6] By 1985, Geraldine Ferraro had run for vice president on the Democratic Party's national ticket and twenty-five women sat in Congress, with a jump to fifty-five in the early 1990s. In 1975, 610 women were serving in state legislatures; ten years later, this number had almost doubled to 1,103, or 14.8 percent of all state legislators.[7]

Until the passage of the 1965 Voting Rights Act, African American representation proceeded more slowly. Only six black men served in the House. And while black representation in the House rose rapidly after the 1970s, almost a hundred years would pass after Reconstruction before another African American took a seat in the Senate. Edward W. Brooke served there from 1967 to 1979, and the first female African American, Carol Moseley Braun, served from 1993 to 1999. Barack Obama entered the Senate in 2005, with Roland Burris replacing him in 2009.

The Voting Rights Act also propelled southern blacks into office. By 1970, 1,469 black elected officials were in office; by 2000, that number had increased sixfold to 9,040. Black representation at state levels showed the greatest growth: according to *Black Elected Officials: A National Roster,* five southern states (Georgia, Louisiana, Mississippi, South Carolina, and Texas) showed a tenfold increase in black representation. Even though the number of these representatives did not adequately represent the number of African Americans nationwide, the progress of the last thirty years or so has been encouraging.[8]

In a related development, beginning in the late 1960s, rising inner-city black majorities helped black men advance into posts as mayors. In 1967, Carl B. Stokes and Richard G. Hatcher became the first African Americans elected to urban executive posts when they won elections in Cleveland, Ohio, and Gary, Indiana. Over the next decades, many other major U.S. cities elected black mayors, including New York City, which elected David Dinkins in 1989. Even cities with majority white populations elected African American mayors. By 1990, 316 African Americans were leading cities across the United States. In 1991, thirty cities with populations over fifty thousand, sixteen of them with white voting majorities, had African American mayors. According to Jeffrey Adler, this rise of black mayors proved to be a "fundamental symbolic turning point for African Americans."[9] Many fewer black women reached mayoral posts, however, indicating continued resistance to women's exercise of executive authority. One black woman, Carrie Saxon Perry, won election in a large city, Hartford, Connecticut, in 1987, but lost her bid for reelection. Also in 1987, Lottie L. Shackelford became mayor of Little Rock, Arkansas. At the same time, some four dozen black women were mayors of smaller cities (populations under fifty thousand), primarily in the South. This represented a major change: ten years earlier, there were only twelve black female mayors in the entire country.[10]

The complementary nature of the rise into political prominence of women and African Americans in the modern era is quite stunning. For both groups, changes began at local levels, where blacks and women new to electoral politics had their strongest connections. The election of African American mayors was, in part, a response to rapid demographic changes taking place in American cities in the decades after World War II, as whites moved out to the suburbs and blacks migrated into the inner cities. Women's political bases depended less on demographics than on their links to local voluntary associations working for woman suffrage, civil rights, municipal-government reform, and general civic and social improvements. Although some of the African Americans and women who won office did so through their participation in civil and women's rights movements, many did so just by working their way up through local party organizations. And for both groups, "crossover" voting was necessary to bring them victory, as a preponderance of black voters was never sufficient to elect a black mayor, and support from women's groups alone could never elect a female. In other words, both groups needed broad-based support in order to succeed, and both groups needed each other.

Over the period from the late 1990s to the 2008 election, the racial, ethnic, and gender diversity of all governing bodies, from city councils and boards of aldermen, to state legislatures and the two houses of Congress, grew steadily. In the process, American government came to "look more like America." President Obama has brought into top executive posts a greater diversity of leaders than the country has ever seen. At this writing, seven women hold key positions: the secretaries of state (Clinton), health (Kathleen Sebelius), homeland security (Janet Napolitano), and labor (Hilda Solis, the first Hispanic woman in the Cabinet); Christina Romer chairs the Council of Economic Advisors, Lisa Jackson administers the Environmental Protection Agency, and Susan Rice is ambassador to the United Nations. Obama appointed two women to the United States Supreme Court, Sonia Sotomayor, the court's first Latina woman, and then Elena Kagan. Other prominent minority appointments include those of Eric Holder (justice), Steven Chu (energy), and Eric K. Shinseki (veterans' affairs).

In addition, as Catherine Rymph points out in Chapter 10, in 2008 "roughly 70 million people voted for a woman to be either president or vice president." The task of diversification is far from complete, but the 2008 campaign has made it highly unlikely that political candidates and appointees of the future will look anything like those pictures of homogeneous men I used to post on my office door. The nation's political landscape has definitely changed.

Women and minorities have done this together. Excluded together, stereotyped together, they achieved change together. Mutually dependent, they advanced together, building incremental changes and standing on the shoulders of those who came before. Much remains to be done. During the 2008 campaign, as Rymph argues, McCain picked a female running mate so as to reignite a sputtering campaign. When Palin began to act as though she was the lead candidate, the media raised alarms about "who was really in charge." And thus McCain had to reassert himself. Female political candidates used to raise alarms about "petticoat politics," a term that referred—critically, of course—to men who appeared to be dominated by women. These kinds of skirmishes over gender stereotypes—who's on top, who's bossing whom, can the man "take it," can the woman keep from "taking over"—will continue for a while but, I hope, will eventually cease to be issues. As Melanie Gustafson insists in Chapter 7, we need to keep on developing strong "counterstories" to head them off.

Some barriers remain high for both women and minorities: as Tiffany Patterson points out in Chapter 2, during the campaign Obama could not show anger, or he would risk being identified as an "angry black man." Hillary Clinton had a double burden: on the one hand, she could not show anger without risking adjectives like "shrill," "aggressive," or "nutcracker" ("unsexed" or "Amazon" were the nineteenth-century labels), all terms historically used against women who push against the constraints of their sex; on the other, if she showed vulnerability, or wept (she did get teary-eyed in one brief moment during the primary season, and miraculously got away with it, as the media said she was showing her "humanity" and that she really cared!), she could be dismissed as too "weak" to be commander in chief.

A Vision from the Past, a Vision for the Future

Now that an African American is in the White House, have we arrived at a place where "difference" no longer makes a difference? Where the race, ethnicity, gender, religious faith, sexual preference, or other ways in which an individual "differs" from traditionally perceived norms for certain roles is irrelevant to that person's ability to serve in that role? Of course not. Do we want to be there? I'm no longer sure. On the one hand, it would be gratifying if, in choosing our leaders, we judged individuals solely on the basis of their qualities of mind, character, heart, and experience. On the other, those qualities are necessarily forged in the crucible of one's life experiences, and those experiences in turn are shaped by race, ethnicity, gender, religious faith, sexual preference, and so forth. How can they not be? How can we not want them to be? A salient point of Obama's "dreams" from his father is the extent to which his sense of his own "difference" critically influenced his development as a lawyer, teacher, community organizer, and politician.[11] And when he became president, one of the first nationally televised events he hosted in the White House was a celebration of the music of the civil rights movement, at the end of which he stood with the performers who sang the black national anthem, "Lift Every Voice," every word of which he knew by heart. How could one fail to be moved by this identification of Obama and his family with the most stirring moments of African American history?

And so I would not wish for issues of difference to vanish from our field of vision. Difference is a key element of identity. The challenge is to keep from turning difference into stereotype. The temptation to do so is enormous. When Governor Alfred E. Smith, a Catholic, ran for president in 1928, he became the target of religious slurs that had nothing to do with his qualifications for office. The nation overcame such stereotypes when it elected John Fitzgerald Kennedy to the White House in 1960. But imagine a presidential candidate who is Native American, or gay, or transsexual. And what about a Jew? This last possibility was actually imagined in a time when many across the entire world thought of Jews as members of a "despised race."

The person who imagined the possibility (and consequences) of an American Jewish president was a magazine writer named Frank Barkley Copley, who in 1912 wrote a short fantasy called *The Impeachment of President Israels*.[12] It tells the story of President David Israels, a lawyer of distinction and a man of wealth and culture, who (according to his longtime secretary and the story's narrator) had a nature "almost as sensitive as a high-strung woman's" and never took to the "game" of politics. "Prejudice against his race" had handicapped him, but he won political support because his party thought he would contribute to its war chest and bring in "Jewish votes." Israels, however, told his co-religionists that if they voted for him "as Jews, they should be ashamed of themselves," and he never contributed a cent to his party.

His presidency went into a crisis after a German warship killed four American sailors. Assuming the United States would retaliate militarily for this crime, Germany mobilized its fleet, but Israels surprised everyone by urging Germany to submit the case to an international court. Press and pulpit railed against him, calling him a "pighead, a stubborn fool, a wild-eyed fanatic, a head-strong lunatic, a sniveling, sneaking, hypocritical coward, a double-dyed traitor and a man without a country." Only his great personal fortune deflected the charge that he was in the pay of the Germans. Socialists and people with blood ties to Germany spoke in his defense, but their words only made things worse. Ministers of the Gospel stirred up "race hatred," yelling for the "blood of this Jew." Anti-Semites shrieked "that lack of patriotism and any stomach for fight was only what was to be expected of a white-livered Jew." The president then shocked the nation further by honoring a long-standing commitment to send the North Atlantic fleet to the Mediterranean to celebrate the birth of Turkey's republic. Horrified at this blow to the nation's defenses, his secretaries of state, war, and navy resigned and Congress impeached the president for "high crimes and misdemeanors."

The remainder of the book recounts the president's defense, which he insisted on making himself. In his speech he explained his view of the relationship between the moral law and democracy. As his goal had always been to represent what was "best" in the people, the call for war had come not "from what was best" but instead manifested "the same animal passion that led the aggrieved street urchin to scream in defiance and threaten with his fists." He was convinced that, had he mobilized, war would have been inevitable. Instead, he had sent the American fleet to Turkey, thereby assuring Germany that he trusted in the sense of honor of the German people, whose civilization and culture he so admired. In return, he concluded, the German emperor had kept his fleet in port, held back by the "moral law."

The president's speech "astounded" the world. Germany offered "splendid" reparation, and the impeachment collapsed. But so did the president. Worn out by his trial, he fell grievously ill and, after lingering a few days, died. The novel ends with a moving paean to "a peculiar people [who] came into being on the eastern shore of the Mediterranean."

Reading this almost hundred-year-old novel in the context of the 2008 campaign was a captivating experience for me. It evoked so many echoes of our recent history. Israels is a president who would rather talk than fight, a "scholar" who insists on negotiating with an enemy instead of bombing them to hell (read "effeminate," "weak"); a party "outsider" who refuses to do the "political" thing just to get elected; an intellectual who reasons before acting (read "nerd," "egghead," "academic") and who appeals to a higher moral law applicable to all civilized people (read "impractical idealist"); a leader tainted with the charge of "socialism" (how enduring this canard, invoked here years before the Bolshevik Revolution of 1917 made it even more popular); an individual whom others insist on identifying by his "race" but who refuses to wear that identity as the sum of his being, the motivator of his actions, or the basis of an appeal to others of his "race" to support him; and finally, vilification because of his "race," here not associated with skin color but with an ancient religion.

Had President Israels not been a Jew, it's possible that his other characteristics—his intellectuality, his insistence on the power of the moral law—would have gotten him into a political maelstrom regardless of his religious faith and cultural identity. But he was a Jew, and this "difference" made him much more vulnerable.

If this novel has anything to tell us, it is that identity and gender politics are hardly new, and if we have learned anything from the campaign of 2008, it is that they will not be vanishing any time soon. Many people believe that those who "differ" from themselves, or from some perceived social norm, might or will do them harm, and that their "difference" is to blame for that harm. While it would be utopian to envision a world without such beliefs, a more reasonable goal would be a world in which difference is acknowledged and respected, but never stereotyped or used rhetorically to deride, belittle, or destroy the other. It may be unrealistic to believe that American elections will ever be free of prejudice and stereotyping. To my mind, however, the "difference" Americans saw so prominently displayed on their television screens during campaign 2008 has made a difference. I can only hope the change is permanent.

NOTES

1. For information on women in high executive and legislative office, see www.cawp.rutgers.edu, the website of the Center for American Women and Politics, Eagleton Institute of Politics, Rutgers University. Sources on blacks include http://www.thecongressionalblackcaucus.com/ and http://www.senate.gov/artandhistory/history/common/briefing/minority_senators.htm, which shows ethnic and racial diversity in the U.S. Senate.

2. See Eric Foner, *Freedom's Lawmakers: A Directory of Black Officeholders during Reconstruction* (New York: Oxford University Press, rev. ed. 1996).

3. These and related issues are discussed in such works as Alison M. Parker, *Articulating Rights: Nineteenth-Century American Women on Race, Reform, and the State* (De Kalb: Northern Illinois University Press, 2010); Glenda Elizabeth Gilmore, *Gender and Jim Crow: Women and the Politics of White Supremacy in North Carolina, 1896–1920* (Chapel Hill: University of North Carolina Press, 1996); George E. Mowry, "The South and the Progressive Lily White Party of 1912," *The Journal of Southern History* 6, no. 2 (May 1940): 237–47; and Jacquelyn Dowd Hall, *Revolt against Chivalry: Jessie Daniel Ames and the Women's Campaign against Lynching* (New York: Columbia University Press, 1979).

4. See Linda K. Kerber, *No Constitutional Right to Be Ladies: Women and the Obligations of Citizenship* (New York: Hill and Wang, 1998), and Elisabeth Israels Perry, "Rhetoric, Strategy, and Politics in the New York Campaign for Women's Jury Service, 1917–1975," *New York History* 82, no. 1 (Winter 2001): 53–78.

5. Some cities and towns today, as well as school boards, still use some form of PR. See http://www.wsipp.wa.gov/rptfiles/Localelections.pdf for a modern assessment of PR's effectiveness in diversifying representatives.

6. For women serving in Congress today, see http://womenincongress.house.gov/ and http://www.senate.gov/reference/resources/pdf/RL30261.pdf. For early representation in state legislatures, see Emmy E. Werner, "Women in the State Legislatures," *The Western Political Quarterly* 21, no. 1 (March 1968): 40-50.

7. In 2010, 1,799 (24.4 percent) of all state legislators in the United States were women; 91 women (17 percent) served in Congress.

8. See David A. Bositis, *Black Elected Officials: A Statistical Summary (2001)* at http://www.jointcenter.org.

9. See David R. Colburn, "Running for Office: African-American Mayors from 1967 to 1996," 23–56, and Jeffrey S. Adler, "Introduction," 15, both in David R. Colburn and Jeffrey S. Adler, eds., *African-American Mayors: Race, Politics, and the American City* (Urbana and Chicago: University of Illinois Press, 2001).

10. *Ebony* 43, no. 6 (April 1988): 62–64. For more on resistance to women executives, see Robert P. Watson and Ann Gordon, eds., *Anticipating Madam President* (Boulder, Colo.: Lynn Reiner, 2003).

11. Barack Obama, *Dreams from My Father: A Story of Race and Inheritance* (New York: Times Books, 1995).

12. I first saw this book on my father's bookshelf when I was a child. *The Impeachment of President Israels: A Story of War and Peace* (New York: Macmillan, 1913) came out first in *The American Magazine* 75 (December 1912): 21–28. A Yiddish translation came out in 1916. Copley (1875–1941) later published the first authorized biography of the famous industrial reformer Frederick W. Taylor. See H. S. Person, "Frank Barkley Copley," *Advanced Management* (July–September 1941): 117.

HISTORICAL TIMELINE

- 1789 U.S. Constitution takes effect; includes Three-Fifths Clause
- 1837 Antislavery convention attended by both African Americans and whites in New York City endorses resolutions opposing racism and supporting women's rights
- 1848 First women's rights convention takes place at Seneca Falls, New York
- 1857 Supreme Court's *Dred Scott* decision holds that enslaved persons of African heritage and their descendants are ineligible for citizenship
- 1861–65 U.S. Civil War
- 1868 Fourteenth Amendment ratified, establishing that African Americans, including former slaves, are citizens. The amendment also explicitly reserved some civic protections for men, the first provision in the Constitution to do so
- 1870 Fifteenth Amendment ratified, forbidding suffrage restrictions on the basis of race or former enslavement
- 1872 Susan B. Anthony arrested for trying to vote
- 1880s–1910 Southern states disfranchise nearly all black voters
- 1896 The People's Party peaks in popularity and nominates William Jennings Bryan as its presidential candidate
- 1920 Nineteenth Amendment ratified, officially enfranchising women
- 1923 Equal Rights Amendment first introduced into Congress
- 1964 Civil Rights Act passed
- 1964 Margaret Chase Smith becomes the first woman to seek a major party's nomination for the presidency
- 1965 Voting Rights Act passed

1968 Shirley Chisholm becomes the first African American woman elected to Congress
1972 Equal Rights Amendment sent to the states for ratification
1972 Shirley Chisholm becomes the first African American to run for president
1973 Supreme Court issues *Roe v. Wade* decision expanding abortion rights
1982 Deadline for ratification of Equal Rights Amendment expires
1984 Jesse Jackson becomes the first African American man to run for president
1984 Geraldine Ferraro nominated as the Democratic Party's vice-presidential candidate
1988 Jesse Jackson again runs for president and finishes second in Democratic primary voting
2000 Hillary Clinton elected to the U.S. Senate from New York
2004 Barack Obama elected to the U.S. Senate from Illinois
2006 Sarah Palin elected governor of Alaska
2008 Senators Obama and Clinton compete for the Democratic presidential nomination
2008 Sarah Palin nominated as the Republican Party's vice-presidential candidate
2008 Barack Obama elected president
2010 Supreme Court issues *Citizens United* decision, lifting restrictions on corporate donations to political campaigns

CONTRIBUTORS

LIETTE GIDLOW (ed.) (PhD, Cornell University), associate professor of history, Wayne State University, is the author of *The Big Vote: Gender, Consumer Culture, and the Politics of Exclusion, 1890s–1920s* (Johns Hopkins University Press, 2004). She is working on a book on the struggle for woman suffrage after the ratification in 1920 of the woman suffrage amendment.

PAULA BAKER (PhD, Rutgers University), associate professor of history at Ohio State University, is the author or editor of four books, including *The Moral Frameworks of Public Life* (Oxford, 1991). She is completing a book on the history of campaign finance.

RONALD P. FORMISANO (PhD, Wayne State University) is the William T. Bryan Chair of American History at the University of Kentucky. He is the author of five books, most recently *For the People: American Populist Movements from the Revolution to the 1850s* (University of North Carolina Press, 2008).

GLENDA ELIZABETH GILMORE (PhD, University of North Carolina), the Peter V. and C. Vann Woodward Professor of History at Yale University, is the author or editor of four books, including *Gender and Jim Crow: Women and the Politics of White Supremacy in North Carolina, 1896–1920* (University of North Carolina Press, 1996), winner of the Frederick Jackson Turner Award, and *Defying Dixie: The Radical Roots of Civil Rights, 1919–1950* (Norton, 2008).

MELANIE GUSTAFSON (PhD, New York University), associate professor of history at the University of Vermont, is the author or editor of three books, including *Women and the Republican Party, 1854–1924* (University of Illinois Press, 2001). She is currently working on a biography of woman suffrage leader Susan B. Anthony.

CONTRIBUTORS

SUSAN M. HARTMANN (PhD, University of Missouri), Arts and Humanities Distinguished Professor of History, Ohio State University, is the author of five books, including *The Other Feminists: Activists in the Liberal Establishment* (Yale University Press, 1998).

TERA W. HUNTER (PhD, Yale University) is the author or editor of five books, including *To 'Joy My Freedom: Southern Black Women's Lives and Labors after the Civil War* (Harvard University Press, 1997), which won book prizes from the Southern Historical Association, the Association of Black Women's Historians, and the International Labor History Association.

MITCH KACHUN (PhD, Cornell University), associate professor of history, Western Michigan University, is the author of *Festivals of Freedom: Memory and Meaning in African American Emancipation Celebrations, 1808–1915* (University of Massachusetts Press, 2003) and co-editor of *The Curse of Caste* (Oxford University Press, 2006).

TIFFANY RUBY PATTERSON (PhD, Minnesota), associate professor of African American and Diaspora Studies, Vanderbilt University, is the author of *Zora Neale Hurston and a History of Southern Life* (Temple University Press, 2005) and associate editor of the sixteen-volume series *Black Women in United States History* (Carlson).

ELISABETH ISRAELS PERRY (PhD, UCLA) is the John Francis Bannon, S.J., Professor, Emerita, of history and women's studies at Saint Louis University. She is the author or editor of five books, including *Belle Moskowitz: Feminine Politics and the Exercise of Power in the Age of Alfred E. Smith* (Oxford University Press, 1987), and is a past president of the Society for Historians of the Gilded Age and Progressive Era.

CATHERINE E. RYMPH (PhD, University of Iowa), associate professor of history at the University of Missouri, is the author of *Republican Women: Feminism and Conservatism from Suffrage to the New Right* (University of North Carolina Press, 2006). She is currently writing a book on the history of the American foster care system, 1935–1980.

KATHRYN KISH SKLAR (PhD, University of Michigan), Distinguished Bartle Professor at the State University of New York, Binghamton, is the author or editor of ten books, including *Catherine Beecher: A Study in American Domesticity* (Yale University Press, 1973; repr. Norton, 1976) and *Florence Kelley and the Nation's Work: The Rise of Women's Political Culture, 1830–1900* (Yale University Press, 1995), each the recipient of the Berkshire Prize, which is awarded by the Berkshire Conference of Women Historians for the best book written by a woman scholar in any field of history.

INDEX

affirmative action, 9, 43, 70, 138
African American men: historical stereotypes of, 74; and jury service, 156; as officeholders, 153–55, 158–59. *See also* African Americans; individual names
African Americans: churches, 17, 26–29, 33, 72; in Congress, 8–9, 153, 158; political appointees, 150; political party preferences of, 6, 8, 59–60; and white feminists, 20, 151, 157, 159; voting behavior of, 53–57. *See also* African American men; African American women; disfranchisement; individual names
African American women: as church members, 59–60, 155; as club members, 59–60; in Congress, 8–9; gains by, 70; historical stereotypes of, 40–42, 44–46; as officeholders, 159; political influence of, 57–58, 151, 154; political strategies of, 58–63; Progressive reform by, 59, 154; as suffragists, 21, 152, 154; voting behavior of, 53, 55–56, 81; and white feminists, 154. *See also* African Americans; individual names; National Association of Colored Women (NACW)
AIDS (acquired immune deficiency syndrome), 31
American Woman Suffrage Association, 20
Anthony, Susan B., 7, 20, 68, 96, 152
antifeminism, 139–42
anti-Semitism, 162–63

antislavery activism, 21, 31, 152
Aquino, Corazon, 90

Baker, Ella, 60, 61
Bartels, Larry, 73, 117
Beck, Glenn, 70
Beschloss, Michael, 95
Bhutto, Benazir, 90
Biden, Joe, 3, 115
Bipartisan Campaign Reform Act (BCRA), 128, 131
Black Panther Party, 67
blogosphere, 26, 28, 40–44, 57, 71, 99, 112, 140
Braun, Carol Mosely, 9, 47, 69, 159
Brooke, Edward W., 158
Brown, Jerry, 130
Brundtland, Gro, 91
Bryan, William Jennings, 109
Buchanan, Pat, 71, 130
Bush, George H. W., 23, 78
Bush, George W.: appointees, 150; campaign fundraising by, 125, 128, 131; and gender stereotypes, 23; and populism, 108; 2000 election, 55, 150; 2004 victory, 77, 80, 150; unpopularity in 2008, 79, 139. *See also* September 11, 2001

campaign finance, 125–35
cell phones (as a campaign tool), 2, 114
Chisholm, Shirley: elected to Congress,

9, 158; founder of National Women's Political Caucus, 67; presidential run, 66–67, 69, 88, 90; principles of, 66, 68, 74, 76, 82
churches, 9, 117. *See also* African American churches
Citizens United, 133
Civil Rights Act (1875), 156
Civil Rights Act (1964), 8
civil rights movement: effects, 15, 68; goals, 8; "long civil rights movement," 58, 62–63, 151; methods, 62; remembered, 1, 161. *See also* Civil Rights Act (1964); Voting Rights Act (1965)
Clark, Septima, 60
Clinton, Bill: Monica Lewinsky scandal, 79, 87; as president, 89, 111, 149; as presidential candidate, 95, 128; relationship with African American voters, 78; role in Hillary Clinton's campaign, 81, 87, 150; support by whites for, 77–78, 80
Clinton, Hillary Rodham: African American support for, 80; aftermath of convention loss, 4, 73, 143; campaign fundraising by, 129, 133; campaign strategy, 1, 69, 80, 143, 150; election results, 145; as a feminist, 143; as First Lady, 3, 39–40, 42, 70, 87, 92; gender-first strategy, 68–69, 71–72; and gender stereotyping, 23–24, 89, 150, 161; and media, 47, 81–82; misogyny toward, 42, 70, 87, 144; and populism, 110–13; as presidential candidate, 42, 131; and race, 20, 70, 78, 90; relationship to feminist groups during 2008 campaign, 10, 69, 89, 143; as Secretary of State, 14, 160; as Senator, 3, 9, 23, 42, 80; as trailblazer, 2, 19–20, 86, 96; white working-class support for, 90, 110, 113, 115, 117
Collins, Susan, 138
Communist Party, 61
conservative movement, 9. *See also* individual names
Cooper, Anna Julia, 56, 154
Copley, Frank Barkley, 162–63

Dean, Howard, 128, 130
Dees, Morris, 129
Democratic Party: African American preference for, 8, 59; campaign fundraising by, 126–28, 131; internal tensions within, 77, 82; national conventions: 1964, 77; 1968, 8; 1972, 67, 75; 2008, 3–4, 114; primaries (2008), 3; rules changes, 8; and women, 8, 138, 142, 146. *See also* individual names
De Priest, Oscar, 154–55
disfranchisement, 7, 56–58, 60, 63, 69, 153
Dole, Elizabeth, 88, 90
Dole, Robert, 128
Douglass, Frederick, 30–31
Dowd, Maureen, 23, 29, 45
Dred Scott, 6
DuBois, W. E. B., 6, 27
Dukakis, Michael, 23, 119

Edwards, John, 3, 80, 108–10, 113
electoral college, 75–76
EMILY's List, 88–89
Equal Rights Amendment (ERA), 9, 138–42

Facebook, 134. *See also* social media
Federal Corrupt Practices Acts, 126–27
Federal Election Campaign Act (FECA), 126–27. *See also* Federal Elections Commission
Federal Elections Commission (FEC), 127, 129, 133
feminists and feminism: among Republicans, 139–43; bipartisanship among, 138; goals of, 137; and race, 21–23, 67, 69, 151. *See also* individual names; National Organization for Women (NOW); National Women's Political Caucus; second wave feminism
Ferguson, Miriam "Ma," 86
Ferraro, Geraldine: elected to Congress, 158; on race, 72–73; and vice presidential nomination, 4, 9, 75, 96, 142–43, 146
Fifteenth Amendment, 6, 20, 69, 152
financial crisis of 2008, 5, 111, 115
First Ladies: Hillary Clinton as, 3, 39–40, 87; Jacqueline Kennedy as, 41; Michelle Obama as, 39, 41; Eleanor Roosevelt as, 40
Ford, Betty, 138
Ford, Gerald, 139
Fourteenth Amendment, 6, 68, 152, 156

INDEX

Fox News, 46–47. *See also* Beck, Glenn
Freeman, Jo, 20
Friedan, Betty, 137
fundraising. *See* campaign finance

gay marriage, 117
gender: discrimination, 66, 68–71, 81, 89–90, 155; gap, 9, 75, 80–81, 142; performance, 23–24; stereotypes, 19, 47, 87, 101
Gandhi, Indira, 90
Giuliani, Rudy, 4, 26
Goldwater, Barry, 23, 115, 129–30
Google, 133–34
Gore, Al, 55, 108, 111, 118–19
Great Depression, 61, 118
Grimke,' Angelina, 21

Harrison, William Henry, 106
Huckabee, Mike, 4, 108–9, 111
Hurricane Katrina, 109–10, 117

immigrants and immigration, 35, 109
Internet (as a campaign tool), 2, 114, 125–26, 129, 132

Jackson, Andrew, 106, 119
Jackson, Jesse, 5–6, 73, 75, 78
Jefferson, Thomas, 30–31, 119
Jim Crow, 6–8, 10, 34
"Joe the Plumber." *See* Wurzelbacher, Samuel
Jordan, Barbara, 8, 158

Katrina. *See* Hurricane Katrina
Kennedy, Jacqueline, 40–41
Kennedy, John F., 95, 162
Kennedy, Ted, 41
Kerry, John: campaign fundraising by, 125, 128, 131; and gender stereotyping, 23; and populism, 108, 110–11, 119; support for, 77, 80
King, Rev. Martin Luther, Jr., 30, 35
Kirchner, Cristina, 90
Kristol, William, 115
Kucinich, Dennis, 108–9, 118
Kunin, Madeleine, 95

Leftwich, Yvonne Scruggs-, 55–56
Lerner, Gerda, 21

Lewinsky, Monica, 79, 87
Lewis, John, 4
Limbaugh, Rush, 141, 144
Lockwood, Belva, 89, 101

Malcolm X, 27
"maverick," 98–99, 114, 140, 144
McCain, John: campaign fundraising by, 125–26; Hillary Clinton supporters, 73, 97; and conservative religious leaders, 29; election results, 146; and financial crisis, 5; as a "maverick," 97–98, 114, 144; and Sarah Palin, 94, 96, 139, 143–44, 160; and populism, 111–17, 120; and primaries, 4; and Theodore Roosevelt, 99; white support for, 80–81; and women, 70, 141, 144
McCain-Feingold (campaign finance legislation). *See* Bipartisan Campaign Reform Act
McCormack, Ellen, 88
McGovern, George, 67, 129–30
Meier, Golda, 91
Merkel, Angela, 91
Mink, Patsy, 88
Mississippi Freedom Democratic Party, 77
Mondale, Walter, 9, 142–44, 146
"[A] More Perfect Union" (Obama speech), 28, 34–36, 71–72
Murray, Pauli, 61

National American Woman Suffrage Association, 155
National Association for the Advancement of Colored People (NAACP), 61, 154
National Organization for Women (NOW), 88–89
National Woman Suffrage Association, 20
National Women's Political Caucus (NWPC), 8, 67, 88–89, 138–39
9/11. *See* September 11th, 2001
Nineteenth Amendment, 8, 69, 73–74, 102, 155
Nixon, Richard, 67, 77, 139–40, 158

Obama, Barack: as antiwar candidate, 24, 89–90; background, 2, 9, 29, 159; campaign fundraising by, 125–26, 129–31, 133; campaign strategy of, 80,

114; effect of 2008 candidacy on AA voter behavior, 54–56, 63; Iowa victory of, 69, 80; and media, 29, 70, 81–82; and populism, 110–20; as President, 14, 160; and the race issue, 10, 32, 89; and racism, 2, 71–72; response to financial crisis, 5; speech, "A More Perfect Union," 28, 34–36, 71–72; Springfield campaign kickoff, 2; victory by, 117; white support for, 81. *See also* Wright, Rev. Jeremiah
Obama, Michelle, 39–46
Onassis, Jacqueline Kennedy. *See* Jacqueline Kennedy

Palin, Sarah: background, 9, 95, 97; convention speech of, 96, 99, 143; and feminism, 4, 10, 96, 102, 137, 139–40; as a "maverick," 99, 114, 144; and John McCain, 94, 160; and the media, 47, 87, 144; misogyny toward, 144; and populism, 114–15; and Ronald Reagan, 99–100; as a Republican leader, 137, 143; and Theodore Roosevelt, 99–100; selection of, 4, 73, 94, 139; and Tea Party, 14; as a western woman, 100, 102, 115
Paul, Ron, 108–9, 130, 133
Pollitt, Katha, 19, 96
populism, 105–21. *See also* individual names
Progressive era, 7–8, 59, 135
Progressive Party (1912), 155. *See also* Theodore Roosevelt
pro-life activism, 5, 88–89, 141. *See also* individual names
proportional representation (PR), 157–58

Randolph, Asa Philip, 61–62
Rankin, Jeannette, 100, 157
Reagan, Ronald, 23, 78, 99–100, 115, 142
Reconstruction Amendments. *See* Fourteenth Amendment; Fifteenth Amendment
Republican Party: and African Americans, 6, 59, 155; antifeminism in, 139–42; campaign fundraising by, 125, 127–28, 131; feminism in, 138–42; and gender stereotypes, 23; national conventions, 96, 115; platform, 1980, 142; platform, 2008, 141; and reproductive rights, 142; and women, 100–101, 137–42, 145–46. *See also* individual names
Richardson, Bill, 3
Romney, Mitt, 4, 109–10
Roosevelt, Eleanor, 8, 40, 157
Roosevelt, Franklin Delano, 118, 157
Roosevelt, Theodore, 95, 97–100, 154
Rowlandson, Mary, 98

Schlafly, Phyllis, 139–42
Schroeder, Patricia, 89–90, 158
second wave feminism, 8, 20, 68, 137, 152
secret ballot, 126, 134–35
Seneca Falls convention, 7
September 11th, 2001, 29, 89, 150
slavery, 20, 30, 33–34, 39, 71
Smith, Alfred E., 162
Smith, Margaret Chase, 86, 88, 138
Smith, Mary Louise, 139–40, 142
Snowe, Olympia, 138
social media, 131. *See also* Facebook
Stanton, Elizabeth Cady, 7, 20, 68, 152
Steinem, Gloria, 67–69, 81, 96, 140
Stevenson, Adlai, 119
Student Nonviolent Coordinating Committee (SNCC), 60
superdelegates, 3
Susan B. Anthony List, 89, 102

Tea Party movement, 14, 35
Thatcher, Margaret, 91
Tillman Act, 127
Trippi, Joe, 130
Turner, Frederick Jackson, 98
Twenty-Fourth Amendment, 57

U.S. Congress: African Americans and, 153, 158; as launching pad for female presidential candidates, 91; women and, 8, 9, 91, 138, 145, 150, 157. *See also* individual names
U.S. Supreme Court: *Citizens United* decision, 133; decision on Civil Rights Act of 1875, 156; decisions on Fourteenth and Fifteenth Amendments, 6; decisions on jury service, 156; desegregated transpor-

tation decision, 61; *Dred Scott* decision, 6; *Plessy v. Ferguson*, 153; *Roe v. Wade* decision, 9

voter turnout in 2008, 53–57
Voting Rights Act (1965), 1, 8, 57, 76, 152, 158–59

Walker, David, 33
Wallace, George, 130
Watergate scandal, 127, 139–40, 158
Wertheimer, Fred, 126
Will, George, 115
woman suffrage movement, 7–8, 20, 152–53, 155, 160. *See also* Fifteenth Amendment; Nineteenth Amendment; African American women; individual names, organization names
women: and affirmative action, 70; antislavery activism by, 21; in Congress, 8–9, 91, 150, 157; conservatives, 9, 139; in Democratic party, 8, 91, 137; discrimination against, 155; and jury service, 155–56; as leaders, 151–52; political progress in the West by, 100–102; in Republican party, 91, 137–40, 142, 145; voting behavior of, 77–78. *See also* feminists and feminism; individual names; organization names; second wave feminism
Women's Christian Temperance Union (WCTU), 154–55
women's rights conventions, 7, 22
Woodhull, Victoria, 89
World War I, 59, 129, 155
Wright, Rev. Jeremiah, 26–34, 36; controversy for Obama campaign, 10, 72, 81
Wright, Richard, 33
Wurzelbacher, Samuel, 116–17

York, Byron, 57
Young Women's Christian Association (YWCA), 59, 155

The University of Illinois Press
is a founding member of the
Association of American University Presses.

Composed in 10/13 Sabon LT Std
by Celia Shapland
at the University of Illinois Press
Manufactured by Thomson-Shore, Inc.

University of Illinois Press
1325 South Oak Street
Champaign, IL 61820-6903
www.press.uillinois.edu

6900144